2004

RECREATIVE MINDS

RECREATIVE MINDS

Imagination in Philosophy and Psychology

Gregory Currie

Ian Ravenscroft

CLARENDON PRESS · OXFORD

OXFORD
UNIVERSITY PRESS

Great Clarendon Street, Oxford OX2 6DP

Oxford University Press is a department of the University of Oxford.
If furthers the University's objective of excellence in research, scholarship,
and education by publishing worldwide in

Oxford New York

Auckland Bangkok Buenos Aires Cape Town Chennai
Dar es Salaam Delhi Hong Kong Istanbul Karachi Kolkata
Kuala Lumpur Madrid Melbourne Mexico City Mumbai Nairobi
São Paulo Shanghai Taipei Tokyo Toronto

Oxford is a registered trade mark of Oxford University Press
in the UK and in certain other countries

Published in the United States
By Oxford University Press Inc., New York

© Gregory Currie and Ian Ravenscroft, 2002

The moral rights of the authors have been asserted

Database right Oxford University Press (maker)

First published 2002

British Library Cataloguing in Publication Data

Data available

Library of Congress Cataloging-in-Publication Data
Currie, Gregory.
Recreative minds: imagination in philosophy and psychology / Gregory Currie, Ian Ravenscroft.
p. cm.
Includes bibliographical references (p.) and index.
I. Imagination (Philosophy) 2. Imagination. I. Ravenscroft, Ian. II. Title.

BH301.I53 C87 2002   128'.3–dc21   2002074928

ISBN 0-19-823808-8

ISBN 0-19-823809-6 (pbk.)

I 3 5 7 9 10 8 6 4 2

Typeset by Kolam Information Services Pvt. Ltd., Pondicherry, India
Printed in Great Britain
on acid-free paper by
T.J. International Ltd., Padstow, Cornwall

To Martha, who said, 'I like the pretend clown, I don't like the real clown'
and

To Max, whose imagination inspires much thought,
and Tamara, who simply inspires

Acknowledgements

We have worked together on this project since 1996. Along the way we have accumulated a great many debts, both intellectual and personal. Among the people we owe thanks to are Derek Bolton, Simon Daniels, Daniel Fresner, Sam Guttenplan, Peter Hacker, Jane Heal, Jim Hopkins, Frank Jackson, Jon Jureidini, Jerry Levinson, Gerard O'Brien, David Papineau, Larry Parsons, Philip Pettit, Mark Sainsbury, Stephen Stich, Tamara Zutlerics, and our editor, Peter Momtchiloff. Martin Davies and Paul Harris deserve special thanks for their advice, support, and encouragement. Thanks also to those who participated in the workshops on simulation and related topics we ran in Australia in 1997–9. At various times the Australian Research Council, the Research School of Social Sciences, Australian National University, Canberra, and Flinders University, Adelaide, supported our work. G. C. thanks the President and Fellows of St John's College, Oxford, for the excellent environment they provided while he was Senior Visiting Fellow there in 1999, and Louis, Pascale, Paul, Rémi, and Simon for making the family so welcome.

Parts of Chapters 1 and 2 draw on material from 'Imagination and Make-Believe', in the *Routledge Companion to Aesthetics*, edited by Berys Gaut and Domenic McIver Lopes (2000), and from 'Desire in Imagination', in *Imagination, Conceivability and Possibility*, edited by Tamar Szabó Gendler and John Hawthorne (2002). Parts of Chapter 4 draw on material from 'Mental Simulation and Motor Imagery', *Philosophy of Science*, 64 (1997). Parts of Chapter 6 draw on material from 'Imagination as Motivation', *Proceedings of the Aristotelian Society*, 102 (2002). Chapter 8 draws on material from 'Imagination, Delusion and Hallucinations', *Mind and Language*, 15 (2000). The material reprinted from the last two of these appears by kind permission of the editors.

G. C.

I. R.

Contents

INTRODUCTION

Philosophers have made ambitious claims for the imagination. Hume used it to account for our belief in enduring objects; for Kant it explained how we unite concepts with sensory experience. These claims take us a long way from imagination as understood by the rest of us. Hume and Kant might have told us how it is that imagination aids the play of infants, the absorption of theatregoers, the daydreams of the idle, *and* makes us metaphysical realists or possessors of conceptual content. They did not. Nor is it likely they would have been successful in the attempt. The best evidence we have is that, where imagination is notably deficient, as it seems to be in people with autism, conceptual competence and the tendency to realism are reasonably intact.

The account of imagination we offer is much more like a folk theory of imagination, spruced up with some philosophical reflection and some results from the relevant sciences: psychology, psychiatry, and neurobiology. We start with what we take to be the obvious function of the imagination: enabling us to project ourselves into another situation and to see, or think about, the world from another perspective. These situations and perspectives are not currently ours, but ones we come to occupy, as we say, in imagination. The perspective taken in imagination might be the perspective of another actual person. It might be the perspective I would have on things if I believed something I actually don't believe. It might be a hypothetical perspective, that of a fictional character of someone else's devising or our own. We will argue that this is the best way to understand the role of imagination in play, pretence, and fiction. Hence our title: recreative minds recreate the mental states of others; their recreation (their 'pleasant occupation, pastime or amusement', as the *OED* puts it) depends on this capacity. Since, as we shall see, 'recreative' contrasts with 'creative', its first syllable should be rhymed with 'pea' and not with 'peck'.

We start by identifying one among the many things called imagination. We call this one recreative imagination. It involves the having of states that are not beliefs, desires, or perceptions but are like them in various ways. Chapter 1 focuses on the similarities and differences between beliefs and what we call belief-like imaginings; we resist the temptation to say that belief-like imagining is a kind of belief. We also argue that there is need for a category of desire-like imaginings. We make a distinction between the character and the content of imagining; this will be important throughout.

Chapter 2 looks at various phenomena that might, or might not, be kinds of recreative imagining. Imagery, in its various forms, is, and so are fantasy and supposition. Supposition is an interesting case, because its nature is clarified by appealing to the idea of desire-like imaginings introduced in Chapter 1. But pretending isn't imagining; we have to wait until Chapter 6 before we get a better idea of the relations between pretence and imagination. Imagining is not a species of introspection, though imagination can have inner states as its object. And a capacity for imagination is no sign that one has a theory about, or special awareness of, one's own inner life.

Belief-like imaginings sound like the 'pretend beliefs' of simulation theory. So they are. But what, exactly, does simulation theory claim? In Chapter 3 we discuss some prominent claims made by simulation theorists, and try to place the theory in a broader context. Simulation has been contrasted with theory; how far is the contrast a real one? We look at two claims. One is that simulation depends on theory; we agree with this and, in doing so, disagree with Robert Gordon. Another claim is that simulation just is theory; we disagree with this one. We say that some simulation is theory, and some isn't.

In Chapter 4 we turn serious attention to mental imagery. For most of this chapter we recount the facts: ways that imagery in various modes—particularly visual and motor imagery—are systematically related to their perceptual counterparts. This helps to make out the claim of Part I that these forms of imagining are genuinely perception-like; it will also help with the argument of Chapter 5, which turns on some differences between imagining in its propositional and perceptual forms. But is motor imagery really much like visual imagery? Is motor imagery a form of perceptual imagery at all? We argue that it is.

We are now ready to tackle the question 'Is there a fundamental difference between propositional forms of imagination and perceptual forms?' We say there is, and that it depends on the idea of *cognitive conservation*. We argue that both kinds of imagining are important for explaining our mentalizing skills. We conclude by tackling another problem: if imagery is perception-like, it should be like perception in matters of content. But, so the argument goes, imagery and perception have fundamentally different kinds of contents. There are more versions of this argument than we can practically deal with; we examine two, and reject them.

Chapter 6 starts a new enterprise: thinking about how imagination develops, and how it might go wrong. We find some complex relationships between imagination and pretence, and speculate on how these different relationships might appear in the different stages of growing up. We ask how pretence and pretending might help us towards a sophisticated concept of belief, and argue that they will not take us all the way.

In Chapter 7 we argue that autism involves a substantial deficit of imaginative capacity. We contrast this view with the metarepresentational theory, against which we offer some objections, and line up beside the executive function theory in the hope that further work might allow a merger of this approach and the imagination-theory. We look at some of the earliest signs of autism, and suggest that they may indicate damage to a system that is more primitive than the recreative imagination.

Delusions are often said to be irrationally false beliefs. Might they be imaginings instead? In Chapter 8 we argue that some may be. We try to show that this hypothesis can explain some puzzling features of delusion, and we draw on work by Chris Frith and others to suggest a mechanism whereby imaginings become delusional. This suggests a new way to think about thought insertion and withdrawal, and about the apparent non-understandability of delusions in schizophrenia.

Our final topic is emotion. We argue that emotion is peculiar in its capacity to cross the boundary into imagination. We suggest that the pleasures, including the pleasant pains, of imagination are dependent on this, and offer an analysis of emotional responses to tragic narratives. We suggest that this involves some complex boundary-crossing: emotions in response to imagined events collide with emotions in response to the real-world narratives that report those imagined events. We end with more speculation, this time on the role of narrative in wickedness.

Part 1

Imagination and its Circle

Chapter 1

PROJECTIONS AND RECREATIONS

"factive attitude"

1.1 TWO WAYS TO THINK

Our thought needs to be constrained by the way things are. We need factive attitudes that reflect the truth. We also need ways to frame our goals, make our plans, and avoid possible disasters turning into actual ones. We can do that by having one kind of factive attitude—belief—and some prefixes—'my goal is...', 'it is possible that...'—to prevent us from confusing the desired or the possible with the actual. So one way to represent goals, plans, and possibilities is to take the attitude of belief towards them all, making sure that we add the prefixes. That way, the distinction between the way things are and the way things might be is reflected in thought at the level of content alone. I believe that P, and I believe that Q is possible; one attitude, two kinds of contents. Prefixing also helps me keep what I believe separate from what (I think) you believe. I believe P and I believe that you believe Q: once again, one attitude, two kinds of content.

We humans have the prefixes, but we also have more than one kind of factive attitude. We can suppose or assume. More generally, we can imagine. That means we have another way to represent goals, possibilities, and the thoughts of others. We can transfer the difference from content to attitude. We are not limited to believing P and believing that Smith believes Q. We can believe P and imagine Q. When we do the latter, we start to put ourselves, in imagination, in Smith's shoes, thinking as Smith thinks, confronting the world as Smith confronts it.[1]

We have two ways of representing the difference: a *content-based* way and an *attitude-based* way. The content-based way is clear enough: believing *P* and believing that Smith believes *P* just are different beliefs, though philosophers notoriously disagree about what the differences between beliefs are. What about the attitude-based way? What is the difference between believing *P* and imagining *P*? While there must be a difference, there ought to be a similarity. Assuming *P* is a substitute for believing it, just as visualizing the cat is a substitute, in some not very clear sense, for seeing it. More on imaginative substitutes for perception in a moment. We take assuming to be a kind of imagining, and we distinguish it from other kinds of imagining in terms of, exactly, its relations to belief. Assuming is what we call *belief-like imagining*.

Belief is just one kind of representational state. Perception, in its various modes, represents aspects of the world to me, and it is these days generally accepted that perception is not belief.[2] And beliefs alone are never sufficient for action. To act I need a picture not only of how the world is, but also of how I want it to be: I need desires. If perceptions and desires represent, there ought to be imaginative substitutes for these as well. In imagination I can desire things I don't actually desire, and perceive things I don't actually perceive. So an account of imaginative projection requires us to give an account of a range of states that are imaginative substitutes for beliefs, desires, and perceptions, and possibly for other things as well. That is what we offer in this chapter and the next.

1.2   CREATIVE AND RECREATIVE IMAGINATION

'Imagining' is used in a variety of ways, and we need to narrow our focus. We are interested in the capacity to put ourselves in the place of another, or in the place of our own future, past, or counterfactual self: seeing, thinking about,

---

[1]   Putting ourselves in another's shoes is usually thought to involve more than simply imagining a proposition. We might need to mirror some more of Smith's beliefs, and perhaps other kinds of attitudes as well. See below, Sect. 1.4. For an extended treatment, see Goldie (2000, ch. 7). Goldie says that empathy involves centrally imagining the other person 'as the narrator' (2000: 178). But while we imagine by narrating, the narrating is usually outside the scope of the imagining. We imagine one who experiences the world, not one who narrates a story about it.

[2]   Jackson (1977) was influential in bringing about this change of view.

and responding to the world as the other sees, thinks about, and responds to it. A great deal of what we call 'imagination' is not concerned with this. Gilbert White said he had too good an opinion of the Romans to 'imagine that they would settle in so barren and dreary a waste [as Wolmer Pond]' (White 1788).[3] White is telling us he would not believe such a thing, and suggesting that such a belief would share salient features with what we would expect from the exercise of imagination: that the gap between belief and reality here displayed would be the result of neglect of reason and evidence.[4]

Since we are interested here in imagination as a capacity quite distinct from belief, we can ignore this 'belief gone wrong' talk. There isn't a distinctive capacity to have beliefs that go wrong; there is a capacity to have beliefs, and that capacity can go wrong. But there are various things we call 'imagination' that are genuinely distinct from belief. One of them is the capacity for perspective-shifting, and that is what we are going to focus on. Let us call the imaginative capacity, whatever it is, that underpins perspective-shifting the *recreative imagination*. What the recreative imagination is, how it works, and what functions it performs are the central questions of this book. Another thing commonly called 'imagination' is important enough to be noted, though we shall put it aside. We see it when someone puts together ideas in a way that defies expectation or convention: the kind of imaginative 'leap' that leads to the creation of something valuable in art, science, or practical life. We will call this the 'creative imagination'.

It is probably true of human beings that their capacity for creative imagining depends in good measure on their capacity for perspective-shifting; if we can place ourselves, in imagination, in situations other than our own, current situation, our capacity to engage with what is merely possible—and hence to make the possible actual—is greatly enhanced. But there is no incoherence in supposing that there can be creative imagination without the support of perspective-shifting. That may be how it is with some of our close relatives. Michael Tomasello has argued that what separates

---

[3] 'That Columbus imagined that he had reached the Indies does not imply that he had any mental images or representations of the Indies' (Hacker 1990: 399). We agree with Hacker that imagining need not involve imagery, but Hacker's example is not, we claim, a case of imagining without imagery, because it is not a case of imagining.

[4] Francis Sparshott says that 'interpretations of events, if reached by bizarre patterns of inference, may be attributed to imagination' (Sparshott 1990: 4).

humans from the other apes is not our capacity for creativity—the capacity to do things in a new way—for other apes have this capacity at least to some degree.[5] Rather, it is our capacity for imitative learning—learning by seeing another's goal, seeing how the other attains the goal, and acquiring from this the capacity to attain the same goal in the same way. Imitative learning enables us to fix innovative practices in the population—to ratchet up from a lower level of technology to a higher one. And it depends, according to Tomasello, on the capacity to 'step into the shoes', in imagination, of a conspecific; to see both the point of what he or she is doing and mentally to rehearse the motor programmes that enable it to be done. In our terms, his point is that apes are capable of creative imagination (to some degree) but not of recreative imagination. They can innovate, but the innovation is not spread to others via imaginative projection. This may or may not be true, but it seems to be a coherent idea; there could be creatures that have plenty of creative imagination, and little or no recreative imagination.[6] The criterion for being creatively imaginative is that you get certain kinds of things done—you make innovations—and it is not essential that you do this in a certain way, namely by using recreative imagination, though it is probable that this is in fact how a lot of human innovation gets done.

There may be some simplification in this. There could be creatures that seem to have creative imagination but really do not; creatures who, if we knew more about how they were constructed, would not count as displaying creative imagination. Consider Ned Block's Blockhead. The Blockhead deals with its current situation by accessing a vast database, which assigns to every possible circumstance an appropriate response (Block 1981). Since Blockhead's responses are just like our own, it may well answer a question in a way we would initially be inclined to say was creatively imaginative. But when we look inside Blockhead and see the uncreative ways it produces its responses, we may well conclude that its way of doing things simply precludes attributions of creative imagination. So inner process seems to

[5]   See Tomasello (2000, esp. ch. 1).

[6]   Suppose that imagination first emerged in the hominid line as a planning tool. Suppose the next stage is to Tomasello's imagining-for-learning. The shift here is to imagine oneself doing not what one plans to do, but what one sees someone else doing. That takes us the crucial distance to 'stepping into another's shoes'. The third stage is where we step into the other's shoes not in order to do what they do, but to find out why they are doing it, or to predict what they are likely to do next. By now we are into familiar territory—imagination as a mind-reading tool (see below, Ch. 3).

have *something* to do with our judgements about what counts as displaying creative imagination. All we want to insist on here is that getting things done by using recreative imagination is not definitive or even criterial for displaying creative imagination. And certainly much use of the recreative imagination is not also use of the creative imagination. People have said that strong mental imagery is no proof that the subject is imaginative—a point we can now put by saying that someone could possess at least one element of the recreative imagination, and yet lack creative imagination.

Hume called the creative imagination 'magical' and 'inexplicable' (see Hume 1902: 24).[7] Certainly, the recreative imagination is more amenable to description and analysis. Unless there is indication to the contrary, the recreative imagination is what we mean by 'imagination' hereafter.

1.3   IMAGININGS AND THEIR COUNTERPARTS

So what is the recreative imagination? Here is our central hypothesis. Imaginative projection involves the capacity to have, and in good measure to control the having of, states that are not perceptions or beliefs or decisions or experiences of movements of one's body, but which are in various ways like those states—like them in ways that enable the states possessed through imagination to mimic and, relative to certain purposes, to substitute for perceptions, beliefs, decisions, and experiences of movements. These are what we are calling states of recreative imagination.[8] Visual imagery, for example, seems to be like visual experience in important ways; we naturally describe its content in terms appropriated from the description of things seen, and many distinctively visual aspects of information processing can be shown to be reproduced in imagery. Auditory imagery stands similarly to hearing things, tactile imagery to touching things, and motor imagery to the experience of moving one's body. Imaginings of these kinds may be called perception-like imaginings. In general, when a form of recreative imagining is X-like, we say that it has state X as its *counterpart*.[9] We shall also

---

[7] On creativity, see Boden (1992), and the well-aimed criticisms in Novitz (1999).

[8] In thinking about this we are indebted to the work of Malcolm Budd, especially his (1989). See also Wollheim (1973a) and Scruton (1974, esp. 104).

[9] 'Counterpart' is Budd's term. See his (1989: 100). Goldman speaks of 'mental facsimiles' which 'share [properties] with their natural counterparts' (2000: 191).

say that vision-like imagining has a visual *character*, that hearing-like imagining has an auditory character, and so on. It will be important to distinguish between the content of a piece of imagining—what it is you are imagining—and the character of that imagining. Imaginings with a visual character need not have vision as part of their contents: their contents need not be such that specification of that content requires deployment of the concept *vision*.[10]

In later chapters we shall say more about mental imagery, or perceptual imaginings. Here we focus on imaginings that have beliefs and desires as their counterparts: *propositional imaginings* will be our generic name for them. Beliefs first. What is sometimes called *imagining-that* is belief-like imagining. An important feature of beliefs is their occupation of characteristic inferential roles; believing something tends to lead to believing other things, depending on what else you already believe. Imagining that you are famous is belief-like partly because it mirrors the inferential role of the belief that you are.[11] There is nothing new in this suggestion. Philosophers interested in belief dynamics assume that imagining is belief-like in this respect when they offer the Ramsey test as a way of deciding whether you should accept a conditional. According to the Ramsey test,

> given an overall state of belief G, you should accept the conditional 'If P then Q' if you should accept Q in the overall state G^*P,

where G^*P is the belief state that results from revising G in the light of P.[12] How do I apply the Ramsey test? If I could add P to my beliefs and settle into a new overall state of belief, I could then just see whether Q seemed reasonable or not. But I can't add to the stock of my beliefs at will. Anyway, I do not wish to take on beliefs irrespective of their truth values just in order to evaluate conditionals. The idea is that instead of adding P as a belief I can add it 'in imagination', and since imagination preserves the inferential patterns of

---

[10]   Apologies to Kaplan for lifting his terminology; our sense of 'character' is different from his. Our distinction between content and character is distinct from, though related to, Millikan's distinction between content and vehicle. Millikan identifies a mistake she calls *content externalizing* 'whereby properties of the vehicle . . . are taken . . . to show up in the . . . content' (Millikan 1993: 258).

[11]   In her account of what she has called 'replication' and now prefers to call 'co-cognition', Jane Heal places much emphasis on the capacity for imagination to preserve the inferential role of belief. See her (1998).

[12]   But the test may not be Ramsey's own. Also, it does not seem to work for certain kinds of conditionals (see Edgington 1995; and below, Ch. 2). For Ramsey's own exposition, see Ramsey (1950); see also Stalnaker (1991: 33).

belief, I can then see whether a new imagining, Q, emerges as reasonable in light of this. If it does, I have reason to think that adding P to the stock of my beliefs would lead me to add Q as well, and so I can add the conditional 'If P then Q' to my beliefs.[13]

It might be objected that we have confused imagining with supposing, for what we do when we assess the truth value of a conditional is to take on the antecedent as a supposition. This is no confusion on our part. In Chapter 2 we shall argue that supposing is (a special kind of) belief-like imagining.

That this kind of imagining is inferentially like belief is further supported by what we know about our imaginative engagements with fiction, backed up by some things that psychologists have recently discovered. If you imagine the novel's hero in London one day and in Chicago the next, you will also imagine that she flew there, unless there is some strong indication in the work that she got there by another means. As readers, we let our imaginings mingle with our beliefs, and further imaginings emerge that, so far as their contents go, are identical with what would emerge from the operation of inference on belief alone. Sometimes fictions defeat our attempts to fill them out via the commingling of imaginings and beliefs; if a story set in 1800 has the character on one side of the Atlantic one day and on the other side the next, I may decide that this is just error on the author's part. My beliefs, together with the kinds of imaginings I think the work entitles me to, don't get me to a plausible scenario. But where interpretation works at all, it works by mixing up beliefs and imaginings and seeing what results.[14] It is this capacity of imaginings to mirror the inferential patterns of belief that makes fictional storytelling possible. If imaginings were not inferentially commensurate with beliefs, we could not draw on our beliefs to fill out what the story tells us, and storytellers would have to give us all the detail explicitly. And that is more than they could ever give, and more than we could stand to hear.

This helps with the problem of truth in fiction. David Lewis once remarked that inferences undertaken by consumers of fictions are peculiar (Lewis 1983: 263–4).[15] Take the inference

---

[13] See Goldman (1993: 192).

[14] There are occasions where we read that the character in 1800 crossed the Atlantic in hours, and are not confused about what to imagine. That's because we have come across some indication in the work that, say, magical modes of transport are available, and we have imagined that as well.

[15] See also below, p. 125.

It is fictional that Sherlock Holmes is human.
All humans are mortal.
So,
It is fictional that Holmes is mortal.

This is an inference in which the conclusion is governed by the intensional operator *It is fictional that*, but where only some of the premisses are so governed. It is not clear that this is in fact the inference we undertake. Rather, the reader's inference might be something like this:

Holmes is human. (Something she imagines.)
All humans are mortal. (Something she believes.)
So,
Holmes is mortal. (Something she imagines.)

Here the inference is perfectly conventional; what is notable about it is the commingling of attitudes—belief and imagination—that it involves. And the general principle that governs the making of such inferences is that, where an inference is from premisses at least one of which is an imagining, the conclusion will be an imagining as well.[16]

Recent work in child psychology has shown that the preservation of inference in imagination emerges early; it is not likely that children first engage in imaginings that are not inferentially constrained and then learn somehow to constrain them. Very young children will spontaneously imagine that an animal is wet if they know that it is part of a pretend game that the animal has had water poured over it, though the animal is in fact dry (since the upended cup was in fact empty) and no one has mentioned the idea of it being wet.[17] It looks as if the child's imagining that the animal had water poured over it mingles with her beliefs about

---

[16] François Recanati makes a similar point about inferences concerning what someone else believes (2000: 334). But in Recanati-type cases, the conclusion and all the premisses lie within the scope of an intentional operator.

[17] See Leslie (1988). Paul Harris and Robert Kavanhaugh found that children from 24 months reliably showed this kind of competence. It was more difficult to elicit it from younger children, but even children around 21 months, when they responded at all, tended to show that they understood which of several animals was wet (Harris and Kavanaugh 1993).

water-pouring situations and leads, belief-like, to the imagining that the animal is wet.[18]

There are other ways that imagination can be like belief. Reasoning can be practical as well as theoretical, and you can undertake a piece of practical reasoning based on what you imagine rather than on what you believe; the result will be a decision, in imagination, to do something. Imagining something can also have consequences for emotion and affect that are very like the emotional and affective consequences of believing it; when we read stories or watch movies and are imaginatively involved with their events, we often experience emotions that are both powerful and apparently continuous with those we experience in response to situations in real life.[19] Fully to understand the mechanisms underlying imaginative practical reasoning and emotion generation, we need the concept of desire-like imagining, and we shall introduce that idea in Section 1.4 below.

All this concerns ways in which belief-like imagining is like belief. But belief-like imagining must differ from belief in various ways, otherwise it is not anything different from belief. And it does differ. One way is that imaginings are doings and believings are not; we discuss this in the next chapter, and make good use of it in Chapter 8. Another way is that beliefs are constrained in various ways in which imaginings are not. It is said that beliefs have to form a rational system in that they must form an internally rational whole, are justified by the perceptual states that lead to them, and justify or rationalize the actions to which they lead. Such constraints can be over-stated: few want to insist that there can never be tensions between one's beliefs; that beliefs are never held in opposition to the evidence; that actions are always rational. But the more a putative belief presses against these constraints, the less confident we should be in attributing it. And beyond some vague boundary, we seem no longer to be talking about belief at all. That is why the various kinds of delusional beliefs that people are sometimes said to possess—that thoughts are being inserted into their heads, that alien

---

[18] Harris says that players of imaginative games engage in ' "looting" of reality to furnish the make believe world ... Pretend events are essentially self-contained; they are not set up as departures from actual events' (2000: 124). But looters choose what to take with them; we say that the decisions of game-players focus almost exclusively on what to leave out. A great deal of reality is inevitably left in.

[19] See below, Sect. 9.3.

forces control their bodies, that loved ones have been replaced by strangers of similar appearance—pose real problems for anyone who takes these constraints seriously.[20] And people who are not suffering from independently identifiable psychopathologies do at least acknowledge that inconsistency in belief is a problem, though they may shelve the problem posed by a known inconsistency because there are more urgent matters to confront or because no obvious solution presents itself. Imaginings are not similarly constrained. We are happy to attribute to someone the imagining that P despite the fact that she never had any perceptual experience that would justify her believing that P; never engaged in any action that would be appropriate if P were true; and possessed many beliefs that contradict P. And we do not expect her to treat the inconsistency between what she imagines and what she believes as a problem she ought to face up to at some stage.

How is this compatible with there being an inferential fit between belief and imagination? Imaginings have limited—usually very limited—duration. When we imagine P, the tendency is for any belief that contradicts P, or which stands in substantial probabilistic tension with P, to fall into the background for the duration and purposes of the imagining. The imagining then combines inferentially with those relevant beliefs that don't contradict or stand in tension with it. When we stop imagining P, our beliefs, including those that were backgrounded by the imagining, are still available for theoretical and practical reasoning. Beliefs are supposed to obey the constraints of inferential rationality long-term and globally; ideally, all our beliefs are always consistent. The most we ask of imaginings is that they carve out a consistent subset of our beliefs with which to connect in the short term. Also, and importantly, imagination does not have the motivating force of belief; we do not act on our imaginings as we act on our beliefs—which is just as well.[21]

That our imaginings need not be consistent with anything other than a small subset of our beliefs explains why we can't assimilate imagining to belief. The attractions of assimilation are summed up in the following response to what we have said so far. 'You have said that belief-like imagining is like belief in some ways and unlike it in others. But you assume

---

[20] See below, Sect. 8.1.   [21] But see below, Ch. 6, especially comments on Velleman.

there is a single conception of belief, and there isn't. One conception is the neo-behaviourist one: whether you believe that *P* is a matter of whether you are disposed to act in a way that is appropriate, given that *P* is true (Mellor 1978; Stalnaker 1984). We can agree that imagining is not believing in that sense. But there are other accounts of belief. L. Jonathan Cohen (1989), for example, says that the belief that *P* is the disposition to feel it true that *P*, and you can have that disposition without being apt to satisfy your desires in worlds where *P* is true. Perhaps these different accounts of belief are not rivals; perhaps they identify different points on a belief spectrum. In that case there is a broad concept of belief that would cover belief as neo-behaviourists understand it, as well as various less demanding conceptions (Morton 1980; Railton 1997). And perhaps we can locate imagining somewhere along this spectrum.

We can't, for the following reason. We can take a liberal view of what counts as a belief, including as beliefs a variety of states which do not meet any version of the neo-behaviourist condition. But belief, however weakly characterized, is normative in that an agent who has contradictory beliefs (in any sense of 'belief') is in a less than ideal epistemic situation. It is no defect in an agent's epistemic condition that she imagines things contrary to what she believes. An otherwise consistent and coherent believer who imagines that Desdemona is murdered while believing that there is no such person is not in any way failing to meet constraints of epistemic virtue. While imagining-that is like belief in various ways, it is not to be classed with beliefs, however weak a sense of belief we opt for.

Don't confuse the false view that imagination lies on a continuum of belief states with the true view that imagination lies on a continuum—or, better, shares a multidimensional space—with belief. The space that beliefs and imaginings both lie in is a space of states which are functional kinds. Beliefs of the kind on which we have been focusing have certain character-istic relations to perception, desire, decision, action, and other states. There may be other kinds of beliefs, with different functional characteristics; perhaps together all these belief states form a vaguely bounded irregular solid within the space. And there might be another irregular solid which includes the states of belief-like imagining that correspond to each of these belief states. At various places these two solids may come very close together. But they do not intersect.

Perhaps there are other reasons why imaginings are not beliefs. The strength of the argument from normativity given above can be brought out by contrasting it with an argument that doesn't work. Beliefs, or at least reasonable beliefs, are context-independent. But imaginings are highly context-dependent; what I imagine relative to one context is quite different from what I imagine relative to another. This argument apes one due to Michael Bratman (1992): acceptance is not belief, because what you accept varies between contexts. The argument is inconclusive; to accept P might be simply (i) to believe P and (ii) to have one's belief that P play a certain role in a given piece of reasoning. And a belief that plays this role in one piece of reasoning need not play that role in another. That way, acceptances could be beliefs, even though acceptance is context-dependent. After all, conscious belief is context-dependent—one consciously believes something in one context and not in another—but conscious belief is belief. *Being an A* can be context-free, while *being an A that is also a B* is context-bound. Imaginings might then similarly be beliefs—beliefs that have characteristics over and above those definitive of beliefs and which make them count as imaginings in some contexts and not in others. The argument from normativity given above blocks this line of thought applied to imagination and belief; if imaginings were beliefs-that-also-occupy-imagination-defining-roles, then in order to imagine things contrary to what one believes, one would have to have contradictory beliefs.

If imaginings are not beliefs but are like beliefs in various ways, should we think of them as cousins, neither much beholden to the other? No. Imaginings are in various ways dependent on beliefs. One kind of dependency concerns content. We tend to think of the contents of imaginings as problematic because of their reference to non-existents; we have imaginings about Sherlock Holmes, Excalibur, Tara, and suchlike fictional things.[22] But beliefs can be about non-existents as well—or rather, we need as intelligible a substitute for the nonsensical 'Belief B is about the non-existent X' as we do for 'Imagining I is about . . .'. The problem of fictional entities establishes no asymmetry between beliefs and imaginings. Now one can imagine that Holmes drinks water, that Excalibur is made of aluminium, that Tara is in London. And imagining these things is different from imagining that

---

[22] For an approach to the semantics of non-existence, see Currie (1990).

Holmes drinks twater, that Excalibur is made of twin-aluminium, and so on. What makes them different? When we answer this question for the case of belief we tend to emphasize facts about the source of the belief and the interactions with the environment to which it leads. By contrast, imaginings look as if they might well lack the epistemic and action-inducing relations that would settle matters of reference.[23] Are we to make do with some kind of 'narrow content' for imaginings? If that were so, there would be a worrying difference between beliefs and imaginings: they could not have the same kinds of contents. We say it isn't so. Imaginings can have wide content, which they inherit from the wide content of beliefs. My imagining is that Holmes drinks water rather than twater because I have the right kind of water-beliefs and do not have the right kinds of twater-beliefs.[24] In general, imaginings are too weak, semantically, to stand up on their own; they need the support of beliefs, with their strong, reference-inducing relations to the world.[25]

The dependence of imaginings on other kinds of mental states should remind us not to expect too much by way of definition of imaginative states. Definitions of belief, desire, and perception have been hard to come by; none of those on offer seem to us secure enough to provide a basis for defining the states that are parasitic on them. Still, unless we are very troubled philosophically, most of us understand well enough what beliefs, desires, and perceptions are. If we understand these things, it should not be too much to ask us to understand their imaginative counterparts.

I.4   IMAGINATION AND DESIRE

We have seen that imagination can be belief-like in respect of inferential role: imagining that *P* leads to new imaginings in the way that believing *P* would lead to new beliefs. Beliefs also enter into practical inferences, where they combine with desires to produce decisions. Imaginative projections can, as we noted earlier, involve the recreation of practical inference: we imagine

---

[23] We will argue later that imaginings need not lack all motivating force.

[24] Or, if I have beliefs of both kinds, the issue is decided by facts about which kinds of beliefs entered into my imaginative project at the appropriate point.

[25] For more on externalism about imaginings, this time in connection with visual imagining, see Abell and Currie (1999).

ourselves in this situation and then, in imagination, we decide to do something. And we may conclude from this that that *is* what we would do in that situation. So it looks as if our list of the forms of recreative imagining is incomplete. Projection can involve more than just a shift of belief; sometimes I need to shift my desires as well, because in the imagined situation I would desire something I don't actually desire. This can't involve *really* taking on a new desire, because desires have connections to actions; if imagining led me to have desires appropriate to a merely imagined situation, I might end up acting inappropriately. The shift of desire must itself be a shift in imagination. There must be desire-like imaginings, as well as belief-like ones.

Postulating desire-like imaginings helps explain the affective consequences of imagination. Sometimes emotional responses are dependent on belief states: I feel envious because of what I believe about your success, and I would feel no envy without those beliefs or beliefs relevantly like them. And my emotional reaction to a fictional situation depends similarly on my belief-like imaginings: Desdemona's death affects me in the way it does partly because I imagine that it is the outcome of a wicked design. But where emotions depend on beliefs, they depend on desires as well; if I didn't desire your success or success relevantly like it, I would not be envious. And so it must be with emotions that depend on belief-like imaginings; to be genuinely belief-like, these imaginings ought to have emotional consequences only in conjunction with states that are desire-like. The phenomenology of spectatorship supports this. Our emotional response to the death of Desdemona is very different from our reaction to the death of Macbeth, a disparity it seems natural to explain in terms of differences of desire: we say that we *want* Macbeth to suffer, and Desdemona to be saved. These are not really desires; they are desire-like imaginings. Desires, like beliefs, face normative constraints, and the constraints on real desire do not govern what we call 'wanting Desdemona to be saved'. Desires can be shown to be unreasonable, or at least unjustified, if they fail to connect in various ways with the facts; the reasonableness of my desiring punishment for someone depends on the facts about what they did. But the reasonableness of my (as we say) wanting punishment for Macbeth—compared to the unreasonableness of wanting punishment for Desdemona—is not undercut by the fact that there is no such person as Macbeth. Desire-like imaginings are constrained, but in different ways. My desire-like imaginings about Macbeth are rationally answerable to facts about what, according to Shakespeare's story, Macbeth did.

It might be replied that the theatregoer's state *is* accounted for in terms of a real desire she has; it's just that we misdescribe it when we say she desires that Othello not kill Desdemona. We should say rather that she has the perfectly respectable real desire that, *in this fiction*, Desdemona not be murdered. Desiring that, in this fiction, someone not be murdered is a real desire, but it is not the desire that someone not be murdered, because *in this fiction* is a propositional operator that behaves like *believes*, or *possibly*. Desiring that *S* believes that *P*, or that possibly *P*, is not desiring *P*, and neither is desiring that, in the fiction, *P*.

This is not a very useful proposal unless it generalizes to other kinds of cases of imaginative projection, as when I shift my perspective in imagination from mine to yours because I want to figure out what you will do. Perhaps those cases can be thought of as involving a little fiction of my own construction, a fiction in which I am in your situation, and which I desire to turn out in a certain way. As we shall see, the proposal won't work even for *Othello*-type cases, so we need not ask whether the generalization really is possible.

One problem with the proposal is that it obscures the distinction between attitudes towards characters, like Desdemona, and attitudes towards fictions, like *Othello*. On the proposal, everything that has the appearance of being a desire-like state concerning fictional characters turns out to be a real desire concerning the fictional narratives that describe them. This would make it difficult to understand the ways we react emotionally to fictional situations. When I am sorry and upset about the fate of Desdemona, I am not sorry that this fiction has it that an innocent and good-hearted girl suffers a cruel fate. One might be sorry about that, deploring that there are fictions with such unhappy outcomes. This is not what at least many of us are sorry about; we are glad that Shakespeare's fiction has it this way, and not the way that a rewritten version with a happy ending would have it. Part of the inner tension one experiences on watching the play derives from the fact that we experience a desire-like imagining that Desdemona flourish, combined with a (genuine) desire that the play be one which will ensure that that desire-like imagining is unsatisfied. In that case desire-like imaginings do not seem to be dispensable, even in those contexts where dispensing with them seems most likely to work, namely where there is an independently acknowledged fiction to appeal to.[26]

Another proposal for doing without desire-like imaginings is this: there is one unified state of imagining, and what we are calling 'belief-like imaginings' and 'desire-like imaginings' are accounted for by saying that in the one case we imagine that we believe something, and in the other we imagine that we desire it. That way we get by with three categories—belief, desire, and a *sui generis* imagining—instead of four—belief, desire, belief-like imagining, and desire-like imagining. The difference between our proposal and this new one is that, on our proposal, I imaginatively project into the situation of one who believes P and desires Q when I have the belief-like imagining that P and the desire-like imagining that Q. On the new proposal what I do is imagine (in some generic way) that

I believe P and desire Q.[27]

This proposal makes all imagining self-imagining, imagining in which one deploys a concept of the self, as well as such psychological concepts as belief and desire. But imagining that there is beer in the fridge surely does not require me to deploy psychological concepts. Also, I ought to be able to imagine that Smith will win the election even though no one believes he will. If this means imagining that 'I believe that Smith will win the election even though no one believes he will'. I am required to imagine something contradictory.[28] Perhaps it is possible to imagine contradictory things, even explicitly contradictory things like this one. But imagining that Smith will win the election even though no one believes he will does not seem to involve imagining anything contradictory, and we should be suspicious of a theory that says it does.

The proposal just rejected confuses content and character. My imagining P has a belief-like character, but belief is no part of its content. And having

---

[26] Notice also that theatregoers often know how the play is going to end; desiring that it not end that way would then seem to involve a sense of hopelessness at odds with the very real tension one feels concerning the outcome. On this issue, see Walton (1990: 263–7).

[27] David Velleman says that the child who imagines being an elephant seeking a drink imagines his thought 'here is a pail of water' to be a belief (2000: 259).

[28] Thanks to Martin Davies for the example.

the desire-like imagining that Q is an imagining with content Q, not with content I desire-Q.

Desire-like imaginings don't seem to figure much in folk-psychological thought and talk about the imagination. If I ask you to imagine so-and-so, you are unlikely to complain that my request is ambiguous between the request that you come up with an imagining that is belief-like and the request that you come up with an imagining that is desire-like. Should this make us suspicious that the latter category is just a theoretician's artefact with no psychological reality? Not at all. When people get down to detail about their imaginings, especially in response to fictions, talk of desire-like states starts to emerge; we say that we wanted Othello to believe in Desdemona's innocence. We've argued that attempts to explain such statements as referring to genuine desires won't work; they have to be understood as referring to desire-like imaginings.

One reason why desire-like imaginings don't figure prominently in our folk theory of imagination is this. When storytellers invite us to imagine things, they generally concentrate on shaping our belief-like imaginings, leaving our desire-like imaginings to follow their natural course. Thus storytellers make it explicit that Desdemona is innocent, that Oliver wants more, that Peter Pan kicks Hook over the side of the ship. These are not things we could be counted on to imagine simply by following our own inclinations; storytellers have to make it clear that these are the things they want us to imagine. On the other hand, they generally don't tell us what kind of desire-like imaginings to have concerning these events; they assume that we will desire in imagination much as we do in real life. For it is harder, much harder, to get people to desire in imagination against the trend of their own real desires than it is to get people to believe in imagination against the trend of what they really believe. So storytelling makes belief-like imagining very salient, and desire-like imagining not very salient. This will be important in the next chapter. In the final chapter we shall have a lot more to say about the tension between my desire-like imagining that Desdemona be saved and my (real) desire that, according to the story, she should suffer a cruel fate.

Chapter 2

FAMILY AND FRIENDS

Chapter 1 introduced the recreative imagination, focusing on cases which are belief- or desire-like. We indicated that the forms of mental imagery should also be included. Is that right? If mental imagery is a form of imagination, should it be described as our imagining seeing or hearing things? And what of pretence, supposition, and fantasy, which have close but so far unclarified relations to imagining: are they also forms of imagining? This chapter answers these questions.

2.1   IS IMAGERY A KIND OF IMAGINATION?

We have said that mental imagery is a kind of recreative imagination. In this respect we agree with the tradition of Aristotle, Hume, and Kant, which placed so much emphasis on imagery. It is also traditional to think of mental images—visual ones, at least—as involving mental pictures. Largely because of the work of Wittgenstein, Ryle, and Sartre, the idea that having a mental image of a mountain is really a matter of seeing a mental picture of a mountain is now universally rejected. But attacks on the traditional view of mental imagery have gone beyond scepticism about mental pictures; some authors claim that imagery is not a kind of imagination at all.[1] We consider four arguments in favour of this conclusion, and reject them all.

The first argument is this:

---

[1] A. White (1990) is an energetic and economical assault on imagery as imagining as well as on the picture theory of imagery. An engaging source for the history is Warnock (1976).

Imagery occurs in dreams, memory, expectation, wishing, illusion and hallucination: all cases where the subject has minimal or no control over the imagery. But imagination is under voluntary control. (A. White 1990: 91)

We all agree that imagery is sometimes under voluntary control. We should all agree that imagination is sometimes not under voluntary control; you can find yourself imagining things you very much don't want to imagine, and be surprised to find that you are imagining something you were previously unaware of imagining (Budd 1989, ch. 5). Perhaps the supposed difference between imagination and imagery is that all cases of imagination could have been under voluntary control, while some cases of imagery, namely the cases of it that occur in dreams, illusions, etc., could not have been under voluntary control. There is a sense in which imagery, as it occurs in dreams and illusions, is not under voluntary control. It does not follow that an image occurring in a dream or an illusion could not have occurred in some other context where it was under voluntary control. And the same can be said about imagination. It is true that there are episodes of imagining that are not under voluntary control. It does not follow that an involuntary episode of imagining could not have occurred in some other context where it would have been voluntary.

   A slightly different argument is this.

While my imagining may, on any particular occasion, be something beyond my control, imagining is always something that I do; imagining something involuntarily is not like having a pain. But having a mental image is not—at least not always—something that I do. (A. White 1990: 91)

Let us agree that imaginings are doings. As the objector notes, they are not always doings that one is able to control, as when one cannot help imagining something unpleasant. We see no reason to think that it is different with imagery. There is a sense in which imagery 'can come and go independently of one' (A. White 1990: 91),[2] but this is just the sense in which unwelcome imaginings can come and go independently of one. The contrast between imagining something and having a pain seems also to hold between having an image and having a pain. We have been given no reason for thinking that imagery is not imagining.[3]

---

[2] The argument we are considering here seems to be one that White endorses, though this is not entirely clear from his exposition.
[3] See also the beginning of Ch. 8.

It may be replied that images have features which indicate that their coming and going is less dependent on the self than is the coming and going of imaginings. For example,

imagery has an objectivity and independence; we can scrutinize our images, which often have unexpected features. But 'One can't be surprised by the features of what one imagines, since one put them there' (A. White 1990: 91).[4]

We can be surprised by features of what we imagine. I can imagine a scheme for murdering someone and then be surprised to discover a flaw in it, and a playwright can be surprised by the richness of her own imaginative construction. I can be surprised when it is pointed out that I was imagining Sherlock Holmes to have a full set of teeth, when I was not conscious of doing so and certainly was not forming an image of them. There may well be potentially surprising features of images that are not potentially surprising features of belief- or desire-like imaginings. That is to be expected on the assumption that these are imaginings of different kinds. Once again there is no reason here for thinking that imagery is not a kind of imagining.

Finally,

imagery is particular and determinate, while imagining can be general and indeterminate. (A. White 1990: 92)

Images are usually indeterminate in some way, as my image of a tiger ascribes to it an indeterminate number of stripes (Lyons 1984). What of particularity versus generality? The claim that imagery is a kind of imagining is, more specifically, the claim that imagery has perception as its counterpart; it is a kind of imagining which apes certain identifying features of perceptual experience. Perceptual experience is always of the particular rather than the general. So we would expect that perceptual imagining would always be particular also. The right conclusion here seems to be that there are kinds of imaginings that are always particular, and kinds of imaginings that are not. Visualizing is one of the former kinds.

If these thoughts are sound, the idea that visualizing is imagining is at least unrefuted. We don't say that we have established that imagery is imagining. The best way to do that is to show that there is explanatory mileage to be gained by putting imagery in the same general category as

---

[4] See also Sartre (1940: 7–8).

phenomena widely agreed to be instances of imagining. We shall attend to that in Chapters 4 and 5. But the question whether imagery is imagination needs to be distinguished from another question: 'Is visual imagery imagining seeing?' (Comparable questions arise, of course, for auditory, tactile, and other forms of sensory imagery.) We turn to that question right now.

2.2   IMAGERY AND IMAGINING SEEING

Our answer to the question 'Is visual imagery imagining seeing?' depends, unsurprisingly, on what we mean by 'imagining seeing'. If it means imagining *that* I am seeing, the answer is no. To think otherwise is to confuse imagery's having a perceptual character (which it does) with imagery's having perception as its content (which it need not). If I have a visual image of a mountain, then the content of my imagining (assuming that imagery is a form of imagination) is the mountain or, if we want to make all contents propositional, there being a mountain somewhere. The concept of perception need play no part in the specification of the content; it must, though, play a part in specifying the character. There is such a thing as imagining that you are seeing something, but it is not imagery; it is the kind of imagining that has as its counterpart believing that you are seeing something. Seeing something and believing that you are seeing something are different things. Since imagery has the first as its counterpart, and imagining that you are seeing something has the second, imagery and imagining that you are seeing something cannot be the same.

'Imagining seeing' might simply be used in a way equivalent to 'visualizing'.[5] That usage is common enough, but it invites confusion. One tends to hear 'imagining seeing *P*' as 'imagining (seeing *P*)', and that takes us back to the false view that seeing always belongs to the content of the imagining. Where 'imagining seeing' refers to visualizing, it needs to be read as 'imagining seeing (*P*)', where 'imagining seeing' names an intentional operator, and 'seeing' modifies 'imagining'. It would be more accurate but less convenient to refer to this operator by means of the expression 'imagining, in a seeing-like way, *P*'. For the same sorts of reasons belief-like imagining shouldn't be

---

[5] Wollheim says that 'to visualize' is equivalent to the 'standard' sense of 'to imagine seeing' (Wollheim 1973*a*: 55).

thought of as imagining believing something, and would most accurately be called 'imagining, in a belief-like way, *P*'.

So we say that visualizing is not, in general, imagining seeing, in any sense of 'imagining seeing' according to which seeing is part of the content of what one imagines. The qualification 'in general' is required because we accept that a case of visualizing could have seeing as part of its content, as would be the case if I visualized you seeing something. What we deny is the automatic inference from '*P* is the content of my visualization' to '*P* involves the concept of seeing'.

That visualizing is imagining seeing has been argued by a number of people.[6] For example, Michael Martin argues that this is required in order to explain how it is that, while sensory imagining has experiential aspects in common with experience, visualizing is not a case of having a visual experience. And we can explain this, Martin says, on the assumption that in visualizing an *F* we represent our seeing an *F*.[7] How could we explain, on this hypothesis, why people are prone to misrecall visualizing as seeing, and in some circumstances will mistake perception for visualization? According to the hypothesis, visualizing an *F* has the representational content, not *F*, but *seeing an F*. Thus the seeing and the visualizing have quite different contents. Why would states with such different contents seem to us to be so similar? Content is just one dimension of similarity; perhaps states could differ in content and be similar in other ways. But the hypothesis offers us no account of what these other similarities might be and how they could, in the face of content-dissimilarity, sustain the overall phenomenological similarity that seeing and visualizing enjoy. On our hypothesis, however, this is much more easily explained: the seeing and the visualizing have the same contents; the visualizing, moreover, has a visual character. We need invoke no more than this to explain our intuition that seeing and visualizing are similar, and the facts about our limited capacity to discriminate between them.

So far we have assumed that visually imagining something is always a matter of having a visual mental image of, or visualizing, that thing. What of, say, filmic imagining? Watching a fiction film, I imagine various things, though I am doing no visualizing, or, if I am, this is irrelevant to the kind of

---

[6] See e.g. Peacocke (1985); O'Shaughnessy (2000, esp. 342).

[7] See Martin (forthcoming, esp. 30 of the widely circulated typescript).

imagining that the film authorizes.[8] Yet there surely is a sense in which I am imagining seeing the characters. We need to acknowledge another kind of visual imagining: one that is not visualizing but has, nonetheless, a visual character. One way to characterize this kind of imagining is to say that an act of seeing can itself be imaginative; imagination invades the perception itself. On that view, filmic imagining involves this: I see the screen image, and the actors and sets recorded on it. In that very act of seeing I visually imagine the fictional characters and locations of the film's story. Thus my seeing, say, a screen image that represents Olivier on a set is a seeing that has another seeing as counterpart. The seeing it has as counterpart is: seeing Hamlet at Elsinore.[9]

Does this idea contradict the supposed encapsulation of perception: its resistance to any kind of control by rational thought processes? The best evidence is that the encapsulation of vision is limited to early vision, that part of the visual system that generates shape representations and is prior to such aspects of vision as object identification (Pylyshyn 1999). Still, even if object recognition is cognition-dependent, it might be worrying to be told that it is capable of being influenced by *imagination*. Indeed, the familiar sorts of arguments to the effect that the evolution of vision is driven by the need quickly to identify predators and prey suggest that any such story about the influence of imagination is most implausible; creatures *that* imaginative are not likely to do well. Much depends on precisely where we draw the boundary between perception and post-perceptual processing; imagination might be thought of as capable of influencing the conceptual spin we give to perceptual contents.[10] Then we could say that imagining is visual in this sense: that its content is tied closely and systematically to the content of the perception, without being part of the perception itself. My imaginings about Hamlet, the details of his movement and appearance, are explicable by reference to the contents of my perceptions, and the information they convey to me about the details of the appearance and movement of Olivier as he is represented on screen. But the imagining does not penetrate the seeing.

[8] For the idea of fictions authorizing certain imaginings, see Walton (1990). But Walton might not accept the account of visual fictions here offered. See Walton (1997a: 66–7).

[9] See O'Shaughnessy (2000: 347) on 'imaginative perceptions'. But his primary examples of the use of imaginative perceptions are acts of seeing in, as when I see the landscape in the photograph. We don't regard seeing-in as requiring imagination.

[10] While Pylyshyn says that early vision is cognitively impenetrable, he also describes the stages at which cognition is influential as 'post perceptual' (1999: 360).

We can think of the kind of imagining we undertake when our visual system is engaged by the source of the imagining (as with watching film) as either perception-penetrated-by-imagination, or as a non-perceptual form of imagining that is, nonetheless, strongly connected to perception. While the first of these views raises awkward questions about the evolution of vision, we prefer to leave the decision between them open. Nothing we say depends on which answer is correct.

Our distinction between character and content helps avoid a difficulty that arises when we consider visual imaginings in response to certain kinds of story events. It might be crucial to the plot that something portrayed on stage or screen is not seen by anyone, and that is clearly what I am to imagine. If visually imagining these events required me to imagine seeing them myself, I would be obliged to imagine contradictory things: to imagine seeing these things, and to imagine that no one sees them. If we say that what is visual about the imagining is its character and not its content, we avoid imputing to the viewer any imagining about herself, and hence any contradictory imaginings.

This is an advantage for our account only if the problem solved really is a problem. Kendall Walton has suggested that it isn't a problem at all, that there is no difficulty in an account of visual imagining that requires of the viewer that she imagine seeing something that no one sees. He makes essentially two points (Walton 1997a: 65–7). The first is that imagining seeing something and imagining that no one sees it is not the imagining of a contradiction, since it is not in general a rule of fictional imagining that imagining *P* and imagining not-*P* results in imagining *P* and not-*P*. No doubt this is so. The problem we hope to avoid is not the problem posed by attributing imaginings with contradictory contents; it is the problem posed by attributing contradictory imaginings. It just does not seem to us that there is any intuitive reason for thinking that one's imaginings in response to a scene which represents unseen events are imaginings that contradict one another. To see this, contrast two scenes, one from the beginning and one from the end of the film *Citizen Kane*. In the first scene the dying Kane utters the word 'Rosebud' while no one is in the room—the nurse enters immediately he dies. Now this first scene is well known to be problematic, for it requires us to imagine that no one was in the room and also to imagine that someone was, since the mystery of Kane's dying words motivates the journalist's quest that constitutes the rest of the film. Note that the problem here is one of contradictory imaginings and not of imagining a contradiction; we need not suppose that the viewer has to bring together, into one imagining, the thought that no one was there and the thought that someone was. The final scene of the film contrasts with this: the camera pulls back to reveal the word 'Rosebud' on a child's sledge, along with the rest of Kane's possessions. It is important for the story that no one is seeing this, and that in consequence the mystery of Kane's dying utterance remains unsolved. But this scene is not problematic. Not only does it not require of me that I imagine a contradiction (that is true of the first scene as well); it also does not require me to have one imagining that contradicts another; it does not require me to imagine seeing something and to imagine that no one sees it. We do well not to adopt a theory of imagining that makes both these scenes problematic in the same way.

Walton's second point might be thought to address this response. It is that, while the final scene of *Citizen Kane* does involve the need to have contradictory imaginings, we hardly notice this because this is just one example of a whole range of incongruities in fictional representations that we take in our stride. Somehow we accept the fact that Othello produces surpassingly beautiful utterances under the most extreme psychological pressures, that dying heroes in opera burst into song, etc. Again, all this is true; there are plenty of incongruities in fiction that we attend to very little and which, if we were to focus on them, would constitute a pointless distraction from what is worth while in the work. Our claim is just that while these things are incongruities, and are recognized by us as such when we are pressed to see them ('That's opera for you', we might say), there simply *is no incongruity* in watching a scene in a movie which represents the events depicted as not being seen by anyone. We say that a treatment of unseen events in stories should avoid attributing to viewers imaginings that collide with one another *just because the events are unseen*. Our account does that.

2.3 PRETENCE

Ryle said that imagining is pretending. Visualizing a mountain is imagining seeing it, and imagining seeing it is pretending to see it. One virtue Ryle saw in this proposal is that it gets rid of pictures in the head; pretending to see a mountain is no more a case of seeing an imagined mountain than pretending to hit someone is hitting an imagined person (see Ryle 1949).[11] Ryle was right to deny, at least in general, that pretending to do F to A is a matter of doing F to an imagined A, and he was right to deny the same thing of imagining doing F to A. Pretending and imagining are similar in other ways. Pretence is adequately describable only by reference to some counterpart, which is what we have said is characteristic of the recreative imagination; when we say what someone pretends to do, we specify something they might really be doing but are not, at least not intentionally.[12] So pretendings and imaginings are both forms of recreative states, in some broad sense. Ryle also held that imagining, like pretending, is something we do, not something that happens to us. Was he right to say that imagining *is* pretending? Perhaps our choice of words here is not especially important, but using some words or others to make important distinctions surely is, and it seems to us that there are important differences between recreative states that are purely mental and recreative states that are kinds of behaviours. We are proposing, pretty much in line with common usage, to reserve 'imagining' for the first—mental—kind of recreative state and 'pretending' for the second—behavioural—kind of recreative state.

If this distinction is granted us, imaginings and pretendings can be distinguished in further specific ways. For example, pretendings are, in principle, directed towards others, and issues about uptake (actual or potential) are relevant to the success of the pretending. Such issues are not relevant to the success of an imagining. Relatedly, while pretending and imagining are things done, there are differences between them. Pretendings are not basic actions—actions one performs, but not by virtue of performing any other action. One pretends to do something by actually doing something else. But many imaginings are basic actions, and where an imagining is not basic it usually depends on an imagining which is basic, as when I visualize Wellington's face by visualizing Goya's picture of him.[13] When you pretend, deceptively or otherwise, you seem to be doing one thing but are actually doing another. What you seem to do is what you pretend to do, and what you really do is the means to achieving the pretence. So you

---

[11] For problems with Ryle's argument and an attempt to improve it, see Matthews (1969).
[12] Someone might pretend to bid at an auction and, by accident, actually bid.
[13] We are indebted to Jerry Levinson for discussion here.

cannot simply pretend to do something; you pretend to do something *by* doing something else. You pretend to faint by really falling to the floor, and you pretend to be a police officer by doing real things like saying 'I am a police officer'. When you imagine that the moon is made of green cheese or visualize the moon, you do not do this by doing something else that is not itself an imagining. One consequence of this is that imaginings are much more intimately connected with subpersonal processes than pretendings are. With pretending there is always at least one other action that stands between the pretending and the subpersonal level; with imagining, the next step down from imagining is almost always to a subpersonal process.

If imagining and pretending are distinct, how are they related? There can be imagining without pretending, since there can be imagining without overt behaviour. And there can be pretence without imagining; neither an actor nor a deceiver need imagine, though it might help them to do so. With children's play, it is natural to assume a close connection: that a child holding a banana to her ear and speaking into it is pretending to make a telephone call when the behaviour is accompanied, or perhaps driven by, the imagining that this thing, actually a banana, is a telephone. Late in Chapter 6, by which time we will have developed the right conceptual tools, we will try to answer the question whether imaginings can play a motivating role in pretence.

2.4   SUPPOSITION

What is the relationship between imagining and supposing? Is supposing just a kind of recreative imagining, or is it an activity of a different kind? Some say it's different. Tamar Szabó Gendler argues that 'imagination requires a sort of participation that mere hypothetical reasoning does not.... What this suggests is that imagination is distinct from belief on the one hand, and from mere supposition on the other' (Gendler 2000: 80–1). We have no problem, she says, in supposing that female infanticide is good, but we do, many of us, have great difficulty in imagining this, and our experiencing this sort of barrier to imaginative participation in alien moralities explains some of our discomfort with certain kinds of fictions. So imagination differs from supposition in the way that imagination differs from belief. I am resistant to believing a moral proposition if it conflicts with what I already accept, and

I am similarly resistant to believing a non-moral one; belief evinces no asymmetric resistance to moral propositions as opposed to non-moral ones. And I am happy to suppose both the moral proposition and the non-moral one; no asymmetry here either. But there is, according to Gendler, an asymmetry in imagining. So imagining is neither believing nor supposing.

We agree that imagining is not belief; we spent part of Section 1.3 arguing for exactly that. But we say that supposition *is* a form of imagining. The kind of imagining that Gendler is contrasting with supposing, and which is, according to her, resistant to alien moralities, is belief-like imagining. Once we see that there is another kind of imagining that often goes with belief-like imagining—what we have been calling desire-like imagining— we see that there is another possibility, namely, that it is desire-like imagining that is resistant. If that is the case, the grounds for distinguishing belief-like imagining from supposing will collapse.[14]

Do not expect us to argue that imaginative resistance is confined to imaginings that are desire-like. We think there *are* cases where belief-like imagining exhibits resistance. But that is because of its connection with desire-like imagining. We claim that (i) resistance is primarily a characteristic of desire-like imagining and only secondarily, or through its relation to desire-like imagining, a characteristic of belief-like imagining; and (ii) supposing is belief-like imagining that does not stand in the kinds of relations to desire-like imagining that tend to produce resistance.

That imaginative resistance is not exclusively a characteristic of belief-like imagining is indicated by the fact that there are cases of imaginative resistance to fictional points of view even where the truth of an alien morality is not at issue. We are often resistant to taking on, in imagination, the point of view of a wicked character, even when the moral world of the fiction itself is not alien, and where the wicked character does not himself believe that his project is moral; Iago would surely be contemptuous of the idea that his plan to destroy Othello was morally admirable. Our difficulty is just that we cannot easily construct for ourselves imaginative replicas of his wicked desires. Indeed, the asymmetry between belief-like and desire-like imagining here is striking. We tolerate astonishing amounts of cruelty and suffering

[14] Alison Denham treats imagination as supposition (2000: 202–4).

being represented in fictions, and are very willing to imagine that innocent people like Desdemona are murdered for no good reason, as long as we are not asked to take on in imagination the desires of the characters who bring about and delight in that suffering.

Isn't it true, as Gendler says, that we are resistant to imagining alien values when that imagining is belief-like? We agree that this is true, but the reason is that there are important connections between moral beliefs and desires, and similar connections between belief-like and desire-like imaginings. Quite what these connections are is hard to determine; we should not say, for example, that believing that F is good always involves desiring F; one can hold F as valuable and not desire F. We can make out a more plausible connection via the idea of an ideal spectator: someone who is sufficiently rational, well informed about, and disinterested in, the action she surveys for it to be the case that, were she to think a certain outcome to the action morally right, she would desire that outcome and, were she to think that outcome morally wrong, she would desire its non-occurrence. Martha Nussbaum has suggested that readers of fiction frequently approximate to the condition of being ideal observers of the fictional worlds they survey: their reason, interest, and moral sensitivities are engaged, but not in the service of their own ends (Nussbaum 1995: 75).[15] So their desire-like imaginings will tend to be in harmony with their belief-like imaginings about the rights and wrongs of the action. And for such a person, resistance in desire-like imagining will translate into resistance in belief-like imagining; if it is difficult for her to have the desire-like imagining that female infants be killed, she can have the belief-like imagining that female infanticide is right only at the expense of the harmony between belief-like and desire-like imagining which is the natural stance of the intelligent and sensitive reader.

On our view, then, supposition is belief-like imagining that is isolated from, or at least not substantially affected by, desire-like imagining. When I am asked to suppose some (possibly alien) moral proposition, I succeed if

---

[15] Nussbaum acknowledges a debt to Adam Smith (1976). It may be that the best way to make this point is not in terms of ideal observers but in terms of one or other of the notions that meta-ethicists have offered us and which play roles in their systems rather similar to that played by ideal observers in the thought of Adam Smith and others like him. We might claim, for example, that readers of fiction approximate to their own ideally rational selves, an idea made use of by Michael Smith (1994). We won't try to decide this issue here.

I manage to restrict my imaginative engagement to the recreation of belief-like states. This turns into an imaginative project that is more than merely suppositional if my desire-like imaginings are engaged as well. I might, by great effort, manage to take on in imagination the desires that conform to this alien moral proposition, desiring female infanticide to flourish, for example. In that case my supposition has become a more richly imaginative project and probably no longer deserves the title 'supposing' (though we are not assuming there is any sharp boundary here). I have, at this point, started 'really getting into' that value, if only in imagination. But if my imagining does start to engage my desire-system at all, it is likely that I shan't be able to summon the appropriate desire-like imagining in favour of female infanticide, and the imaginative project will be derailed.

Desire-like imaginings will play an important part in imaginative projections that do not seek to explore value. Take the project of thinking through how you might react to a particularly difficult predicament. If Mary merely assumes that her child is very ill, she probably will not conclude from this that God exists. But, as critics of the Ramsey test have noted, it may still be true that, were Mary to believe that her child is very ill, she would come to believe in God. Mary can't find this out by merely assuming that her child is ill, but if she took this as the starting point for a more thoroughgoing imaginative project that engaged her desire system as well as her belief system, she might come to see the attractions that religious belief would have for her in that situation. This is one of the ways in which imagining yourself in a situation is more than just doing bits of reasoning.[16]

Whether and to what extent we succeed in insulating belief-like imagining from desire-like imagining, and thus engage in an act of supposing, will depend on a number of factors, including natural capacities that vary between persons. But one important factor will be the rhetorical and descriptive features of that which prompts the imagining in the first place. If I simply ask you, without embellishment, to suppose, for the sake of the argument, that female infants should be killed, you may well succeed in forming the relevant belief-like imaginings without bringing the desire system into play. If I create, as novelists and film-makers do, a vivid and detailed world in which to situate these circumstances and into which

---

[16] See below, Sect. 5.2.

I encourage you to place yourself in imagination, this mental partitioning will be much more difficult. We cannot say, therefore, that this or that proposition is something I can suppose, while some other proposition is beyond my suppositional powers. The most we can say is that this proposition, in this context of presentation, given my natural inclinations, present thoughts, recent experiences, etc., is or is not something I can insulate from desire-like imagining.

There have been some simplifications here. We have spoken as if people are always resistant to alien desires, and to the values which, as ideal spectators, they would take on in imagination only if they took on correspondingly alien desires. Neither is strictly true. Sometimes we find evil attractive and wish to explore, in imagination, an evil outlook. Sometimes we are simply drawn into desiring morally alien things by subtle rhetoric that makes us unaware, or less than fully aware, of what we are doing. And we might be rationally persuaded that imagining the alien perspective is something we should strive for; by taking on in imagination values and desires that are abhorrent we may be better able to understand why people take them on in reality, and perhaps we can thereby come up with sensible suggestions for preventing the spread of evil ambitions. Also, belief-like imagining is not infinitely biddable. Stories sometimes ask us to imagine, in a belief-like way, things we may find it difficult to imagine. In *Ivanhoe* Walter Scott has one of his characters, a colourful fellow called Athelstan, struck dead by a blow that the narrator clearly sees as fatal; later the character reappears, having recovered from what we are now told was a superficial wound. Readers find this difficult to integrate with the imaginative project they have been engaged in up to that point. And Scott, evidently, did not expect them to imagine it; he says in a footnote that the character was revived at the insistence of the printer, who refused to set the work until it was done. So the asymmetry between compliant belief-like imaginings and resistant desire-like imaginings is not absolute. But it does require a special effort, and we feel it needs a special justification, consciously to take on alien desires in imagination, simply because they are alien desires. And there is no comparable resistance to taking on alien beliefs of a factual kind, except for special reasons like those that move us in the *Ivanhoe* case.

We have been claiming that suppositions are imaginings. In Chapter 7 we return to this theme, while speculating about what might be wrong with imagination in autism. In the course of doing so we suggest a way forward for anyone keen to argue that *some* suppositions are not imaginings.

2.5   FANTASY

We rejected the distinction between imagination and supposition, saying that supposition is a certain type of imagining. What about fantasy? Some writers take imagination and fantasy to be distinct; Roger Scruton says that while imagination aims to grasp reality 'in the circuitous way exemplified by art', fantasy is a flight from reality (Scruton 1983: 127). No doubt there is a distinction here, but it sounds to us more like a distinction between imagination put to one use and imagination put to another. Accordingly, we treat fantasy as a species of imaginative project, and concentrate on describing some of the ways in which imagination can be fantasy. But we don't rule out the possibility that fantasy extends beyond the boundary of imagination, and that there are things other than imaginings that can count as fantasy. In ordinary speech, 'fantasy' can be used to refer either to an imaginative response, or to the object of that response. People speak of 'fantasy literature', for example. We will use 'fantasy' exclusively to refer to the response. The reason is that, in so far as one can say that an object of a response is a fantasy, that is because it is apt to call forth, or is designed to call forth, a fantasy response. And there are works that it would not be right to call fantasy but to which people sometimes respond in a way which exhibits fantasy. So the response sense seems to be the primary one.

Roughly, we take fantasy to be indulgent imagining. There are various ways in which imagining can exhibit indulgence, and one can be indulgent to varying degrees, so there will be cases of imagining that are fantasy for one reason, and cases of imagining that are fantasy for quite other reasons, and there will be cases of imagining that are fantasy to a considerable degree as well as cases that are marginal. In what follows we focus on three ways in which imagining can be indulgent, though we are not claiming that these are the only ways; there may be indefinitely many such ways.

According to the first way, one's imaginings count as fantasy if they exhibit one's preference for comparatively effortless imagining over effortful imagining. Ernst Gombrich once contrasted the too-easy-to-read eroticism of Bouguereau's *Birth of Venus* with Botticelli's depiction, where one has to work against the geometry of the figure to make imaginative contact with its beauty. With Bouguereau, one's imagining falls out effortlessly from the visual content of the picture (Gombrich 1963: 37). It is fantasy in this sense that Peter Lamarque has in mind when he makes a distinction between works that encourage us to make decisions about our imaginative stance, and those (melodrama and horror are the kinds he cites) where we simply find ourselves responding in a certain way (Lamarque 1996: 147). This distinction is especially useful when we focus on desire-like responses to fictions. As we noted earlier, shifting one's desires in imagination is difficult compared with shifting one's beliefs in imagination, and one way for works to indulge fantasy is for them to present situations to which we can respond with only a minimal shift of desire. When works force us to acknowledge propositions about character and motive that are unfamiliar to us, they often ask us to have desires in imagination for which our real beliefs and desires leave us to some extent unprepared.

The idea of fantasy as easeful imagining accounts for at least some of what Scruton calls 'fantasy', and which he takes to be a property of desire. Scruton gives this example.

A morbid person may reflect intensely and aimlessly on the subject of human death and suffering. The image of agony may rise frequently before his mind and begin to exert its fascination. There is born in him the desire to witness such a scene. At the same time fear, sympathy and respect for human life makes it abhorrent to him to realize his desire . . . The effect of this prohibition is to turn his desire towards a substitute: he begins to seek the 'realistic' portrayal of death and destruction—for example, in a waxworks museum, or in the cinema . . . The desire for this perfect image of suffering is an example of fantasy. (Scruton 1983: 129)

It seems odd to use this example to contrast fantasy with imagining, since it is surely undeniable that the person here described imagines, of the wax-works scene or the cinematic image, that this is a scene of real death and destruction. And Scruton's description of the case makes it clear why this is a case of fantasy as well as of imagining; the realism of the image brings forth the imagining: this is death and destruction, without the need for interpretative work.

Lamarque contrasts two fantasy genres, melodrama and horror, with the case of tragedy. The contrast is instructive. It shows that it would be wrong to identify our first kind of fantasy with escapism. Escapism we take to be a preference for imaginings that protect us from uncomfortable truths. This can be fairly classed as indulgent imagining, and hence as fantasy, but it is not fantasy in the sense of easeful imagining. It might be argued that some of the greatest works of the literary canon—works that certainly require imaginative effort—provide opportunities for escapist imaginings. On this view the great tragedies, with their sometimes harrowing representations of suffering, present a vision of moral disasters, their causes, course, and consequences, that is wildly at odds with the depressing facts of human existence. For example, these works place a great deal of emphasis on the role of character in the determination of moral choice, but the best evidence we have is that character plays only a marginal role in determining people's moral choices.[17] Emphasis on character is just one way in which the tradition of tragedy romanticizes suffering so as to make it palatable to a society obsessed with the development of personal qualities.

We don't need to assess this argument here. Correct or not, the argument ought not to be rejected on the grounds that its conclusion is conceptually false. We must leave a space for representations that, while certainly requiring imaginative work and therefore not fantasies in our first sense, are escapist in virtue of the comforting falsity of their presuppositions, and so are fantasy of the second kind.

The third way that imagining can be indulgent, and therefore exhibit fantasy, is by being an imaginative project the aim of which is to satisfy all, or as many as possible, or the strongest, of one's desire-like imaginings. The kind of imaginative project associated with reading formulaic romances on the Mills & Boon model would fall into this category. Notice that horror and melodrama, along with tragedy, would not. For in horror and melodrama things often turn out badly so far as the characters are concerned, and the appeal of these genres cannot therefore be fully explained in terms of their satisfying our desire-like imaginings. In these cases, we take it, the appeal is to be explained by their capacity to satisfy real desires concerning narrative. We have the desire-like imagining that Desdemona live, but also the (real) desire for a narrative according to which she does not. We have a desire-like imagining that Stella Dallas (Barbara Stanwyck) be present at her daughter's wedding, but desire a narrative according to which she is shut out. We say

---

[17] See Campbell (1999a); Harman (1999).

more about the contrast between desire-like imaginings concerning characters and desires concerning narratives in the final chapter.[18]

2.6 THOUGHT EXPERIMENTS AND THE DIRECTION OF GAZE

In one respect our account of imagination may appear too restrictive. We
have focused on the recreation in imagination of mental states only. The
idea is that states of recreative imagining are states that mirror many of the
properties of the mental states which are their counterparts. Having states of
recreative imagining enables us to model the having of those other, counterpart states. It does not enable us to model states and processes which are
not themselves mental states; in particular it does not enable us to model
the worldly states and processes that may be the objects of our imaginative
thoughts. To think otherwise would be, again, to confuse counterparts and
contents. Belief-like imaginings simulate beliefs, not the states of affairs that
they and those beliefs may have as their objects. And visual imagery does not
involve the replication, in the head, of that which would be seen in the
external world were one seeing rather than merely visualizing.

People have said that thought experiments in science involve the mental
modelling of the situation that the experiment describes, and such situations are typically not mental processes but rather processes involving part-
icles and light waves, falling bodies and rolling balls.[19] This is not recreative
imagining according to our usage. It may be true that we are capable of
mentally modelling physical processes, and that our capacity to do this
underlies some of our experience with thought experiments in science. The
evidence one would need to find in order to establish this is quite different
from the evidence which supports the idea that there are states of recreative
imagining. We have no idea where this further evidence might be found, and

---

[18] Imaginings can be fantasy in several ways. Jim, who imagined quelling mutinies and keeping
up the hearts of despairing men, had imaginings that count as fantasy by all three criteria
described above (Conrad 1900, ch. 1).

[19] Nancy Nersessian says that a thought experiment involves a mental model which is a
'structural analogue of the situation described [in the experiment]' and which is manipulated
using 'simulative model-based reasoning' (Nersessian 1992: 296–7, 291). For a 'theory-theory'
account of thought experiments, see Norton (1991). Thanks to Rachel Cooper for drawing our
attention to this material.

do not include the explanation of thought experiments among the ambitions of our theory.

Does the fact that the recreative imagination is thus restricted in its scope mean that acts of imaginative projection are essentially inward-looking: activities that direct our attention to the mental states we are recreating, rather than outwards to worldly things? People who have recently offered imagination-based explanations for various human capacities have denied that they are offering a means of introspection.[20] They are partly right to deny it, as we can see by appealing again to the distinction between content and counterpart. The question 'What things can be imaginatively recreated?' is answered by finding out what sorts of things are the counterparts of states of recreative imagining. Since those counterparts are themselves mental states, the things that can be imaginatively recreated are mental states. The question 'To what is the subject attending during acts of imagining?' gets the answer 'To those things, whatever they are, that figure in the contents of the mental states being recreated'. If I want a beer and believe there is one in the fridge, I am focused on the beer and the fridge, not on my mental states. So if you want to project yourself into my situation, you will also end up focused on the beer and the fridge, and not on your own imaginings.

Though it is a mistake to infer that you are introspecting from the fact that you are modelling the mental states of another, it is possible to be doing both. We can, after all, have thoughts about our mental states. If Jones is wondering how to rid himself of a desire he thinks is immoral, he may have to think about his desire and not, at least not primarily, about the object of his desire. Your modelling of Jones's thinking will need to be just as inward-looking as his thinking is. This is a case of thinking about one's mental states as states with a certain content; presumably what worries Jones is that he has a desire with an undesirable content. But there are other 'inner' aspects of one's mental states, and simulations can give us important insights into some of them. A vivid and imaginative projection into someone's situation can sometimes tell us what it would feel like to be in that situation.[21] The

---

[20]   See e.g. Heal (1986); Blackburn (1992); Gordon (1992).

[21]   See Ravenscroft (1998). As Richard Holton and Rae Langton point out, moral philosophers have sometimes overestimated our ability to discover, by imaginative projection, what the situation of another being is like; see their discussion of R. M. Hare's claim that empathy can settle matters concerning the welfare of bears and trout (Holton and Langton 1998).

project need not be an essentially inward-looking one; I start by imagining the world as it appears to someone trapped in a narrow cave. Nonetheless, I might end up knowing something about how being thus trapped feels—an example we take up again in Chapter 5.

2.7 NADIA AND THE REINDEER MAN

The same point about direction of gaze needs to be kept in mind when thinking about other uses of imagination. Simon Baron-Cohen suggests that we can put a least upper bound on the development of human mind-reading skills, using the evidence from imagination-based artefacts like the cave painting of the Reindeer Man at Trois-Frères. Such things, he says, are 'necessarily representations of the artist's mind, of the artist's thinking about his or her own thoughts . . . So, we can say with some confidence that a full theory of mind must be at least as old as 30–40,000 years' (Baron-Cohen 1999: 269).[22] While such products may be evidence of an imaginative capacity, they are in no sense evidence for the possession of a theory of that capacity. We no more need a theory of mind to imagine objects than we do in order to have beliefs about them. The master of the Reindeer Man needed to think about peculiar hybrid creatures, not about his own mind.

Perhaps the Reindeer Man does tell us something about the modernity of the human mind 30,000 years ago. In a brilliant and provocative essay Nick Humphrey argues that the example of Nadia, an autistic and mentally retarded girl who produced astonishing sketches at the age of 5 and credit-able work at 2 years old, indicates that cave art (some of it remarkably similar to Nadia's work) is no evidence for the modernity of the human mind 30,000 years ago (Humphrey 1998).[23] If so unusual a mind as Nadia's can now

---

[22] Steven Mithen says, 'The presence of imaginary beasts in Upper Paleolithic art, together with associated evidence of ritualistic activity—an activity that normally involves pretence—appears conclusive evidence that those cave painters were also mind-readers' (2000: 495).

[23] Nadia's drawing was not in any way typical for a child with autism. Children normally start by drawing what they know is there; only at the age of about 5 years do they move to 'visual realism', picturing likenesses of what they can see. Nadia's case is extraordinary partly because she seems to have missed out the early 'intellectualist' phase altogether. Results of Charman and Baron-Cohen (1993) suggest that autistic children make the same shift as normally developing children do, that the earliest detectable time of the shift is about the same as for normals, but that many autistics do not make the shift until much later than the normals.

produce work like this, the minds of the cave-dwelling folk then may have been, by our standards, just as alien. However, *creative* cave art like the Reindeer Man, which corresponds to no actual thing, surely indicates that these artists were mentally dissimilar to Nadia, at least in so far as they possessed imagination. There are various reasons to be wary of this conclusion.

One thing to say is that it is unlikely that the Reindeer Man dates from 30,000 years ago; it may be as recent as 15,000 years. This may not matter to the argument, since there are candidate hybrids, such as the Bison Man at Chauvet, which certainly do pre-date 30,000 BP. More significantly, depictions such as the Bison Man may represent real shaman figures in animal dress and not hybrids at all. But let us assume they are hybrids. That makes the cave folk different from Nadia only if she didn't draw hybrids. In fact some of her figures look very much as if they are hybrids. Humphrey puts this down to her having lost track of an original project and simply starting a new one, putting the head of another animal atop the body of a giraffe she had begun earlier.[24] And he says that figures 'of this kind' are to be found in cave art as well, implying that apparent hybrids in cave art are similarly unplanned. Anyone looking at the illustration of the Reindeer Man given by Baron-Cohen is likely to object that this figure is obviously a planned and integrated hybrid figure—it is not simply the head of a reindeer stuck on the body of a man. Baron-Cohen's illustration is taken from a sketch of the Reindeer Man by the Abbé Breuil done in the mid-nineteenth century; it has been argued that Breuil was an enthusiastic over-interpreter and that the original is much less obviously an intended hybrid.[25]

An alternative would be to argue that Nadia, for all her disability, was able to use imagery creatively, and that her hybrids *were* intentional. To us, her giraffe–donkey appears to be of this kind, though Lorne Selfe, who spent much time with Nadia during her prolific drawing phase, seems to have thought that her hybrids were not intentional. What sort of imagination would be required to produce an intentional hybrid? Visual imagery is the

[24] Humphrey cites this as an example of what has been called 'lack of central coherence' in autism, a notion due to Uta Frith (1989). It is at least as plausible to suppose that losing track of the picture (if this is indeed what happened with Nadia's hybrids) was due to faulty executive function. See below, Sect. 7.2.

[25] You can get some idea for yourself by turning to Bahn (1997: 165).

obvious answer, and Fiona Scott and Simon Baron-Cohen have argued that children with autism are impaired on the production of visual images of non-existent things (Scott and Baron-Cohen 1996); the children they tested were very poor at producing pictures of 'impossible objects' though they were well enough able to draw, and matched normal controls produced two-headed men with ease. The children with autism did badly when instructed to draw a monster with two heads, even when various prompts were given in the drawing process ('now draw another monster head on the body'). But experiments of Leevers and Harris (1998) indicate that autistic children *can* produce impossible pictures; their failure to do so in the experiments of Scott and Baron-Cohen were probably due to the high executive demands of the test situation.

So it is possible that Nadia and the artists of 30,000 years ago were similar in that both had, by our standards, extraordinary drawing ability but little or no visual imagination, and that the hybrids of both were simply failures to keep to the plan. It is also possible that they were similar in that, for all their, by our standards, diminished intelligence and lack of self- and other-awareness, they had strong visual imagination and the capacity to represent hybrids. But nowhere in this is there evidence that the master of the Reindeer Man had a theory of mind. The issue of autistic imagination is one we take up in Chapter 7.

Part II

Simulation in a Generalized Setting

Chapter 3

THE SIMULATION PROGRAMME

3.1 IMAGINING AS SIMULATION

A good way to describe the relation between a piece of imagining and its counterpart is to say that imagination *simulates* this other thing. That implies likeness, and asymmetric dependence: when *A* simulates *B*, *B* does not simulate *A*. One objection to the term's use here would be that simulation is a relation between one *process* and another, and not everything we would call simulative imagining is a process; how, for example, could belief-like imagining simulate belief, since having a belief is not a matter of undergoing a process? The answer is that the imagining simulates the role of belief *in* inferential and other processes; its likeness to belief is, exactly, similarity of role in certain processes. If the model is apt to play an important and reliable role in the process of simulating the effects of wind on the bridge, it is not stretching concepts very far to say that the model simulates a bridge. It is in that sense that an imagining would simulate a belief. But note that the asymmetry is between occasions of use of enduring objects, not between enduring objects. On one occasion the wind tunnel simulates the behaviour of the wing on take-off; on another it might be the other way round, with the wing in flight serving to inform us about what would happen in the wind tunnel.

'Simulation' has recently acquired a special sense in the philosophy of mind.[1] Robert Gordon, Jane Heal, and Alvin Goldman have argued that to understand and predict the behaviour of others we need not depend on the possession of an apparently rather complex psychological theory; instead we can draw on our capacity to simulate other people's reasoning and decision-making. Beyond this elementary statement of the view, we have to acknowledge divergences between its proponents: Gordon, as we shall see, credits simulation with a capacity to substitute for theory that is more thorough-going than anything endorsed by Heal or Goldman; Heal insists, as we shall also see, that the philosophical point to be made on behalf of simulative methods is a narrow one concerning thoughts only, while Goldman has emphasized the similarity between the simulation of reasoning and the reuse of perceptual processes that occurs with mental imagery.

Divergent views of these and other kinds about simulation have prompted the suggestion that simulation exhibits no coherence, and should be retired from the philosophical scene. But simulation theory is said to contrast with theory-theory: the belief that we understand people's psychological states by appeal to a psychological theory. There are widely differing conceptions of what this theory is and in what ways we have access to it; many assume that it is internally represented, though there are differences of opinion about how: in a language of thought according to some; in a connectionist system or in a mental model according to others. Some think it is acquired while others take it to be innate. Some suppose that it is modularized while others take it to be part of general beliefs. Some suppose it is unavailable to conscious inspection, while others take it to be capable of being made explicit. Some assume that it has properties commonly associated with scientific theories such as involving nomological generalizations; others mean no more by 'theory' than 'propositional belief', and do not even assume that beliefs, or all of them, need be internally represented. This

---

[1]   Simulation theory is generally regarded as having been invented independently by Robert Gordon (1986), Jane Heal (1986), and Arthur Ripstein (1987). The idea is suggested in Morton (1980) and is pretty clearly expressed in Humphrey (1980). It goes back to Adam Smith (1976). See also Harris (1988) for developments of the idea within psychological theory. The idea has been further developed by Gordon and Heal in later work (Gordon 1992, 1995, 1996; Heal 1994, 1995, 1996a,b, 1998); by Alvin Goldman (1989, 1992, 1993, 2000), and by Stephen Stich and Shaun Nichols (Stich and Nichols 1992, 1997; Nichols et al. 1996), though Stich and Nichols have been critical of the theory. Many of these papers are collected in Davies and Stone (1995a,b).

ought not to encourage us to abandon the idea of theory altogether. Rather than abandon the idea of simulation, we prefer to think of it in programmatic terms: an idea with certain distinctive features capable of being developed in different ways. The central commitment of the simulation programme is this: a belief in the existence of states of recreative imagining, their role in our everyday understanding of minds, and their capacity to reduce the amount of psychological theorizing that we need to attribute to people in explaining their mentalizing capacity. The view has three components: an existence claim, an explanatory claim, and a claim of economy. We take them in turn.

How is the existence claim to be understood? We have postulated a broad range of states of recreative imagining that divide naturally into two classes: propositional imaginings and perceptual imaginings. Simulation theorists have tended to concentrate on just the former kind. In fact most of the discussion has focused on belief-like imaginings, which simulation theorists have called 'pretend beliefs'. Should simulation theory be construed in such a way that it encompasses imaginative states of other kinds as well? Later we will argue that considerations of economy exert a pull in the direction of limiting simulation theory to being a theory of propositional states.

The explanatory claim is that mentalizing depends to a significant extent on, and can be at least partly explained in terms of, our capacity to project ourselves in imagination into the situations of others, and to generate within ourselves states of imagining that have as their counterparts the beliefs and desires of someone (hereafter 'the target') whose behaviour we want to predict or understand. And having provided ourselves with those imaginings, we are then able to use them so as to mirror the inferences and decisions that the target makes.

Simulationists say that the explanatory claim is to be preferred to the hypothesis that mind-reading is done by appeal to a folk-psychological theory. There is some uncertainty about quite how the opposition between these two approaches is to be understood. Is the simulation theorist claiming that we *always* predict and explain the behaviour of others by using recreative imagination? If so, it is not very plausible; there are times, surely, when we base our predictions on empirical generalizations, or simply on considerations about what the rational thing to do in that situation would be. Is it supposed to be a claim about how we predict and explain others in certain independently specifiable circumstances? No one has said what those circumstances are, though some theory-theorists have argued that, in certain situations where it is likely that simulation would be used if it ever is used, the evidence suggests that we use a theory (actually a false one) and not simulation.[2] Particular attention has been paid by both sides of the debate to questions about cognitive development, and there have been conflicting claims about the role of simulation in the child's progress towards full mind-reading competence. Simulation theorists disagree among themselves concerning how much of a role simulation plays in this. We shall say more about the role of simulation in development in Chapter 6. In Chapter 7 we offer systematic support for the explanatory claim, though we do so indirectly. One way to see how important a faculty is for performing a certain task is to examine what happens when the faculty is lacking or damaged. We will argue that autism is partly characterized by an incapacity of recreative imagining—an incapacity that explains much about the mentalizing and other difficulties that people with autism face.

The claim of economy is that simulation reduces the burden of theory: if we cannot assume that people use simulation when mentalizing, we have to credit them with implausible amounts of theory. Put this way, the claim of economy is a modest one. It does not seek to dispense with theory al-together, or to suggest that theorizing is unimportant for mentalizing. Yet some writers have suggested that failure to eliminate theory altogether means that the theory-theorist wins the debate. Here is Frank Jackson:

to answer what K—where K may be an electron or a human being or a planet or . . . —will do in S, you should draw on what you think K will do in S. Now, views about what K will do in S is a theory of that K—maybe a rather simple one, maybe a highly complex one. It will be a theory that connects inputs to K with outputs from it. So the general point is that we should answer questions about what K will do in terms of our own theory of that K. What else could we sensibly do?

---

[2] There is by now quite a literature devoted to this issue; see e.g. Greenwood (1999); Heal (1996a); Kuhberger et al. (1995); Nichols et al. (1995, 1996); Ravenscroft (1999); Stich and Nichols (1992, 1997). Greenwood's paper contains a valuable distinction between active and passive simulations, along with some impressive evidence that active simulations can reproduce surprising behaviours, and a distinction between a subject's verbal predictions of another's behaviour and his or her anticipations of that behaviour—two things that we have good reasons to think will often come apart.

It is this line of thought that makes me hold that the theory-theory account of how we should predict human behaviour and human mental states must be the correct one. (Jackson 1999: 78)

There are two things that can be meant by the claim that an answer to the question 'What will K do?' must draw on a theory. The first is that the answer is the expression of, and hence draws on, a belief—the belief that K will do S—and a belief is a theory. We agree. But the simulation theorist who contrasts simulation with theory is making a point about how we get to the answer, not a point about the answer itself. The other thing that could be meant is that we must arrive at the answer by means of theory. Without agreeing that all answers to all questions depend on theory, we are happy to agree that answers to questions about people's mental states, arrived at on the basis of simulations, do so depend. If I wonder whether you will choose X or Y, I may project myself into your situation, giving myself the relevant belief-like and desire-like imaginings, and find myself choosing X. I then conclude that you will do the same. I may not be assuming anything here about why you would prefer X, and indeed have no view about why, so it seems, I would prefer it myself.[3] But I have to assume that you and I are relevantly alike, even though I may not be aware of making this assumption—the assumption, if it is there, is implicit. And it will be easy enough for you to convince me that I *am* implicitly assuming this by pointing out that if I thought that you and I were *not* relevantly alike, I would not have drawn the conclusion that I did draw.[4] And if I simply had no opinion about whether we were relevantly alike, I would either not draw the conclusion or I would give it a lot less credence than I do in fact give it. In the light of these true and indeed rather obvious counterfactuals, there is nothing controversial or mysterious about the claim that I am assuming a relevant similarity between us, and that that assumption constitutes dependence on a theory. We do not have to assume that the theory is buried very deep, in the way that a Chomskyan theory of grammar is said to be, or that it is in any sense a protoscientific theory.[5]

To agree with this is to make no great concession to what theory-theorists have generally claimed. The simulation theorist's point is that simulation

---

[3] Later we discuss these kinds of cases again; see Ch. 5.

[4] We follow Jackson (1999) here.

[5] See Feagin (1996: 92) for a similar view.

lightens the burden of theory; she need not claim that it does away with the burden altogether. Take an analogous case. In the film *Apollo 13* (and, for all we know, in reality as well) the team at Houston need to find a way to reduce the power demands of the stricken craft. They might have tried to do this by calculations based on premises drawn from the relevant physical and engineering theories, together with statements of relevant initial condition. They did it another way: by having an astronaut play with the power system of a comparable craft on the ground, until he found a way to run the craft on power known to be available to *Apollo 13*. No doubt the astronaut used theories of various kinds, including a theory that says that this craft and *Apollo 13* are relevantly similar. But it seems reasonable to say that the method he used was *less* dependent on theory than the way of calculation would have been—and probably quicker and more reliable as well.

We need here to identify a possible source of confusion. 'Simulation', as currently used, is ambiguous; it has a narrower, and a broader, meaning. Suppose I try to predict your behaviour by imagining myself in your situation. There are three things that must go on if I am to get the answer by simulation. The first is to acquire some knowledge, or at least some beliefs, about your situation. The second thing is for me to place myself, in imagination in that situation, and to see what, in imagination, I decide. The third is to draw a conclusion from this about what you will do. Sometimes 'simulation' refers to the whole three-tier process, sometimes just to the bit in the middle. It is just that bit in the middle that is, properly speaking, simulation; the other, framing parts of the process are not part of what I do when I simulate your decision-making, though the first is essential to get the simulation going, and the third essential to make predictive use of it. Now suppose someone asks, 'Can simulation take place without any psychological theorizing?' To get an answer, we have to decide how 'simulation' is meant in the question. As Jackson puts the question, it seems that 'simulation' must have its broader sense. His point is that I can't make use of the simulation proper without appeal to psychological theorizing at the third and final stage. We agree: simulations never work without assistance from theory. Robert Gordon does not agree; he holds that simulation is especially economical in that it is capable of delivering insight into the mental states of others without the intervention of theory-based inferences at all. In the next section we examine Gordon's argument.

3.2   SIMULATION AND THE INFERENCE FROM ME TO YOU

In Section 3.1 we pointed out that when I simulate your decision-making processes I assume—perhaps only implicitly—that you and I are relevantly alike. Is there a form of simulation which does away with this assumption? Recall our three-tier account of prediction or explanation by simulation: I start with a view about your situation; I imagine myself in that situation as I understand it; I draw from the imaginative process a conclusion about what you will do or why you do it. That last bit involves an inference, an inference from me to you. Robert Gordon (1995) has argued that simulation does not need that step.

Gordon's argument depends on a distinction between two kinds of imaginative projects. In a project of the first kind what I imagine is myself in your situation. In a project of the second kind I imagine being you in that situation. Gordon's claim is that a project of the first kind involves our third, inferential step, but that a project of the second kind does not. So we can do simulations without inference from me to you as long as we do simulations that involve just the second kind of imaginative projection. In the case where I merely imagine being myself in your situation, I do my imagining and find myself deciding to F; I then have to infer that you would do F. But in the case where I project myself into a situation where it is you who is acting, no inference is required. For in this case the upshot of the imagining is already that *you* do something. As Gordon puts it, 'once a personal trans-formation has been accomplished, there is no remaining task of mentally transferring a state from one person to another, no question of comparing [the agent] to myself' (Gordon 1995: 56).

Before responding to the argument, we make two points. The first is that Gordon is quite right to say that there are two kinds of imaginative project here. The fact that there is a substantial difference between them was pointed out, in another context, by Richard Wollheim: merely imagining myself in Smith's shoes, without going so far as to imagine being Smith 'leaves it open to me at any moment to imagine myself brought face to face with [Smith]. And that is something that the imaginative project I have in mind [i.e. being Smith] clearly rules out' (Wollheim 1984: 76). Secondly, as Gordon points out, the second kind of project need involve no inconsistent imagining. I need not imagine that I, Jones, am Smith. I just imagine that

I am Smith, where the reference of 'I' has shifted to Smith as part of the conditions of the imaginative project itself. 'I' as used by Jones within the scope of his imagining refers to Smith, not to Jones.

So we have no objection to the idea of simulations of the second kind. Do they give us mind-reading that is less dependent on inference than the 'analogical' kind of simulations that require me merely to imagine being in Smith's shoes? To answer this question we must distinguish two senses of 'dependent on inference'. In the first sense my belief is dependent on inference just in case I do actually go through a process of inferring the belief from what I imagine, along with other premisses. In this sense it may be the case that simulations of the second kind are not dependent on inference. I might have a tendency, when I imagine myself to be Smith and to be Φing, simply to form the belief that Smith will Φ, and do this without going through any inference, as I might immediately form the belief that P when I hear you utter 'P'. But this cannot be what is at issue, for I might equally have the disposition to believe that Smith will Φ when I imagine myself, in Smith's shoes, Φing. The question here must be one about justification. This is the second sense of 'dependent on inference': dependent on inference for a justification of your belief. Perhaps, when I have a perceptual experience with the content P, I am immediately and non-inferentially entitled to the belief that P—except in special circumstances. Can it be that way with beliefs formed on the basis of what I imagine? It is hard to see how any imagining could, in any circumstances, immediately and non-inferentially justify any belief. But fortunately, we do not have to show that no imagining can ever do this. Gordon's case rests on the claim that, of two kinds of imaginings, one and not the other allows us a justified, but non-inferentially justified, belief. We deny this. Suppose I imagine being in Smith's shoes, and form, on the basis of this, a belief about what Smith will do. According to Gordon, this is an inferentially based belief. Suppose now that I change my imaginative project in just this way: that instead of merely imagining being in Smith's shoes, I imagine being Smith. According to Gordon, I am now entitled to believe, without inference, that Smith will do such and such. But how could this change in the nature of my imaginative project have produced any epistemically relevant change to the relation between the imagining and my belief? Changing the imaginative project in this way does not make the imagining a more reliable guide to what Smith will do; the reliability of the project depends on whether, in imagination, I am getting my mind to work like Smith's. Adding the stipulation 'I am Smith' does nothing to ensure that my mental processes are more like Smith's than they were before the stipulation—except in the unusual case where the thought 'I am Smith' plays a part in Smith's own decision-making.[6]

Perhaps Gordon is moved by the thought that a project of the second kind—I imagine being Smith—might be so continued that, when you ask me 'What will Smith do?' I answer 'Φ', staying in character. And I could, again staying in character, simply say to myself 'I, Smith, will Φ'. And all this could be done without any inference from me to Smith, or any thought about whether Smith and I are relevantly similar. But this establishes nothing about whether I can gain non-inferential knowledge of Smith from my imagining. My saying to myself or to anyone else 'Smith will Φ' as part of a pretence does not constitute my acquiring a belief about what Smith will actually do, and it certainly does not constitute my acquiring any knowledge; that can happen only outside the scope on my role-taking.

So much for the claim that simulation can do without theory. In the next section we look at an argument that says that simulation, even in the narrow sense (what we will call 'simulation proper'), just *is* theory.

3.3   THE THREAT OF COLLAPSE

We agreed with Jackson that mentalizing based on simulation involves—at least tacitly—a psychological theory to the effect that the target's psychology is akin to the simulator's. We can think of this as the minimal psychological-theoretical commitment of mental simulation: mental simulation involves at least that much theory. It has been argued that simulation cannot avoid a rather more substantial commitment to psychological theorizing. We will look briefly at the debate provoked by this claim. We then give what seems to us to be a straightforward and quite general account of the relations between simulation and theory.

Jane Heal has argued that, under certain conditions concerning the causal regularities that prevail within the thinking subject, simulation will

---

[6] See also criticism of Gordon's position in Botterill and Carruthers (1999: 86–7).

collapse into psychological theorizing (Heal 1994: 132). This argument depends on an independently motivated account of what it is to possess a (tacit) theory, which we will briefly explain.

Suppose that a subject's thoughts obey the rule of &-elimination: when the subject has a thought of the form $A \& B$, she has a further thought of the form B. Under what circumstances does this transition involve tacit knowledge of the &-elimination rule as opposed to merely conforming to that rule? Following Evans (1981), Martin Davies has suggested that the subject has tacit knowledge of the &-elimination rule only if there is a common causal explanation of all the subject's transitions from representations of the form $A \& B$ to representations of the form B.[7]

Now consider Neil, who wants to predict the conclusion Sue will draw from her belief that $A \& B$. According to simulation theory, Neil begins by forming a representation with the content $A \& B$. His own reasoning processes lead him to form a representation with the content B. Neil therefore predicts that Sue will come to believe that B. Moreover, let us assume that there is in Neil a state which figures in the common causal explanation of all such predictions; there is, in Neil, a state which figures in the explanation of all of his transitions from beliefs with content of the form 'S believes that $A \& B$' to beliefs with content of the form 'S believes that B'. Call this the T-state. Then, by the account of tacit knowledge sketched in the previous paragraph, Neil has, and here deploys, tacit knowledge of the psychological generalization 'If S believes that $A \& B$ then S believes that B'. Neil's simulation thus counts as an exercise in psychological theorizing, if there is in him the T-state.

A natural response here is that this result is more apt to be taken as a refutation of the theory of tacit knowledge from which it is derived than a serious objection to simulationism.[8] Is there a plausible way to amend the theory so as to block the derivation? Here is a proposal for amendment based on a suggestion of Peacocke's (Peacocke 1994, p. xxiii). Let's assume that

---

[7] See Davies (1981a,b, 1987, 1989, 1995) and Davies and Stone (forthcoming). Strictly speaking, there being a state common to all the transitions will not be sufficient to establish tacit knowledge since there must in addition be a background of what Davies has called 'enabling conditions'. Enabling conditions include an adequate supply of oxygen and nutrients to the neurobiological state which figures in the common causal explanation. See Davies (1987). Henceforth when we say that some state S is sufficient to explain some transition, we should be taken to mean that S plus enabling conditions is sufficient to explain that transition.

[8] A suggestion made in discussion by Kim Sterelny.

there is in Neil a state—call it R—which figures in the common causal explanation of his transitions from beliefs with content of the form '*S* believes that *A* & *B*' to beliefs with content of the form '*S* believes that *B*' (hereafter the belief–belief transitions). Then R has the content 'If *S* believes that *A* & *B* then *S* believes that *B*' (hereafter G) only if R's having *that* content explains, in a way that makes rationally intelligible, Neil's battery of belief–belief transitions. But R's having content G would *not* explain those transitions. Recall that Neil begins with the belief that Sue believes that *A* & *B* and then obtains a representation with the content *A* & *B*. It is *that* representation which is transformed by a simulative process which involves R. So R must have a content which renders intelligible the transformation of a representation with the content *A* & *B* into a representation with the content *B*. The content G is *not* a content which renders intelligible that transformation. It is utterly mysterious how a state with content G could transform a representation with the content *A* & *B* into a representation with the content *B*. In that case attributing to R the content G cannot be sufficient to explain the battery of belief–belief transitions. So R does not embody tacit knowledge of G. What Neil does have is tacit knowledge of the &-elimination rule. For attributing to R that content *does* provide an explanation of Neil's transitions from representations with content of the form *A* & *B* to representations with content of the form *B* and, consequently, an explanation of his belief–belief transitions.

Perhaps we can, in this way, fend off the claim that simulation is itself a form of psychological theorizing. And on reflection, it can be seen that the claim should never have been framed as a reductive one. For the argument was always premised on a contingent thesis about the presence of some or other causal regularity in the mechanisms that underpin certain mental processes. At most, it was an argument to the effect that, for an individual or group of individuals with certain causal innards, an act of simulating is an act of theorizing.[9] Let us now ask the more general question 'How, in general, is what we do when we engage in simulation related to what we

[9] We are puzzled by Heal's claim that this result is dependent upon taking facts about subpersonal processing as constitutive of the simulation thesis. What the result seems to be dependent on is what the facts about subpersonal processing are, not on whether one regards these facts as constitutive of or in any other way related to the idea of simulation itself. On the other hand, her objection might be construed as an objection to the idea, prominent in the Evans–Davies theory, that facts about subpersonal processing are constitutive of facts about the possession of tacit knowledge.

do when we theorize? Is it generally the case that what we have been calling simulating is just theorizing under another description?' Note that the question is not whether simulating is always *psychological* theorizing; we take it that the argument just given shows that it is not. The question is whether it is theorizing of any kind. We say that simulation is sometimes theorizing, but sometimes not. We will now offer an answer to the question 'When is simulating theorizing?'

3.4 WHEN IS SIMULATION THEORY?

We need to be clear, for a start, about what we take theorizing to be. Here is a very straightforward account. I theorize when I go from one or more propositions to some other proposition by using mental processes that are apt to track relations of logical or evidential dependence between the propositions concerned. I might start with some propositions I believe and end up with some new proposition which I did not previously believe but do now believe exactly because I got it in this way from previous beliefs. It is crucial to note that the propositions in question might not be believed; they might instead be assumed. When we assume something we treat it, in some ways, as if we believed it; we let the assumed proposition mingle with our real beliefs and we come to some new conclusion on the basis of the assumption and what we already believe. And the new conclusion isn't believed either; it is just a conclusion arrived at on the basis of a mixture of belief and assumption. And we take it that this sort of thing is just as much theorizing as when we are operating exclusively on the basis of what we believe.

We have said that when we theorize we pass from one or more propositions to some other proposition via mental processes that are apt to track relations of logical or evidential dependence. This proposal can be understood in a weak and a strong way. According to the weak reading, the input and output propositions are linked by evidential or logical relations. According to the strong reading, not only are the input and output propositions thus linked; so are any intermediate propositions. For reasons that will become clear, we intend the stronger reading.

Notice that we are not here assuming that theorizing is necessarily something that is conscious, or that theorizing is based on assumptions or beliefs that are mentally represented in some specific way, or even that they are mentally represented at all. Nor are we assuming anything about the contents of the beliefs or assumptions that are involved. These propositions can have contents of all kinds, so that I can theorize about rocks and planets and people, depending on the contents concerned.

Now it looks as if simulating is just theorizing, for simulation involves having imaginative counterparts of the other person's beliefs, and we have agreed that those imaginative counterparts are just assumptions. So simulation is just theorizing from assumptions. To take an example, suppose it is important to me to know whether Poirot thinks I killed Roger Ackroyd. I happen to know that I did, but that is not the issue. I know things Poirot doesn't, and must do my best to adjust for his ignorance. So I reason, not from what I know, but from what I think he knows about the crime, and see where my reasoning gets me. Suppose it gets me to the conclusion that Jones (me) did not in fact commit the murder; I may then conclude that Poirot does or will think that I'm innocent: a reassuring result, though this is not part of the simulation proper.

If part of what is going on here is simulation, it is hard to see how it is not also theory. In fact it seems to be the kind of theorizing we called reasoning from assumptions. It might not be theorizing in the rather grand sense of reasoning from some highly articulated and well-defined set of assumptions which are unified, counterfactual-supporting, and all those other good things that theories sometimes are. There is grand theory and ordinary theory; all we are saying is that my bit of simulation was ordinary theorizing.

The result generalizes: whenever a simulation is a simulation of a bit of thinking that counts as theorizing, the simulation ought to count as theorizing as well. The only difference between the original bit of thinking and the simulation of it is that, with the simulation, the premises are not believed by the one doing the thinking. It is just the familiar phenomenon of reasoning from assumptions rather than from things believed.[10] That can't be the difference between theory and non-theory.

Notice that my simulation of Poirot might not be theorizing of a psychological kind; it might involve no assumptions with psychological content, except at the final step, when I assume that he and I are relevantly similar. It might just have gone like this:

---

[10] In Goldman's terms this would be 'theory-driven simulation'. See his (1992: 196).

The murder was committed in London.
Jones was in Australia at the time.
So,
He couldn't have done it.

This does not concern psychological matters. But we have agreed, for the moment, that the issue is not whether simulation is psychological theorizing; the question is whether simulation is theorizing, full stop. It seems that it is.

However, it was always the aim of simulation theory to explain, not merely how we come to know what beliefs people derive from their other beliefs, but what decisions they make.[11] And if we turn now to simulated decision-making, we can quite easily see that this is not theorizing. For what one decides to do depends not merely on what one believes, but on what one desires. Take a simple case where I make a decision based on things I believe and desire. As I leave my room, I see the dean in the distance walking my way; I know that the dean wants to ask me awkward questions about Philosophy's budget and my recent holiday in Barbados. Knowing this, I want to avoid the dean, and believe that I can effectively do so by ducking down the stairs. I have the desire that

(Des) I avoid the dean

and the belief that

(Bel) I can avoid the dean by ducking down the stairs

and so my decision is that

(Dec) I duck down the stairs.

But if we take these three propositions, (Des), (Bel), and (Dec), it is hard to see how the first two provide any kind of evidential or logical support for the third. As Velleman puts it, 'When the agent's attitudes towards [the first two] propositions move him to [duck down the stairs], he is not responding to any action-justifying property of the propositions themselves; he is simply manifesting the valence of his attitude towards the former proposition' (Velleman 2000: 101). Of course, there are cases where we theorize and things go wrong, and we end up with premises and conclusion that are not appropriately related by logic or evidence. But we don't want to assimilate decision-making

---

[11] See e.g. the trail-walking example in Gordon (1992).

(especially, as in this case, decision-making that has gone right) to theorizing that has gone wrong. And if decision-making isn't theorizing, then surely simulated decision-making isn't theorizing either. When I simulate your decision-making I have some simulated beliefs, some simulated desires, and I get from them to a simulated decision. This isn't theorizing.

Again, the result generalizes. Simulation is theorizing if and only if what it is a simulation of is theorizing. If there is simulation of stuff which isn't theorizing, then some simulation is not theorizing, and simulation does not collapse into theory.

A theory-theorist could at this point say that she never claimed that simulation is just theory in disguise; what she said was that, as a matter of fact, all we ever use when we are mentalizing is theory. That is, of course, an empirical question; she happens to think that the empirical evidence supports her view.

We don't think that this is an adequate response. For one thing, we could sensibly question whether the systematically acquired evidence we have really does support the proposition that we only ever use theory in our men-talizing.[12] For another, the admission that there is a possible kind of simula-tion that isn't theory surely puts paid to the idea that simulation *collapses* into theory. A proof of collapse would be a proof that simulation could never be anything other than theorizing. More than this, the theory-theorist's pos-ition looks inherently unstable. If we think about simulation of the kind that we have agreed to be theory—namely, the kind of simulation where what I simulate is your theorizing—then it is surely just very implausible to say that we *never* do that kind of simulating. This, in itself, gets us exactly nowhere against the theory-theorist, because we have already agreed that this sort of simulation actually is theory; the theory-theorist can admit that we do this kind of simulating all the time. But having admitted this, the theory-theorist is in an uncomfortable position. For if she admits that we sometimes simulate theoretical reasoning, why should she deny that we ever simul-ate decision-making also? If she agrees that we do (even occasionally) simulate decision-making, then she agrees that not all mentalizing is theory.

One objection to our proposal runs like this. Jane Heal has pointed out that all inquiry begins and ends with belief:

---

[12] See below, Ch. 6 and 7.

Unless I lose grip on the distinction between myself and others, I do start, and must start, from a representation having the content 'So and so believes that p'. My subsequent imagining that p . . . is only part of a total thought state which remains a thought about another's thought. And what is delivered out at the far end of my deliberations is likewise an explicit representation of the other's future thought or action. (Heal 1994: 136)

Very often there will be evidential relations between the contents of the beliefs with which a simulation begins, and the content of the belief with which it finishes—what we have called the first and third stages of a simulation in the broad sense. Jones might begin his simulation with the belief that Smith desires to avoid the dean and the belief that Smith believes that the best way to avoid the dean is to duck down the stairs, and end it with the belief that Smith will decide to duck down the stairs. That Smith desires to avoid the dean and believes that the best way to do so is to duck down the stairs provides eviden- tial and rationalizing support for the idea that Smith will duck down the stairs. So the simulation of decision-making has, after all, collapsed into theorizing.

This depends on taking theorizing in the weaker of the two senses distin- guished earlier. We endorse the stronger reading, which requires that inter- mediate propositions in the sequence be related in a theorizing way to those next in the sequence. And this condition is not met by Jones's simulation. Here, the simulation proper proceeds from (Des) and (Bel) to (Dec), and we have seen that this transition fails to be a theorizing transition.

The theory-theorist has a further objection. Go back to our decision- making case:

(Des) I avoid the dean

and

(Bel) I can avoid the dean by ducking down the stairs

so

(Dec) I duck down the stairs.

Call this *Transition 1*. We said that the propositions in Transition 1 are not related in the right ways for (Dec) to be describable as obtained from the other two by theorizing. Now suppose that decision-making occurs in a different way, by our undertaking Transition 2:

(Bel*) It is desirable that I avoid the dean

and

(Bel) I can avoid the dean by ducking down the stairs

to

(Dec) I should duck down the stairs.

Here the first two propositions can be thought of as rationalizing the third; they provide a kind of support for it, though the support is neither evidential nor logical. This is what has been called deliberation,[13] and perhaps it should count as theorizing. If it does, my simulation of it counts as theorizing also, and so we can agree that theorizing is used to figure out what people will do, without having to deny that simulation is theory.

Presumably there are many occasions when our efforts to project ourselves imaginatively into the situations of others result in our undertaking a bit of deliberation of this form; we imagine ourselves in the situation and try to think about what it would be best for us to do. Is it always like this? Surely not. There are times when we have a feel for what we would do in a situation, without having any idea, or any good idea, what desire is motivating us, or whether in doing what we turn out to decide to do, we are doing what it is best for us to do. Consider the centipede game. At each stage player A has the choice of grabbing, which ends the game and deprives him of further winnings, or investing, which leaves him vulnerable to a grab from B on the next move; this would mean that A got slightly less than he would have done had he grabbed on the previous move (see Morton 1995). How do you work out when that is likely to be? A backwards induction argument indicates that we will all defect on the first round; in fact we don't. Better than calculation is an empathetic feel for the point at which the other player is likely to defect. You can have that feeling without being able to say what it is that is driving the decision, or whether defection at that stage is the right thing to do. I may know that you and I tend to make similar kinds of decisions in a certain area, without knowing why we do; putting myself in

---

[13] See Pettit and Smith (1990) and Smith (1994: 132): the intentional and the deliberative perspectives.

your shoes I simply find myself, in imagination, making that decision.[14] That sounds much more like my simulating Transition 1 than my simulating Transition 2. Go back to Mary (see Section 2.4), wondering how she would react to the serious illness of her child. She may get some illumination from vividly imagining herself in the situation; she will probably not be helped by asking what, in that situation, would be the best thing for her to do.

In general, and as we would expect, simulation takes on the character of what is simulated. When what is simulated is theorizing, the simulation is theorizing also; when it isn't, it isn't.

3.5   MECHANISMS AND CAPACITIES

A basic insight of simulation theory is that we proceed from imagined or assumed premises in just the same way that we proceed from our beliefs (Heal 1995: 35). That is what makes belief-like imaginings apt to substitute for beliefs; for those who believe in desire-like imaginings, the same holds for their relation to desire. This is a hypothesis about mental capacities; it says that there are not two capacities here but one. Reasoning is sensitive to content, and content does not distinguish beliefs from assumptions.

Sameness of capacity does not entail sameness of mechanism. An agent might exercise the same capacity in reasoning both from beliefs and from assumptions, but have distinct mechanisms for doing these things. Some simulation theorists have offered a hypothesis about the mental mechanisms involved; according to this hypothesis there is just the one mechanism as well as the one capacity. Consider practical reasoning. There is, let us assume, a mechanism dedicated to forming decisions on the basis of our beliefs and desires. 'Mechanism' here means a physical system, a part (though possibly a very widely distributed part) of the body, something that might be damaged or fail to develop. When it operates solely on the basis of beliefs and desires as inputs, we have practical reasoning that delivers decisions. This mechanism can then be run 'off-line', disconnected from action-generating systems. When operated this way, it takes as inputs belief-like and desire-like imagin-

---

[14] This emphasis on the knowledge to be gained from 'uncomprehending' simulations contrasts sharply with the idea, suggested by Bill Brewer, that simulations give us access to a kind of rationalization of action that depends on experiencing the subject's own 'seeing why [he] is right in doing as [he] does' (Brewer 1995: 247 and n.).

ings and delivers imaginary substitutes for decisions. And the mechanism is thus able to do double duty partly because it is sensitive only to those aspects of its inputs that reflect content (or perhaps just syntactic structure). The off-line version of simulation theory says that systems designed to give us the capacity to form new beliefs and make decisions can be reused to enable us to model belief formation and decision-making.

Call this hypothesis of reuse I_1. This is a claim about the *implementation* of imagination. What are the alternatives to I_1? One alternative is hinted at in the literature.[15] We will call it the *two-mechanisms view*, or I_2. This is the claim that there are in fact two distinct but similar mental mechanisms, one which takes real beliefs and desires as inputs and gives real decisions as outputs, and another which takes the corresponding imaginings as inputs and gives decision-like imaginings as outputs. These mechanisms would be similar in that they both ensure the preservation of inferential relations between the inputs, and obey the constraints of rationality (whatever you assume them to be) on the relations between inputs and outputs. But they are distinct mechanisms. In particular, they are realized in distinct neural systems. I_1 and I_2 are competing implementation hypotheses.

Should the simulation theorists be committed to either I_1 or I_2? There are two reasons, neither of them utterly compelling, why the simulation theorists should prefer I_1, at least for the case of simulations of decision-making. The first reason is that the postulation of two mechanisms is less economical than the postulation of one, especially when we all accept the need to postulate the one, whether we agree with any of the claims of simulation theory or not. The second reason for preferring I_1 is this: we have very good reason to think that imagination-based decision-making does not operate in isolation from the subject's real beliefs and desires. One of the supposed advantages of simulation as a way of understanding other people is that one does not need to make a vast number of assumptions about what the target believes and desires, even though the subject has a vast number of beliefs and desires that may be relevant to what she will decide. You just put yourself in her shoes, assume you are relevantly similar to her except in the ways already adjusted for by the introduction of imaginings into your mental set, and let your own beliefs and desires model hers (Heal 1996*b*). And the same is true of

---

[15] See Heal (1994). But Heal is not endorsing this or any implementation hypothesis.

theoretical reason; we saw in Chapter 1 that the imagination-based inferences of even very young children (some as young as 21 months) draw on knowledge of, or at least beliefs about, the real world. The child who witnesses the pretend act of 'pouring water over Teddy' will, without instruction or the provision of any general rule, imagine that Teddy is wet. The child is basing her inference not merely on the imagined proposition that Teddy had water poured over him, but on her belief that things that have water poured over them get wet. If imagination and belief operated under a system of inferential apartheid—as the two-mechanisms view has it—how could this happen? One defence of I_1 would be to say that the inference-from-imagination mechanism takes inputs from the subject's beliefs as well as from her imaginings. But in that case this mechanism would do perfectly well, on its own, to run inference from imagining *and* inference from belief.[16]

However, I_1 is bound to need some qualification. There must be, for example, a special pathway *into* the decision-making system for inputs which are not beliefs but imaginings, and there must be a special 'sideways exit' from the system so that one can get from the result of a simulation—an imagined decision—to a conclusion about what the target of the simulation will do. In the present state of knowledge it would be very difficult to make confident suggestions about what parts of the brain might be implicated in these tasks. We shall see in the next chapter that a similar question about the existence of a single operating system arises for cases of perceptual imagining, and that here we may be able to draw upon empirical research. We conclude, however, that these results are less than decisive.

Earlier we contrasted mechanisms with capacities. Not all simulation theorists have wanted to endorse I_1 or any other claim about mechanisms. Jane Heal takes the simulation hypothesis to be about capacities only. It is the claim that we bring to the project of understanding the reasoning of others just the capacities they themselves deploy in that reasoning (Heal 1998: 477). When I am thinking about what Smith will decide, I imagine myself in Smith's situation, facing the problems he faces, and apply my capacity for decision-making to the problem. And we can see, says Heal, that this is how

---

[16] We remarked that the two reasons just given are not utterly compelling. One source of doubt is the difficulty of making parsimony judgements about hypothesized biological systems. Ravenscroft (1999) offers an analysis of what it is for one biological system to be simpler than another.

we do normally approach a mind-reading problem, without having to do empirical studies. There is, of course, the further question of how this capacity is implemented, and empirical studies may help us to answer this question. But that is not a question we need to answer in order to decide whether simulation theory is true.

Can we be confident that our use of capacity categorizations will never be affected by our judgements about sameness and difference of mechanism? Surely not. Is visual object recognition one capacity or many? We are less likely to think it is one now that we know that people with selective damage to the visual system sometimes recognize one class of objects and not another. Is conditional reasoning one capacity? Empirical results have persuaded some people that we need to distinguish between the capacity to reason condition-ally in a deontic context and the capacity to reason conditionally in a non-deontic one. Does understanding minds depend on a general-purpose capacity to understand representations? One reason to think that it does not is that people with autism are good at understanding non-mental representations. We take no stand on the three examples, merely noting the possibility that capacity identities can be undermined by results about mechanisms. And capacity identities can be supported by information about mechanisms. Suppose we were able to identify a mechanism M—a neural circuit, say—that was an essential and central component in the chain of systems active when we make decisions; we might discover that damage to M dramatically affects decision-making performance but leaves other capaci-ties intact.[17] And suppose we could show that M is significantly engaged when we are trying to predict someone else's decisions. Perhaps it even turns out that damage to M affects performance on this task as well. If both these things were true, we would have support for the simulationist's claim that the prediction of decision-making depends on decision-making capacity.

We would not in that case have *proof*. Apart from the difficulty of getting the right kind of evidence about brain mechanisms, there would be other ways to explain the result. A neural system implicated in one task might play a quite different role when contributing to another task. All we are claiming is that the activation of the same brain areas in decision-making and in decision prediction would be evidence in favour of the simulation hypothesis.

---

[17] Or all bar one—see text immediately following.

Suppose, however, that it were true that the simulationist's claim about capacities needed no support from the evidence for mechanisms, and could never be undermined by such evidence. You could then afford to be a simulationist with no interest in mechanisms, and no interest in making connections between the philosopher's and the scientist's pictures of the mind. Since we are interested in those connections, we shall have quite a lot to say about mechanisms in the rest of this book.

In the next chapter we consider the issue of capacities and mechanisms in the context of thinking about perceptual imaginings. Before we get to that, a final point about the off-line version of simulation theory. As usually formulated, this version of simulation theory postulates a two-stage process: taking as inputs to the decision-making system imaginative substitutes for beliefs and desires, and taking the system off-line. We say that there are not two distinct things that need to be done here. To use the decision-maker to simulate decision-making we do not need to employ states of recreative imagining as inputs *and* ensure that the resulting decision does not lead to action. Doing the first of these things is sufficient, because something is a state of recreative imagining only if it lacks the action-provoking powers of beliefs and desires. Consider this analogy. You use a sieve with a certain gauge of mesh to sort stones. Let us stipulate that 'big stones' are those that will not go through the mesh. If I pour only big stones into the sieve, I know that they are not going to pass through, and I do not have to do anything to 'bring the sieve off-line' to prevent them from passing through; they fail to pass through merely by virtue of being big stones.

Abandoning the idea of bringing the decision-maker off-line has some advantages. People have worried that simulation theory is uneconomical because it postulates a mechanism for, exactly, bringing the system off-line.[18] Whatever grounds there are for thinking that simulation theory is uneconomical, this is not, on the present proposal, one of them. Secondly, the whole notion of bringing the system off-line is problematic because it is an obvious fact that people are able to do mind-reading tasks while performing other actions. If mind-reading severed the connection between decision and action, we would always fall in a heap when we mind-read.

---

[18] See Stich and Nichols (1992: 138). Several times in this article Stich and Nichols say that the child who is learning to simulate has to learn to do two things: 'to take the decision making system off-line and provide it with some pretend inputs' (1992: 149; see also 142).

Chapter 4

IMAGERY: CAPACITIES AND MECHANISMS

In this chapter we focus on perceptual forms of imagining: visual imagery because its rich phenomenology and physical basis have been extensively investigated, and motor imagery because it has some characteristics that make it hard to classify; it has also been the subject of ingenious experiments in recent years. We take up again the theme of capacities and mechanisms, bearing in mind what we have said about mechanisms providing evidence for capacities. We have seen that one basic insight of simulation theory was that we exercise the same capacity for reasoning, whether we start from beliefs or from imaginings. Generalizing, we can think of belief- and desire-like imaginings as allowing us to exercise capacities for information transformation; what is distinctive of them is that they enable us to undertake propositional transformations, by practical and theoretical reasoning. We can think of perceptual imaginings in much the same way; there are distinctively visual ways of representing and transforming information, and visual imagery enables us to represent and transform in just those visual ways. To get more or different information about something while looking at it, we may have to move towards it, or rotate it, or view it in a different part of the visual field. Visually imagining things is partly characterized by being a form of imagining that mirrors these modes of transformation, sometimes in surprising ways.

This is our least philosophical chapter. Earlier claims about the likeness between imagery and perception are given some support from the sciences, and the picture we build up will be made use of in Chapter 5, when we return to the question 'What sorts of recreative states are proprietary to simulation?' But there is light before the end of the tunnel; we conclude with an attempt to resolve a puzzle about the nature of motor imagery.

4.1 IMAGERY AND PERCEPTION: COUNTERPARTS

One thing would have to be established before we could feel secure about thinking of perceptual imagining as recreative: that perceptual imagining stands in the right kind of relation to perception—a relation appropriately analogous to that in which belief-like and desire-like imaginings stand to genuine beliefs and desires. Whether this is so is made somewhat complex by the fact that beliefs and desires are rather different kinds of states from perceptions. In particular, beliefs and desires have, and perceptions do not have, the capacity to enter into inferential relations with other beliefs and desires for purposes of theoretical and practical reasoning; we have argued that this is a feature which the corresponding states of recreative imagination mimic. Perceptions, on the other hand, are largely distinguished by the characteristic ways in which they present us with information about the real world: vision in one way, audition in another, and so on. And many of these characteristic ways are available to the experiencing subject who can discriminate between different kinds of perceptual experience and to some extent describe the differences. It is these characteristic ways of presenting information, with their attendant phenomenology, that states of perceptual imagining mimic, as we shall see.

The subjective experience of visual imagery is strikingly similar to that of vision, and we spontaneously and non-collusively describe visual imagery in visual terms.[1] It is not easy to say exactly what these similarities are, and it is equally evident that there are important differences between them as well. But the reality and the importance of these similarities are well attested by experimental evidence. We know, first of all, that our ordinary ways of identifying both imagery and perceptual experience are similar enough for

---

[1] This is true even when people describe the difference between imagery and vision. Here is a response to a survey of imagery carried out by Galton: 'Dim and not comparable in brightness to the real scene. Badly defined, with blotches of light; very incomplete; very little of one object is seen at one time' (Richardson 1999: 12).

us occasionally to mistake perception for imagery.[2] Indeed, there have been reports of patients who deny they are blind because they mistake imagery for perception (Goldenberg *et al.* 1995). People can also find it difficult to remember whether they have seen something or merely formed a visual image of it.[3] It is not comparably difficult to discriminate having seen something and having imagined hearing it.

Modes of perceptual access like sight have characteristic patterns of facilitation and constraint; the success with which information about an object can be obtained by looking at it is substantially determined by the object's size, shape, and orientation, and by the distance and point of view of the observer. The same patterns often show up in visual imagery. In vision, information about shape and about orientation are presented as a package deal; consequently, it is much easier to decide whether two objects have the same shape once they have been brought into the same orientation. The same factoring out of orientation seems to be required to perform this task in imagery, as Shepard and colleagues showed in classic experiments that gathered what is called 'chronometric' data: information about the time it takes subjects to perform tasks in a variety of conditions. Times for judgements of shape similarity in imagery are proportional to the difference in orientation of the objects concerned, indicating that subjects imagine the two objects brought, at a constant speed, into the same orientation.[4] It is more difficult to discriminate oblique lines than it is to discriminate lines in the horizontal or the vertical. This effect is also present—in fact it was more pronounced—when subjects have to form images of the patterns (Kosslyn *et al.* 1999*b*). A given object will overflow the visual field of imagination at about the same distance (the distance it is imagined to be from the imaginer) as it will overflow the real visual field as we approach it with eyes open.[5] Objects

---

[2] In a classic experiment which has been reproduced with better methodology, the American psychologist Perky asked people to visualize a banana. These people did not know that there was in fact a just visible image of a banana on the screen that they were looking at. It was clear from their own descriptions that what they took to be mental images were in fact percepts of a banana depiction. See Segal (1970).

[3] See Kosslyn (1994: 55). This is especially true of vivid imagers; see Reisberg *et al.* (1986); Reisberg and Leak (1987).

[4] See Shepard and Cooper (1982); Shepard and Metzler (1971). The same kind of effect seems to hold for differences of location; see Cave *et al.* (1994).

[5] See Kosslyn (1994: 100) for a description of this experiment and a response to criticism of it.

blur as they move towards the periphery of our visual field; it is the same with objects imaged as at the periphery.[6] It occurred to us that there might be evidence that synaesthesia is reproducible in imagery.[7] The issue is somewhat complicated because synaesthesia is itself a phenomenon involving imagery; in a typical case, the perception of a sound invokes the image of a colour. Our question is whether people who experience synaesthesia on hearing a sound would experience it if they, say, imagined hearing the sound instead of really hearing it. From what we can see, this question has not been subject to experimental tests.[8]

Our visual access to the world occasionally produces some peculiar effects of which an attentive subject may become aware. These are visual illusions. They don't seem to be inevitable concomitants of vision, and one can imagine sighted creatures not subject to illusions, or at least not subject to the ones we are subject to. A good test of how well our visual imagery corresponds not merely to vision in some generic sense but to human visual experience is to see how much of this illusory baggage comes with our imagery as well as with our vision. The answer seems to be: a quite surprising amount. Among the best-known and simplest visual illusions is the Müller-Lyer illusion: two parallel lines of the same length appear to be of different lengths when differently oriented arrowheads are added. There is evidence that this illusion is reproducible in imagery.[9] As complex an effect as the McCullough Effect, where viewing black bars on a coloured background produces an after-effect in the complementary colour, seems to be to some extent reproducible in imagery.[10] It has even been claimed that imagery can create faint after-images (Kunzendorf 1990).

[6] See Finke and Kurtzman (1981). In one important respect chronometric testing reveals important differences between vision and imagery. Imagery tasks that involve comparing patterns take much longer when they involve high spatial resolution than when they do not; but there is very little difference in the time taken when the tasks are performed using perception. One explanation is that high resolution is obtained by cells lower down the visual system, and that the activation of such cells in imagery requires extra effort (Kosslyn *et al.* 1999*b*).

[7] Synaesthesia is sometimes described as involving 'tasting shapes' or 'seeing sounds'. More neutrally, it seems to involve at least involuntary simultaneous experiences in different sense modalities, both caused by a property normally experienced through just one modality. It seems that about 1 in 2,000 people, mostly female, have these experiences. See Baron-Cohen *et al.* (1996).

[8] Thanks to John Harrison for discussion here.

[9] Finke and Shepard (1986). But see also Reisberg and Morris (1985).

[10] See Finke (1989: 47) for review.

People taking part in chronometric studies of imagery often report a sense, not merely as of seeing objects rotate or change their locations, but of rotating and moving objects.[11] Chronometric studies have now been undertaken which focus particularly on motor imagery. Because motor imagery involves the sense of moving one's body, change over time is even more central here than it is with visual imagery, and the question of how similar motor imagery is to the experience of actual movement is one that chronometric studies have a special place in answering.

Chronometric studies show that imagined hand movements are substantially constrained by the same internal, bodily factors that constrain real hand movements. When subjects were asked to imagine moving their hands into the position of a hand on a displayed target, their response times were a function, not simply of the angle of separation between their own hand orientation and that of the stimulus, but of the factors affecting the durations of the corresponding actual movements: handedness of subject, origin of movement, length of trajectory, and awkwardness of target position (Parsons 1994). Indeed, the duration of the actual movement and that of the corresponding imaged movement were very similar. The correlation is almost perfect for simple movements, although more awkward imaged movements take a little less time than their actual counterparts. Even in the case of more awkward movements, though, the durations of the actual and imaged movements remain proportional. Experiments with real and imagined walks generated similar correspondences of duration (Decety et al. 1989).

Many of the movements that we make are constrained by external factors, and we cannot expect that whatever bodily resources are devoted to the generation of motor images (on which, see below, Section 4.2) will always be able to take them into account in the absence of the real forces those factors would impose on the body. We would not expect that the performance of someone asked to imagine rotating her hand in a pot of jam would display the chronometric and other properties displayed by actual hand rotation in that medium—unless the subject knew something relevant about the properties of jam, and was able to use that knowledge for realistic motor planning. We noted that real and imagined walks take almost exactly the same times for a given subject and distance; but when people were asked to shoulder heavy

---

[11] Kosslyn (1999) suggests that rotation tasks in imagery can involve either imagining rotating the object manually or imagining seeing it rotated by an external force.

packs and imagine walking with them, their imagined walks generally took significantly longer than their real ones.[12] This raises a standard theory-theorist's suspicion: that what people here describe as an 'imagined walk' is not something dependent on recreative imagination at all, but is simply a process by which they arrive at an answer to the question 'How long would such a walk take?' on the basis of their (false) belief that walks with heavy packs take longer than walks without (Pylyshyn 1981). If this theory adequately describes the present case, it cannot easily account for the many other cases where time of action depends on factors people are generally unlikely to comprehend. For example, because the velocity of movements involved in writing and drawing increases with their amplitude, the time taken to write a signature is not much affected by its size; this far from obvious 'isochrony principle' seems to hold for imagery as well (Decety and Michel 1989). In fact the theory-theorist's answer in the case of the imagined walk with the pack is also implausible because, prior to undertaking the imagined walk, the subjects undertook a real walk with the pack, and their times for this walk were very similar to their times on the unencumbered walk. Marc Jeannerod offers another explanation: it is the common experience of agents that the duration of a movement increases with the force applied, because one typically applies a greater force in order to move a greater distance. Now suppose that, in both the real and the imagined pack-walking situations, a greater force was centrally programmed by the agent. In the real case, where an actual load is encountered, the programmed extra force simply compensates for the increased resistance, and the duration is as it was without the pack. In the imagined case, with no actual resistance, the increased load is interpreted by the agent as a sign of increased duration (Jeannerod 1997: 102). Jeannerod's explanation certainly does appeal to the general beliefs of the subject, just as the theory-theorist's does, but unlike the theory-theorist's, it does not dispense with the imagined walk; it claims instead that the result of the imagined walk is misinterpreted in the light of the agent's beliefs.[13] We say

---

[12] Notice that in this case the subjects did not have also to imagine the weight of the pack; they were really feeling the weight while they imagined walking.

[13] Jane Heal (1996a) has emphasized ways in which a simulation can be misinterpreted in the light of the subject's beliefs. Jeannerod makes the point that, since we do not perceive the extent of temporal intervals directly, subjects' estimates of the time of an imagined action are especially likely to be theory-laden (Jeannerod 1997: 101).

more about the role of knowledge and belief in imaginative processes in Chapter 5, when we discuss the issue of cognitive penetrability.

Unconstrained hand rotation in air largely banishes external factors, so it ought to be the simulationist's flagship example, with real and imagined performance in very close accord. So it is, except that awkward imaged movements of the hand take a little less time than their actual counterparts. What is the explanation? There are performance-affecting factors at work even in hand rotation that are absent in the imagined counterpart. Real motor actions receive corrective feedback from the visual and proprioceptive systems—feedback which is absent in the case of movements which are merely imaged. It has long been hypothesized that such feedback slows down the performance of movements by placing additional processing demands on the movement control centre. So perhaps the shorter duration of imaged awkward movements relative to actual ones is due to the absence of corrective feedback in the case of imaged movements. This argument gains support from the fact that the discrepancy between real and imagined performance times is significant only for awkward movement, which is also the kind of movement we would expect to be dependent on visual and proprioceptive feedback.

If imagined movement is constrained by the factors that constrain our real movement, it follows that imagining impossible movements is itself impossible. Yet people often say they can imagine—in the kinaesthetically vivid way appropriate for recreative imagining—such impossible movements as extending their arms so as to touch a light fixture in a high ceiling.[14] We reply that one might easily have the sense of being able to imagine doing this while in fact not being able to. For one thing, kinaesthetic imagery is sometimes difficult to distinguish from visual imagery, and there is, on our view, no objection to imagining *seeing* an arm being thus extended. While extendable arms may be inconsistent with our biology, perception of extendable arms is not incompatible with the structure of human vision. More importantly, we grant that it is possible to imagine in a kinaesthetic way *parts* of the process of extending your arm to the ceiling: you imagine stretching upwards, straining to reach the ceiling; you then imagine actually touching it. Neither of these is biomechanically impossible, but taken

---

[14] This objection was put to us by Graham Nerlich.

together they do not amount, strictly speaking, to imagining stretching all the way to the ceiling. We are prone to describe partial imaginings in terms strictly applicable to the whole: people who imagine swimming 100 yards rarely undertake the whole episode in imagination. It may therefore be that we take a sequence of possible, partial imaginings to be the completion of an act of imagining which, taken as a whole, is impossible.

4.2   IMAGERY AND THE IMPLEMENTATION CLAIM

Is it true, as I_1 claims, that the various modes of imagery depend largely on the cognitive mechanisms that underpin the corresponding mode of perception? For evidence that supports this idea we turn to situations where there appears to be competition between perception and imagery, to visual pathologies, and to brain imaging. Let us take these in turn.

If visual imagery employs mechanisms of the visual system itself, then visual imagery and vision, when occurring simultaneously, should affect one another in ways that, say, visual imagery and audition do not. It is known that the requirement to use vision in reporting the results of an imagery task degrades performance on the task, while reporting verbally does not (Brooks 1968). And forming images can reduce accuracy on a visual task (Craver-Lemley and Reeves 1987). But same-mode interaction between perception and imagery does not always degrade performance; imaging a given letter of the alphabet enhances detection of the same letter when visually presented, and the enhancement is greater than that which is transferred when imaging one letter and seeing a different one. Stephen Kosslyn (1994), whose views we shall return to, has argued that imagery is recruited to the performance of visual tasks in a variety of situations where the visual input is degraded.

Damage to brain areas that produces deficits in vision sometimes also produces comparable deficits in imagery: loss of colour experience and difficulties locating or identifying objects have been offered as examples of this.[15] In Parkinson's disease impaired recognition of the emotional expression on a face goes with impaired ability to image an emotional facial expression (Jacobs et al. 1995). Patients with damage on the right side of the

---

[15]   For review, see Farah (2000, sect. 9.6).

brain sometimes fail to respond to, and apparently to notice, objects in the left visual field; this is called unilateral neglect (UN). When asked to imagine being placed in a familiar location (the Piazza del Duomo in Milan was the location for the original experiments), the descriptions given by UN patients showed systematic neglect of objects on the left side of the imagined scene.[16]

However, not all the evidence from brain damage supports the implementation hypothesis I_1. There are reported cases of intact visual imagery in patients who are cortically blind or who have serious visual deficits.[17] And there are subjects with UN in imagery but not in vision (Gauriglia *et al.* 1993). It might be replied that the implementation claim is not the claim that the neural substrates for vision and for imagery are exactly the same, but rather that they substantially overlap. There is good evidence that they do.[18] With the development of precision techniques, the evidence has become more impressive. Recall the assumption that judgements of shape identity in imagery involve imagining the objects being rotated into the same orientation. When subjects are performing these tasks, a visual area of the brain which is sensitive to motion (V5) is activated (Cohen *et al.* 1996). Activity in the primary visual cortex (area 17) of the brain has been detected, and found to be inversely proportional to the time it takes subjects to answer a question about a letter they are asked to image (Kosslyn *et al.* 1996). By disrupting activity in this area and observing the effect on performance, Kosslyn's group found strong evidence that activation in this area actually contributes to performance on an imagery task (Kosslyn *et al.* 1999a).

The acknowledgement of overlap is not good enough to establish the implementation claim. For one thing, the kinds of overlap detectable by even the most discriminating modern techniques do not rule out the possibility that perception and imagery tasks are being undertaken in subtly different ways. And much depends on where the overlap is. The implementation claim suggests that perception and imagery are related as the two sides of a partly closed zip fastener: the inputs are from distinct sources, but

[16] Bisiach and Luzzatti (1978); see also Bisiach *et al.* (1979).

[17] Bartolomeo *et al.* (1997); Berhmann *et al.* (1994); Chatterjee and Southwood (1995); Servos and Goodale (1995). For methodological criticisms of some of these studies, see Butter *et al.* (1997). See also Farah (2000: 271).

[18] Goldenberg *et al.* (1989a,b) showed that the occipital and inferior temporal regions were active both during tasks which required visual perception and during tasks which required visual imagery. See also Farah *et al.* (1989); Kosslyn *et al.* (1993).

higher-level processing is the same in both. To test this hypothesis strictly the place where the inputs come together would have to be specified, and for this we need a theory of how vision and imagery actually operate.

One such theory has been developed by Stephen Kosslyn. As we shall see, Kosslyn has made a claim that approximates very closely to the implementation claim. While Kosslyn's theory is unlikely to be precisely correct, it is sufficiently well developed and tested to be used as an initial model. He has also made other claims about the representational form of imagery: that visual imagery involves the internal manipulation of 'quasi-pictures'. We reject this part of Kosslyn's view, but it is independent of his views about implementation. So here we ignore his pictorialism.[19]

Kosslyn's model of higher vision involves several interrelated components. First, there is a *visual buffer* consisting of topographically organized areas in the occipital lobe that are used to segregate figure from ground. Information from here goes to a number of different areas that carry out different processing tasks and some of which have access to 'top-down' information which helps with object identification. In vision, activation of the visual buffer, which is the first step in higher visual processing, occurs as a result of inputs from the retina which have been processed by low-level visual operations. Imagery occurs when there is activation in the visual buffer which is *not* due to retinal stimulation, but which derives from visual memory. Kosslyn has said that 'Once a pattern of activation is evoked in the visual buffer, it is processed the same way, regardless of whether it was evoked by input from the eyes (perception) or from memory (imagery)' (Kosslyn 1994: 74). If this were true, we could regard the implementation claim I_1 as vindicated, it being understood now that the two sides of the zip join at the level of the visual buffer. Is it true?

Prompted by the various dissociations between vision and imagery previously described, Kosslyn and colleagues undertook to assess the extent to which imagery and vision activate the same areas of the brain (Kosslyn *et al.* 1997). Activation in the visual buffer was found to be the same in both vision and imagery. But while both vision and imagery activated areas associated (according to Kosslyn's theory) with all the other subsystems of the visual system, there were differences in precisely which parts of these areas were

---

[19] On which, see Abell and Currie (1999).

activated. The researchers conclude that 'most of the information process-ing functions are accomplished in slightly different ways in imagery and perception' (Kosslyn *et al.* 1997: 330). This appears to be a drawing back from Kosslyn's earlier and more optimistic claim quoted in the previous para-graph. However, we need to note that the visual and imaging tasks under-taken by subjects in Kosslyn's study were in many ways very different. The visual task involved identifying an object from an unusual point of view (a picket fence seen from almost directly above, for example), while the imagery task involved seeing a lower-case letter, forming an image of the corresponding upper-case letter, and then deciding whether an *X* would fall on or off the imaged letter. It would be interesting to see whether two comparably distinct visual tasks produced patterns of brain activation that were as distinct as those found when one task is visual and the other imagistic.

Summarizing, we may say that there is plenty of evidence that imagery is like vision in important and sometimes surprising ways; that imagery is subject to the same pattern of breakdown as vision; and that there are close anatomical relations between imagery and vision. But while vision and imagery occupy pathways that substantially overlap, we lack convincing evidence that they are identical at any stage, except possibly at that of the visual buffer. In the next chapter we consider the possible implications of this. Before we get to that, however, we need to remind ourselves that visual imagery is not the only kind of imagery. What are the prospects for the implementation claim as applied to motor imagery?

Many brain areas involved in motor behaviour seem to be active during tasks involving motor imagery.[20] If the mechanisms that govern imagined hand movement are those that govern real movement, they ought to show lateralization: the right side of the brain controls the left (contralateral) hand, not the right (ipsilateral) hand, and vice versa. It seems that people make judgements about whether a left or right hand has been presented by imagining moving their own hand into the orientation of the presented hand. Larry Parsons and colleagues looked at patients who had undergone separation of the hemispheres of the brain. Presenting a left hand to the left visual field meant, in effect, that one was presenting a contralateral hand to

---

[20] See Parsons *et al.* (1995); Stephan *et al.* (1995).

the right hemisphere; presenting a right hand in the same way meant presenting an ipsilateral hand. Hemispheric disconnection meant that the motor functions of the other hemisphere could not be recruited to the hand identification task. The patients performed normally when identifying contralateral hands, but were at chance for ipsilateral hands. This is predicted by the theory that motor systems for controlling movement also control imagined movement; the subjects could perform the required rotation when the hand was contralateral, but not when it was ipsilateral (Parsons *et al.* 1998). Since subjects rarely report mentally moving the wrong hand when identifying a presented hand, it seems that at some level a decision about whether the hand is a left or a right has occurred *before* performing the mental movement; Parsons's experiment shows that the imagined movement is not epiphenomenal—remove the opportunity for mental movement and performance collapses.

We noted that simultaneous visual imagery and vision affect each other in ways that suggest they compete for processing resources in the same system. Is there any evidence that the same holds for motor imagery and actual movement? We have not found experiments that test this proposition directly, but there are some indications that interference effects would be found.[21] Recall that people make judgements about whether a left or right hand has been presented by imagining moving their own hand into the orientation of the presented hand. It seems that the position from which they imagine moving their hand is its actual current position, and not a fixed canonical position (Parsons 1994). From this, one would expect that concurrent limb movement would interfere with left–right judgement. There are also indications that remembering one's body position is interfered with by later body movements (Smyth *et al.* 1988).

What of the relation between deficiencies in motor performance and motor imagery? Once again the evidence suggests a strong connection. Right-side affected patients with Parkinson's disease who performed a simple finger sequencing test were significantly slower with the affected hand than with the other; this asymmetry was matched very closely by an asymmetry in their imagined performance of the task (Dominey *et al.* 1995). One patient, unable to perform the sequence with the affected hand, was equally incap-

---

[21] We are indebted here to Larry Parsons, personal communication.

able of carrying out the task in imagination; medication restored both real and imagined performance.[22]

There seems to be an important difference between motor imagery and the other forms. Motor imagery seems to work by operating the motor system as if one were initiating action, but in such a way that action itself is blocked. Why should this give rise to processes which, when consciously experienced, appear as perceptions as of moving one's body? Normally, these perceptions would arise as consequences of bodily movement itself. Why do they arise when movement is inhibited? In other words, visual imagery activates perceptual mechanisms, but motor imagery activates action initiation mechanisms. Why would this produce an experience as of moving?

There are a number of reasons for thinking that the motor system employs what Rick Grush calls an 'emulator': an internal device that models actual body movements and provides feedback to the motor system to enable motor instructions to be modified as the movement is undertaken.[23] Why do we need an emulator when feedback is available from the moving body itself? Because the speed of messages from the limbs to central systems is too slow to provide effective feedback in many cases of movement. The emulator, being located much closer to central motor areas, can provide feedback in a timely way.[24] Thus the emulator is a 'forward model', enabling prediction and control of a system by mimicking that system's dynamics. Such a model will, of course, be prone to errors of its own, and support for the existence of such a model is found in studies of errors people make in assessing the position of their hand after movement in darkness. Subjects in these studies consistently overestimated movement. The specific pattern of bias and variance shown can be accurately modelled on the assumption that there is 'a trade-off between the inaccuracies

---

[22] But lesions in the parietal lobes seem to interfere with the ability to predict movement from mental performance (Sirigu et al. 1996).

[23] See Grush (1995) and Clark and Grush (1999). There is independent evidence that part of the function of the cerebellum is to provide such a model. One function of the model might be to represent what is called the 'efference copy' of a motor command, which is then compared with the actual sensory outcome of the movement; this enables the subject to distinguish between perceptual changes due to the environment and perceptual changes due to movement of the body (Von Holst 1954). For recent studies, see Blakemore et al. (1998); Wolpert et al. (1998). We say more about efference copying in Sect. 8.3.

[24] See e.g. Paulignan et al. (1991).

accumulating in the internal simulation of the arm's dynamics and the feedback of actual sensory information' (Wolpert *et al.* 1995: 1882). Attempts to explain the pattern that do not use a forward model do not correctly predict the observed results. If the emulator hypothesis is true, then motor instructions which are prevented from being transmitted to the limbs might still activate the emulator, the operation of which then gives rise to those processes we recognize as the perception of bodily movement.

4.3   IMAGINED PERCEPTION OR IMAGINED ACTION

We said that motor imagery differs from other forms of imagery. There has been some uncertainty as to whether motor imagery should be categorized as a form of imagined perception, or as imagined action (Annett 1995). In our terms, the issue is this: what is the counterpart of an incident of motor imagery? Is it an experience of movement, or the movement itself? If we want to treat motor imagery in just the way that we treat visual or auditory imagery, we shall have to say that the counterpart is an experience of movement, and not the movement itself.

However, this view faces a difficulty. We see this when we consider the issue of what we might call *non-cognitive constraint*. We have noted that visual imagery is subject to constraints that are very like—and in some cases identical to—the constraints on perception; this is one of the reasons we have for saying that visual imagery is vision-like. Evidence for this included the reproducibility of visual illusions in imagery, and effects such as the differential discriminability of vertical and diagonal gratings, and of gratings at different places in the visual field. These effects occur in both perception and imagery, and do not seem to be explicable in terms of the recruitment of the subject's knowledge about perception to imagination, because people generally do not know about these effects. What seems to be happening is that visual imagery uses the human visual system, and these effects are explicable in terms of features of the system itself, rather than in terms of features of the objects in the world being perceived. That is why we call these *non-cognitive* constraints: they operate independently of what we know or believe, since most of us know little about the operation of the visual system. In general, we expect that when a form of imagery is X-like, it will be constrained by features of X, whether the subject knows about those features or not. For the rest of this section 'constraint' always means 'non-cognitive constraint'.

So being constrained by features of X is one reason for saying a form of imagination is X-like. Another is that the imagining and the X are not always easy to tell apart. We have seen circumstances in which people can misrecall a visual image as a veridical perception, and can even mistake a perception, at the time they are undergoing the experience, for a visual image. Let us call these two kinds of reasons 'discrimination-based' and 'constraints-based' reasons. In the case of visual imagery, these two kinds of reasons pull together; they both favour the view that visual imagery has a (visual) perceptual character. The problem with motor imagery is that these two kinds of reasons pull, apparently, in different directions.

Take discrimination-based reasons first. The reason we spontaneously describe certain mental events as motor images is because those events seem, in various ways, like perceptions of movement, not because they seem like the movements themselves. Having had a mental image, we can then be confused about whether the event imaged actually occurred or not. But if the image was a visual one, you did not confuse your image of a cat with a cat; you allowed your image to confuse you into thinking you had seen a cat. Just so in the case where the source of the confusion is a motor image. You did not mistake the motor image for a movement of your body; that would be like mistaking the middle of next week for the cat. Rather, you came mistakenly to believe that you had moved your body because the motor image was misrecalled as an experience of bodily movement. Discrimination-based reasons support the view that motor imagery is imagined perception.

Now consider constraints-based reasons. It seems that the most significant non-cognitive constraints on motor imagery are constraints on motor *performance*. Thus the chronometric data on imagined hand movements shows that the constraints on these imaginings are things like handedness, difficulty of the movement, initial position of the hand, and the condition of the subject's action initiation systems—remember the patient with Parkinson's disease whose imagined finger sequencing was distinctly slowed. So constraints-based reasons seem to support the view that motor imagery has a motoric character.

We hold that motor imagery is perceptual and not motoric in character; we take the discrimination-based reasons at face value. But we do not take the constraints-based reasons, as we have stated them, at face value. We think they need to be restated. And when they are restated, they will support the perceptual account of motor imagery. If motor imagery has a perceptual character, and not a motoric one, how do we explain why it is that the constraints on motor imagery seem to be motoric? Note first that, if the time taken to imagine a finger sequencing operation is constrained by facts about the time it takes to perform the operation, it is equally constrained by facts about how long it takes to experience the operation. Perhaps facts about motor perception *do* constrain features of motor imagery. We need, here, to distinguish mediate and immediate constraints. The immediate constraints on motor imagery are facts about motor perception; the immediate constraints on motor perception are facts about movements of the body. Since *constraint* is transitive, facts about movement are mediate constraints on motor imagery. But they are mediate, and are not immediate, constraints. And if the immediate constraints on motor imagery are facts about motor perception, we can hold to the view that motor imagery is perceptual in character; when a form of imagery has an X-like character, we expect it to be immediately constrained by facts about X.

Two questions naturally arise in response to this thought. The first is: 'What makes us say that the immediate constraints on motor imagery are not facts about movement but facts about motor perception?' The answer takes the form of an empirical prediction, corresponding to an intuition about counterfactuals. Suppose that there were cases where our sense of moving our bodies systematically misled us about the duration of the movements themselves. Then we would expect that a motor image of just that movement would be similarly misleading. In other words, were the chronometric data for motor performance and for the perception of motor performance to come apart, we would expect that the chronometric data for motor imagery would track those for motor perception and not those for motor performance.

The second question is this: 'What is the explanation for the fact that (so we claim) motor imagery is mediately constrained by facts about bodily movement?' After all, visual imagery of cats is not mediately constrained by facts about cats. It is, as we have remarked, constrained by facts about the subject's beliefs about cats. The question is an empirical one, and we are not sure what the answer is. The best hypothesis seems to be one that appeals to

the emulator mentioned in the previous section. The brain activity productive of motor images activates the emulator; the emulator is so designed
as to mirror the actions of the body; the activity of the emulator triggers
feelings as of moving one's body in the way that real movements of the body
would. Put all that together and you get an explanation for why the time it
takes to imagine performing an action depends, to the extent that the
emulator is reliable, on the time it takes actually to perform it.

There are other arguments that can be put in favour of the view, here
rejected, that motor imagery is imagined movement rather than imagined
perception of movement. We will consider just one of them here. When
we ask someone to imagine (perceptually) an object external to the body, we
have to specify (unless it is clear from context) what sensible form the
imagining is to take. I can imagine the object visually, or through an
auditory or olfactory image. But when I ask you to imagine moving your
body, I do not have to make any such specification with respect to sense. In
the sense that this claim is true, it is consistent with our view. In what sense is
the claim true? There is a familiar distinction between moving one's body
and one's body moving. Unmindful of this distinction, I could take your
instruction to imagine moving my body to be satisfiable by my having a
visual image of myself moving, or an auditory image of the same—assuming
that my body makes a distinctive noise. But there is a sense in which this
would not, in itself, be imagining moving my body; the image would not
capture the sense of effort that goes with moving your body. If we assume
that the instruction to imagine moving is an instruction that, at least
implicitly, requires imagining the effort of movement, the only way to
satisfy the instruction is through motor imagery. So when we take the
instruction in this way (as we normally and sensibly do), there is no further
specification to be got of what form the imaging is to take. This is because
there is only one sense by which we directly detect our own effort of
movement, while there are many senses by which we can detect the
movement of our body or of any other body. In that case the difference
between being asked to imagine moving your body and being asked to
imagine a cat cannot be pressed into service as an argument for saying that
motor imagery is imagined movement rather than imagined perception.

If, as we claim, motor imagery is imagined perception of action, it is not
imagining that you are perceiving action. Nor is it imagining that has

perception as part of its content. What you are imagining is, exactly, moving your body, just as what you are imagining when you visually imagine a cat is a cat. A motor image is an imagining of movement. We have put this in terms of the content–counterpart distinction. To repeat: motor images have as their counterparts perceptions of bodily movement. They have as their contents active movements of one's body.[25]

---

[25] While we claim that motor imagery is the simulation of experience, we don't say that motor imagery is always consciously experienced. Imagery in all its modes can occur, we take it, without being conscious, just as perceptual experience can fail to be conscious.

Chapter 5

CONTENT AND CONSERVATION

5.1 COGNITIVE CONSERVATION

In Chapter 3 we laid out some central claims of the simulationist programme. We took this to be a set of proposals about the role of recreative imagining in mentalizing and about the relations between imaginatively recreating people's mental states and theorizing about them. One dispute within the simulationist camp is whether the theory applies only to propositional states like beliefs and desires, or more generally to other kinds of states like perceptual states.

This could easily degenerate into a disagreement over terminology; there is no reason to insist that 'simulation' be used exclusively to apply only to the use of propositional forms of imagining rather than in a more inclusive sense. And we will argue that a proper account of our mentalizing capacity needs to include recreative imaginings that are perceptual as well as those that are propositional. But we shall see that the simulationist's interest in economy, or the reduction of the burden of theory, naturally gives special emphasis to the role of propositional recreative imaginings.

Discussions of how genuinely economical simulation is have often appealed to an idea called 'cognitive impenetrability'. This idea was introduced by Zenon Pylyshyn. A process is cognitively penetrable in Pylyshyn's sense if and only if it is rationally sensitive to the semantic properties of its inputs.[1] Decision-making *is* cognitively penetrable since we expect that what people will decide to do displays a rational dependence on the contents of the beliefs and desires that are inputs to the decision-making process. But vision, it has been argued, is not cognitively penetrable.[2] What I see when I open my eyes displays no rational dependence on my beliefs and desires. It is dependent instead on what happens to be in front of me. We will argue that cognitive penetrability is not the notion that we need, but considering it will lead us to a better one.

Shaun Nichols and Stephen Stich once argued like this. We do not predict people's actions by simulating their decisions, because our predictions are cognitively penetrated: experiments show that they depend on beliefs, some of them false, about what is and what is not relevant to making certain kinds of decisions (Stich and Nichols 1992). And this is exactly what we would expect if we made our predictions on the basis of a less than fully reliable folk-psychological theory. Now it is clear that in Pylyshyn's sense the simulation of decision-making (if there is such a thing) is cognitively penetrated, because decision-making is cognitively penetrated. Indeed, decision-making is a flagship example of cognitive penetrability; we expect people's decisions to be rationally related to their beliefs. So the success of a decision simulation depends partly on the simulator having the *same* rational sensitivity to the contents of the input thoughts as did the person whose decision she is simulating. Acknowledging this, Nichols and colleagues, in the course of setting out constraints on simulative processes, give the phrase 'cognitive penetration' a new meaning: 'The notion of cognitive penetrability important to the simulation debate is rather that a capacity is cognitively impenetrable only if the subject's cumulative knowledge or ignorance of the domain is irrelevant to the subject's performance on tasks exploiting the capacity' (Nichols *et al.* 1996: 46).

Everyone agrees that decision-making depends on knowledge of various things; Nichols and colleagues are saying that it does not depend on

---

[1] Pylyshyn says that a behaviour pattern is cognitively penetrable if it 'can be altered in a way that is rationally connected with the meaning of certain inputs' (Pylyshyn 1981: 159), and that a function is cognitively *impenetrable* if it 'could not be altered in a way that exhibits a coherent relation to the meaning of its inputs' (1981: 167).

[2] See Pylyshyn (1999). But Pylyshyn argues that it is just early vision that is 'impervious to cognitive influences' (1999: 342).

knowledge of decision-making. And so the simulation of decision-making should also be independent of our knowledge of decision-making. Nichols and Stich then claim that the empirical evidence favours the idea that our predictions of other people's decisions are influenced by a (false) theory about decision-making. They base this claim on evidence from a version of the so-called 'illusion of control' experiment, which purports to show that people irrationally value a lottery ticket more if they chose it rather than having been given it. Nichols and colleagues carried out an experiment of their own designed to encourage subjects to predict, by simulation, the behaviour of others involved in a situation designed to elicit the illusion of control. Their subjects failed. They conclude that decision prediction is not done by simulation.

Others have questioned the data on which Nichols and Stich's argument depends.[3] We won't do that here. Instead, we focus on the general claim that a simulative process must not display rational sensitivity to information about the process being simulated. This can't be right. While making a decision (a non-imaginary decision, that is) you might draw on the theory that, say, decisions like the one you are currently making should be made randomly, or while drunk, or only after talking seriously to an expert in decision theory. If you do, your decision is informed by a theory of decision-making (though not necessarily by a good one). To simulate the decision-making that you engage in here I cannot afford to put aside theories of decision-making. In fact I ought to draw on the same ideas about decision-making that you draw on. How could the sort of information your decision is based on be crucial to whether your decision is simulable or not?[4]

[3] For a debate on the validity of their results, see Kuhberger *et al.* (1995); Nichols *et al.* (1995); Ravenscroft (1999). In more recent work Stich and Nichols have abandoned this general argument, saying that simulation mechanisms can be cognitively penetrated. They now urge that the term 'simulation' be retired (Stich and Nichols 1997). We examine their earlier argument because it is a useful way to see how better to understand the correct constraints on simulation.

[4] Stich and Nichols note that the rule 'simulations may not have recourse to a theory of decision-making' would be problematic if, as Jerry Fodor apparently believes, people normally make use of such a theory when they make decisions (Stich and Nichols 1992: 154). They propose as a remedy that the prohibition be restated: 'simulations may not have recourse to a theory of decision-making except where that theory is stored in the practical reasoning system'. Our example above indicates that the restatement will not do; I can simulate your decision-making even when that decision-making drew on general beliefs you have about decisions.

Still, claims to the effect that some task is done by simulation can be exposed as bogus by showing that the performance on the task depends on having certain kinds of information. Nichols and Stich's results concerning the illusion of control—assuming their results are correct—are anomalous for a simulative account of decision-making because, in the case being considered, there is no reason to suppose that the people whose behaviour is being predicted would, in this particular situation, be taking account of a theory of decision-making. The question is how to distinguish between legitimate and illegitimate appeals to theory in simulation. The answer is as follows. When you simulate S's reasoning or decision-making, you should appeal to *just the same* theories or beliefs or information that S appeals to in his reasoning or decision-making. Call this the condition of *cognitive conservation*. The suspicion in the case of those people asked to predict the behaviour of subjects in an illusion-of-control experiment is that they got the wrong prediction because they drew on information that the subjects did not draw on.

Suppose we say that simulation theory is intended to apply only to imaginative states that meet the condition of cognitive conservation; simulations that use such states alone will, if the simulation goes well, not draw on more information (i.e. theory, in our broad sense) than is drawn on by the target of the simulation. The question would then be 'What states of recreative imagining, if any, meet the constraint?' Unfortunately, we must introduce a further complication here, because the quite *general* requirement of cognitive conservation as just stated is too restrictive. Stich and Nichols give a relevant example:

consider one of the standard examples used to illustrate the role of imagery in thought. Suppose we ask you: 'How many windows are there in your house?' How do you go about answering? Almost everyone reports that they *imagine* themselves walking from room to room, counting the windows as they go. What follows from this about the cognitive mechanism that they are exploiting? Well, one thing that surely *does not* follow is that off-line simulation is involved. The *only* way that people could possibly answer the question accurately is to tap into some internally represented store of knowledge about their house; it simply does not make sense to suppose that off-line simulation is involved here. (Stich and Nichols 1992: 140)

Generalizing the thought here, we can say that a piece of perceptual imagining will always draw on information that perception does not draw on, namely, knowledge of the visual, auditory, or other appearance of the object perceived. This would be sufficient to show that sensory imagining is not simulation if simulative processes require satisfaction of the condition of cognitive conservation. In response we argue that, while perceptual imagining fails to be wholly cognitively conservative, this is not a ground for thinking that perceptual imagining is never simulation. For it is not in general reasonable to demand of any simulation process that it is cognitively conservative *at the input stage*. Let us distinguish between the information needed to run the process, and the information needed to generate the right inputs to the process. And let us consider a case simulation theorists have been apt to present as a paradigmatic simulation in the non-mental realm, and on which they model their idea of mental simulation: the wind tunnel. Once you have set up the wind tunnel you want it to recreate, as nearly as possible, the conditions of flight. For that you need knowledge that you don't need in order to bring about those conditions in flight, namely how to create an artificial airflow of the right force and direction, changing over time to match, say, the flow of air produced by take-off. Similarly, someone bent on simulating another's decision might legitimately depend on knowledge of a certain special kind which the target lacks. Suppose that when Mr Forgetful is making decisions he always forgets that he is due to pick up his son at 3.30.[5] If I am going to simulate his decision-making, I might need to know that he forgets this, so that I can leave out a very natural candidate for an input to the decision simulation I want to run. But Mr Forgetful may not know that he generally forgets to pick up his son at 3.30—he has probably forgotten it. It seems harsh to say that when I use this bit of knowledge to adjust for Mr Forgetful's idiosyncratic epistemic take on the world, I am thereby prevented from simulating his decision-making. All we must insist on is that the knowledge I use to generate the right inputs does not get reused later on in a way that would violate cognitive conservation.

The same argument applies to the case of visual imagining; just as I cannot get the right inputs to simulate Mr Forgetful without knowing that he forgets to pick up his son, so I cannot get the right inputs for visualizing my house—inputs that come from visual memory—unless I know what my house is like. But in order for visual imagery to be successful simulation it must be the case that this knowledge plays no part *beyond the selection of inputs*.

---

[5] For the career of Mr Forgetful, see Hargreaves (1976).

That is why we emphasized (in the previous chapter) the results of Kosslyn's recent study which indicate that there are various subtle differences of processing at higher levels as between imagery and vision. If it turns out that those differences reflect the fact that imagery draws on 'top-down' information that vision does not draw on, then imagery fails the relevant test of cognitive conservation. That this is so is certainly not established by Kosslyn's recent experiments; at most those experiments suggest that it may be true. If it is true, it may also still be true that imagery is partially simulative—a patchwork of simulation and non-simulative processes perhaps.

Now let us say that an episode of recreative imagining I is a successful simulation of mental process M iff

(1) the component states in M are counterparts to the component states in I;
(2) after the input stage, I is cognitively conservative with respect to M.[6]

Perceptual imagining is recreative imagining that may or may not have the capacity to be simulative; whether it is depends on whether perceptual imaginings are cognitively conservative beyond the input stage. Given our current uncertainty about the extent to which vision and visual imagery share mechanisms, we cannot say with any confidence that visual and other forms of perceptual imaginings pass the relevant test of cognitive conservation, that they are cognitively conservative beyond the input stage.

The situation is very different with propositional imaginings. Here we know a priori that the condition of cognitive conservation is capable of being met. We do not, of course, know a priori that there are such things as propositional imaginings in the world of human psychology, or that such imaginings are used for specific purposes. But we do know a priori that, if there are propositional imaginings, they meet this condition. The reason we know this is that the concept of a state of propositional imagining is the concept of a state from which we reason in the same ways as from beliefs and desires. And 'reasoning in the same way from' means reasoning from the same premises to the same conclusions by the same inferential route. The belief-like imagining that P just *is* that imaginative state that has the same

---

[6] Although cognitive conservation is always with respect to some target process, we will occasionally say just that something is cognitively conservative, assuming it is understood what it is cognitively conservative with respect to.

inferential liaisons as the belief that P. Getting from imagining P to conclusion Q cannot take more or different auxiliary premises than getting from the belief that P to the conclusion Q does; otherwise the imagining in question simply would not be the imagining of P. And this characteristic is essential in order for imaginative states to play the sorts of roles in mentalizing that simulationists have suggested for them. Suppose you believe P and I don't. I want to see what you will conclude from P. I take on the belief-like imagining that P, and see what I conclude. My doing this would not be illuminating of your mental state if I had to depend on supplementary premises that you did not depend on, or if it made no use of a supplementary premise that you did depend on. I need to reason just as you do, and from just the same premises; otherwise I would have no grounds for concluding that you will draw this conclusion. The whole point of inferences from imagined propositions is that they should be cognitively conservative with respect to inferences from beliefs.

We may doubt, of course, whether propositional imaginings *fully* meet the constraint of cognitive conservation. There probably are factors that prevent belief-like imaginings from mirroring *all* the inferential liaisons of beliefs. But to doubt that belief-like imaginings play these roles even approximately is to doubt the very existence of such imaginings. With perceptual imaginings, on the other hand, doubt about their capacity for cognitive conservation is not tantamount to scepticism about their existence. The sorts of considerations that hold our concept of, say, visualization in place have to do with the idea of a state which reproduces, in significant ways, the phenomenological aspects of vision. Questions about at what stage, if any, the process of visualization depends on knowledge impact not at all on our concept of visual imagination.

It would be reasonable, therefore, for a simulation theorist to insist on a principled distinction between propositional imaginings and other kinds of imaginings, confining the claims of simulation theory to imaginings of the former kind. But there is a price to be paid for this restriction in terms of explanatory power. We shall argue that imaginings of various non-propositional kinds play an important part in mentalizing. This role is then not accounted for by simulation theory, and so that theory's claim to explain our mentalizing capacity is compromised. Moderate simulation theorists have hoped to divide the territory: to explain our mentalizing capacity in terms of simulation plus some measure of theorizing. What we shall suggest is that the territory does not divide neatly in this way. There is a third element to be taken account of: non-simulative imagining.

5.2   MAKING AND UNDERSTANDING DECISIONS

Modelling the beliefs and desires of others is an important part of modelling what goes on in them when they make decisions, but it is not by any means the whole story; we need to model many of their perceptual states as well. One reason is that perceptually based demonstratives play an important role in an agent's thought: I don't want to be able to dance in way *F*, where *F* is to be specified by giving some description of the dancing; I want to dance in *that* way. Similarly, I believe that my walls are *that* colour.[7] In cases like this we could not fully model the target of our imaginative project without also having imaginings that seek to recreate the contents of her perceptions. In cases like that one, perception scaffolds thought.

Sometimes a subject's perceptual experiences have to be accounted for in our imaginative projection because of their capacity to *interfere* with thought. You might not do very well in predicting the actions of someone being charged by a bull if you attended to thoughts alone and failed to get any sense of how the bull's terrifying appearance derails thinking about how to get out of danger.[8] It is not that the perception of the bull itself is in conflict with the subject's thought; rather, the perceptions generate an emotion of paralysing fear. An account of the emotions and their relations to the imagination will have to wait until Chapter 9; for now we say just that real emotions, and not just imaginative states that have emotions as counterparts, can occur within the scope of an imaginative project. And these emotions can be generated by perceptual imaginings as well as by belief- and desire-like imaginings, and sometimes by complex combinations of these types of imaginings. Fictional narratives, as we shall see, hold us largely because they prompt us to imaginings that have powerful emotional consequences.

[7] See Heal's own intriguing account of perceptual demonstratives in her (1997).

[8] Gordon gives a similar example: when wondering about how you would react to ominous noises in the basement indicative of an intruder, vividly imagining the actual sound would be important to getting a right answer (Gordon 1986).

The combined role of perceptual imaginings (including, incidentally, motor imagery) and emotions in the recreation of another's mental state is nicely illustrated in a little story by Kendall Walton:

Imagine going on a spelunking expedition. You lower yourself into a hole in the ground and enter a dank, winding passage. After a couple of bends there is absolute pitch darkness. You light the carbide lamp on your helmet and continue. The passage narrows. You squeeze between the walls. After a while you have to stoop, and then crawl on your hands and knees. On and on for hours, twisting and turning and descending. Your companion, following behind you, began the trip with enthusiasm and confidence; in fact she talked you into it. But you notice an increasingly nervous edge in her voice. Eventually the ceiling gets too low even for crawling; you wriggle on your belly. Even so there isn't room for the pack on your back. You slip it off, reach back and tie it to your foot; then continue, dragging the pack behind you. The passage bends sharply to the left, as it descends further. You contort your body, adjusting the angles of your shoulders and pelvis, and squeeze around and down. Now your companion is really panicked. Your lamp flickers a few times, then goes out. Absolute pitch darkness. You fumble with the mechanism . . . (Walton 1997*b*: 39)

Reading this you probably undergo uncomfortable sensations of darkness, confinement, and a rising sense of panic as things get worse. If this experience was induced by an act of imaginative projection, it is not adequately described by saying that you take on the belief-like imagining that you are confined in a dark space.[9] Your starting point is phenomenally richer and more specific. It is as if you are peering into the gloom, moving your hands before you, wriggling through the space; it is these perceptual imaginings that are productive of your rising sense of confinement and panic.

Walton's story emphasizes the role of motor imagery in the creation of a phenomenologically rich imaginative experience. Such imagining, even where it is not phenomenologically salient, may play an important and phylogenetically ancient role in predicting another's behaviour. Rizzolatti and his group have found that neurones in the macaque brain fire prior to

---

[9] We are not assuming that propositional states never have associated phenomenology. We agree that occurrent conscious propositional attitudes are often subjective states (Peacocke 1999: 206). Simulation of such attitudes can have an associated phenomenology, quite apart from the phenomenology of associated perceptual imaginings and emotions. But one's response to the Walton story is not accounted for in terms of the phenomenology of occurrent propositional attitudes alone.

and during reaching and grasping actions performed by the creature, and also when the creature observes an experimenter performing those same actions (Rizzolatti *et al.* 1996). There is indirect evidence for the existence of these 'mirror neurones' in the human brain.[10] It has been argued that the firing of mirror neurones in response to the behaviour of another constitutes the simulation of the other's motor plan, from which a prediction about movement can be derived (Gallese and Goldman 1998).

There is a further non-propositional aspect to decision-making that is hard to specify but which imaginative projection seems, in favourable circumstances, to be capable of mirroring. Very often it seems that we decide on the basis of a *feeling*, by which we mean the sort of phenomenological state that indicates to us the rightness or wrongness of a certain state of affairs. No doubt this is true in the realm of moral decision-making, but it operates in many other areas. How would Smith arrange the furniture in this room? Having taste in interior decoration much like Smith's, I can put myself in his shoes and work through the changes. But I don't do this by reasoning about what makes for stylish placement. I go on until the room feels right, and then stop. This can be important in social contexts. In certain situations of interlocking decisions (like the centipede game, described in Chapter 3) people cannot simply decide what move is rationally dictated by the information and preferences they have. A feel for what the other person will do is often important, though hard to justify as rationally mandated. Thinking about what the other person will do, I start to feel uneasy after a certain number of moves, and the unease increases with further moves. It seems that I am getting an empathetic sense that they will bail out soon, so it is time I did so. That requires putting myself into the other's shoes and sensing, from within that imagined position, the pull of a certain option. That cannot be done by appeal to a mechanism sensitive only to rational inferential and evidential connections.

Arguments like these might be countered by insisting that, while the domain of simulation is a restricted one, there are times—plenty of times perhaps—when consideration of rational connection alone will do the trick. Recent work in neuropsychology challenges this idea. Antonio

---

[10] See Hutchison *et al.* (1999). See also Berthoz (1996). Trevarthen (1998) supposes that such imagery is the basis of intersubjectivity.

Damasio has examined cases of damage to specific areas of the brain which seem to involve a loss of appropriate emotional response (Damasio 1994).[11] These people do not lack knowledge of their situations and of the facts relevant to the decisions they need to make, but typically they are extremely bad at making decisions, and may suffer bankruptcy and family breakdown as a result. Damasio suggests that they illustrate the importance of emotion in rational decision-making; far from being at odds with rationality, emotions, on this view, are a vital ingredient in practical reason; without cues from one's emotion system as to the appropriateness of a proposed course of action, one is apt to get lost in endless consideration of possibilities. If this is right, then the project of examining another's decisions from the point of view of content alone runs the danger of being as indecisive as the reasoning of Damasio's patient Elliot, who could explain in exhaustive detail the relevant factors, and then note that he still had no idea what to do.

As originally conceived, the idea of mental simulation did double duty: it was meant as an account of what it is to 'step into another's shoes'; it was also presented as an alternative to theorizing about minds. Earlier in this part of the book we agreed that simulation must go along with theorizing, but defended simulation against the idea that it collapses into theory. We have admitted also that there are kinds of recreative imagining which may well turn out not to be kinds of simulation, because they fail to respect the constraint of cognitive conservation. If we think that simulation and theory exhaust the field, we must conclude that these (perhaps) non-simulative forms of imagining turn out to be forms of theorizing. But we shouldn't say that simulation and theory exhaust the field. There are mental resources we bring, and must bring, to the project of understanding others that may not be simulative but are not instances of theorizing either. In Chapter 3 we argued that the simulation of X is theorizing just in case X is theorizing. The result holds good for recreative imaginings generally; a piece of recreative imagining is theorizing if it has theorizing as its counterpart. But perceptual imaginings don't; they have perceptual states as their counterparts.[12] Perceptual imaginings are cognitively penetrated, and may fail the test of

---

[11] For discussion, see Blackburn (1998: 125–34).

[12] We have agreed, of course, that perceptual imaginings may depend on theorizing in various ways. This is a different issue from whether perceptual imagining *is* theorizing.

cognitive conservation; but such imaginings, however much they are influenced by theory, do not themselves constitute acts of theorizing. We do not show that a mental process is a process of theorizing by showing that it is cognitively penetrated or, if it is an imaginative process, by showing that it is more cognitively penetrated than its counterpart. In the final chapter we shall have a lot to say about emotion. Here we just note that emotions are cognitively penetrated. Very often they display a rational sensitivity to our beliefs, as when we cheer up on learning that the news is not so bad after all. Yet to have an emotion is certainly not to theorize. Given the ways in which perceptual imaginings are similar, phenomenologically and chronometrically, to perceptions, share resources with perceptual systems, and suffer similar patterns of disorder, there is as much reason to place these kinds of imaginings alongside perceptions as there is to place other kinds of imaginings alongside beliefs and desires. The only people who should think that perceptual imagining is theorizing are those who think that perception itself is theorizing. We are not among them.

Instead of a simple simulation–theory divide, we need a more complex picture: the basic distinction is between theory and non-theory. Simulation crosses that divide, since some simulation is theory and some isn't. And simulations are a subset of a wider class of acts of imaginative recreation; the members of that larger class that don't count as simulations don't count as theory either.

5.3   NON-CONCEPTUAL CONTENT

We have found important differences between kinds of recreative imaginings; the suspicion that perceptual imaginings do not satisfy the condition of cognitive conservation makes them not apt to be treated in the same way that propositional imaginings are. Still, there is nothing here to cast suspicion on the idea that perceptual imaginings are genuinely recreative imaginings. After all, we have seen many ways in which perceptual imaginings and same-mode perceptions are alike. But in one important regard we have simply assumed that they are alike: in regard to content. We have assumed, that is, that a visual image can have the same content as a visual experience can have, just as a belief-like imagining and a belief can have the same content. Now we confront the suggestion that this assumption is wrong.

The argument is this: because of its relations to the knowledge on which it depends, imagery has conceptual content and so fails to be like perception, which has non-conceptual content.[13] And failing to be like perception in this crucial respect, imagery thus fails to have perception as its counterpart. How could one kind of state have another as counterpart when they don't even have the same kinds of content?[14] In recent years discussion of this issue has been dominated by some empirical results which purport to show that imagery is 'conceptually fixed' in a way that perception is not. Before we come to the philosophical issues that are central to the question whether imagery is conceptually richer than perception, we'll briefly take a look at these empirical results.

Chambers and Reisberg (1985) claim that such classical examples of perceptual reinterpretation as the 'duck-rabbit' are unavailable in imagery.[15] In their experiment subjects were shown the figure under conditions prompting just one interpretation, and were then asked to form a mental image of the figure. No subjects were then able to achieve the other interpretation by focusing on the image, whereas it is known that many would quickly achieve the other interpretation if they were looking at the drawing.

Further experimentation suggested that the matter is not so straightforward. It was found that the duck-rabbit figure is reversible in imagery given the right kind of instructions to subjects.[16] Further, there is evidence that even uncued reversal is possible (if somewhat unusual), at least for subjects with superior visualization abilities (Kaufmann and Helstrup 1993). But such reversal is considerably rarer in imagery than in perception. Is this support for the claim that imagery is conceptually fixed in a way that perception is

---

[13] Richard Wollheim says that 'In imagination, unlike perception, the imagery (roughly) receives its content from the thought, not vice versa' (Wollheim 1973b: 52). Martha Farah argues that the use imagery makes of perceptual pathways undermines the distinction between perceptual and cognitive systems (Farah 2000: 254). But Wilfrid Sellars suggested that imagery is non-conceptual; he says that imagination is a 'blend' of imagery and conceptualization (1978, sect. 11).

[14] According to Kosslyn (1994, ch. 3), imagery processing at the higher levels involves the application of information which might be described as conceptual; on Kosslyn's view this is a feature common to both imagery and vision. The issue here is not whether the processing of images is conceptual at some level, but rather whether at the lowest level of processing common to vision and imagery, imagery—but not vision—is conceptual.

[15] Reisberg et al. (1989) found a similar result concerning auditory images.

[16] See the discussion in Kosslyn (1994: 336–9).

not? We think not. On no one's account are perception and imagery the same. In particular, imagery is action, and needs significant mental resources to be sustained. These 'performance' features of imagery may well be sufficient to explain the difficulty of inducing the shift in aspect perception in imagery, without our needing to invoke differences of content. We'll assume, therefore, that the empirical evidence is equivocal at best. So let us turn to more directly philosophical methods.

There is a history of defences of the view that perception has, after all, conceptual content, and its most distinguished recent advocate is John McDowell.[17] If perception does have conceptual content, then we could concede that imagery does as well, with no damaging consequences for the view that imagery has perception as its counterpart. But we are doubtful about McDowell's arguments, one of which we'll comment on below.[18] Anyway, it seems best to make things more difficult for ourselves by accepting the non-conceptual nature of perception and then seeing whether we can avoid the conclusion that imagery is conceptual.

The basic non-conceptualist's point is that an experience can carry information about a certain state of affairs, and hence represent that state of affairs, without the subject of that experience possessing the concepts necessary adequately to characterize that state of affairs.[19] And this point is consistent with the fact that many concepts are acquired on the basis of experience. As McDowell notes, on the basis of an experience of a certain shade of blue, a person may acquire a concept of that colour, being able to have thoughts of the form 'X is that shade of blue', even in the absence of the sample that originally gave rise to her capacity to refer to that shade (McDowell 1994: 57–8).[20] But we should not draw from this the conclusion drawn by McDowell himself, that experience is already and necessarily conceptualized. One's experience may represent an object as having a certain complex pattern of unfamiliar shades of colour on its surface, yet

[17] See McDowell (1994, lecture III); also Brewer (1999, ch. 5).

[18] We are also unsympathetic to his motivation: to find a way to make perceptions reasons for beliefs, by placing them in the realm of concepts. For deflationary comment, see Fodor (1998, ch. 1).

[19] It may be that carrying information about P does not directly entail representing P because other conditions have to be met as well (see Dretske 1997: 7). But we can assume that the perceptual system is such that these extra conditions are satisfied.

[20] As McDowell points out, the condition that the thought be available in the absence of the sample is necessary in order to avoid trivializing the criterion of concept possession.

one may simply fail to register one or other of the shades to the extent necessary to be able to have, after the experience of the object, thoughts of the form 'X is that shade'. This does not undermine the claim that the experience did indeed represent the object as having that shade on its surface.[21]

So let us assume that perception has non-conceptual content; what, then, of imagery? We ought to see whether the arguments for saying that perception is non-conceptual also apply to imagery. Here's an argument of Tim Crane's (1992). Beliefs have conceptual content because possession of a belief requires the possession of certain inferential dispositions; one who believes that a is F and also that $a = b$ is disposed to infer that b is F. And, at least under some circumstances, the subject who believes the first proposition ought to believe the third. Now the capacity to make such inferences depends on the ability to discern a structure within the thought that a is F, and this ability constitutes the speaker's possession of the concepts which structure the thought that a is F. So having beliefs entails having inferential dispositions, which in turn entails having concepts. But perceptions are not related by inferential dispositions in the way that beliefs are. Further, while there is a sense in which a subject with certain beliefs ought to have certain others, there is no comparable demand that a subject with certain perceptions ought to have certain others. This is a reason for thinking that possession of the concepts essential to characterize the state's content is necessary in the case of belief, but not of perception.[22]

Crane's argument applies just as well to imagery. Images are not related to one another by inferential dispositions, nor is the having of one or more images ever grounds for saying that the subject ought to have certain other images. If these features, when they occur in perceptual states, are to be explained in terms of those states lacking conceptual content, then it would seem that the same explanation ought to be applied to their occurrence in imagery as well.

How is the claim that imagery has non-conceptual content consistent with our admission that we depend on our knowledge of things in order to

---

[21] See also Martin (1992) for an anti-conceptualist argument based on the idea that one can fail to notice how things appear to one.

[22] A similar case for the conceptual nature of the content of desire can be made by appeal to the role of desires in practical rather than theoretical inference.

generate images of them? Note first that one's possession of the concept of an F does not rule out the possibility that one can be in a state which represents the state of affairs '*a* is *F*', but represents it non-conceptually. The claim that perception is non-conceptual, as argued for by Crane, is not the claim that when the subject lacks the relevant concepts, perception is non-conceptual. It is the claim that perception is non-conceptual *whether the subject possesses the concepts or not*. The difference between the person with the experience and the concepts, and the person with the experience but lacking the concepts, is not, on this account, a difference that shows up at the level of experience itself. It is a difference in what is true (perhaps merely counterfactually true) about the impact of their perceptions on their beliefs; the one who possesses the concept of an *F* is apt, when perceptually confronted with an *F*, to believe that there is an *F* in front of her, and the one who does not possess the concept is not apt to do this. Nor does experience gain conceptual content when the subject's possession of the relevant concepts is causally implicated in the experience. Having the concept of an aardvark and wishing to find one, I might go out looking for one. My search is successful, and I see an aardvark. It was because I had that concept that I had the experience of seeing an aardvark. But the experience isn't conceptual, even though it was caused by a state the possession of which required possession of the concept *aardvark*. The connection between concept possession and conceptual content is not given by co-occurrence, or by causation, but by metaphysical necessity; you simply *can't have* beliefs without concepts.[23] So if *conceptual* and *non-conceptual* are to dissect the field of contents, non-conceptual content must be content which it is metaphysically *possible* for you to have without possessing the relevant concepts, and that is a pretty weak condition. We have agreed that it is very often true that image formation draws on conceptual knowledge. If I intentionally form an image of an *X*, I must have the intention to form one, and that requires that I have a concept of an *X*. But images can be formed in ways other than by intentional image formation. Images, especially hypnagogic ones, often have at least the

---

[23] This point is taken into account in the following definition of non-conceptual content, due to Tim Crane and based on earlier work by Adrian Cussins (1990): For subject *X* in state *S* with content *P*, *P* is *non-conceptual* iff *X*'s being in *S* does not entail that *X* possesses the concepts that canonically characterize *P*, where the concepts that canonically characterize *P* are the concepts which appear in a specification of the way *P* presents the world. (See Crane 1992: 143.)

appearance of coming to us unbidden and representing strange, sometimes hard to describe objects in the same way that unfamiliar and unexpected perceptions do. Images can represent to us colours and shapes we have seen fleetingly and forgotten—items of which we have no concept, even in the very weak sense of concept possession used by McDowell.

All this has been formulated within the scope of an assumption: that the question whether perception is conceptual is a question about whether perception has the same kind of content that belief has. On this way of seeing it, to say that perception has non-conceptual content is to say that the content of a perception is not the same kind of thing as the content of a belief, and hence that a perception and a belief can never have the same content. We suspect that this is the wrong way to see the issue. We would rather say that when we form beliefs directly on the basis of our perceptions, our perceptions and our beliefs can have the same content. I see that P, and I come to believe that P. Indeed, the possibility of the coincidence of content would seem to be a necessary condition for the fulfilment of a condition emphasized by McDowell, namely that our perceptions can justify, and not merely cause, our beliefs. Crane actually agrees: perceptions and beliefs can, he says, have the same contents.[24] Unfortunately, he also claims that the contents of beliefs, being conceptual, are 'composed of concepts', while the contents of perceptions are not. But this is not a possible combination of views. If a perception and a belief have the *same* content, whatever the components of the contents of the belief are, they are also the components of the contents of the perception. How to avoid the difficulty?

One can believe that P and desire that P: same content, different functional roles. Similarly for believing that P and perceiving that P: same content, different functional roles. To meet the demands imposed by the functional role of belief, including the role of belief in inference, a believer

---

[24] Actually, Crane says, 'when a perception that p causes a belief that p, the *whole* contents of these two states are of the same type—p' (Crane 1992: 155). So we might take Crane to mean that the contents of the perception and of the belief are not strictly identical but merely of the same type, in which case it might be possible for him to hold that the content of the one has constituents different from those of the content of the other. But a content *is* a type; when we both believe *p*, what I believe and what you believe are literally the same thing, though of course our believings are different. So to say that the contents of two beliefs are of the same type is to say that they have the same content. The same holds for the relations between the content of a belief and the content of a perception.

must have concepts. But meeting the demands imposed by the functional role of perception does not, in itself, require concept possession. So perceptions and beliefs differ at the level of functional role, and it is that difference which makes beliefs conceptual and perceptions not. It is not a difference which gives them essentially different contents. The content of a perception is a proposition, and so is that of a belief. This will be important later on.

If we see the issue that way, it makes little difference to what we have said about the non-conceptual nature of imagery. What we shall now want to say is that imagery is non-conceptual, not in the sense of having an especially non-conceptual content, but in the sense of being a state, the functional role of which does not require of its possessor the kind of discriminatory and inferential powers that in turn depend on concept possession. We can rest the case for the non-conceptual nature of imagery on the argument of Crane already given, without falling into the difficulty occasioned by thinking that this is a matter of having a special kind of content.

However, we don't want to take on commitments over and above our needs. It may be that there are perfectly good senses in which perception is conceptual as well as senses in which it is not. All we need is to be able to say the same thing about imagery. Here is a thought about perception which suggests a sense in which its contents are conceptual. According to Milner and Goodale (1995) visual experience arises from a pathway distinct from that which guides fine motor action. Various evidential trails converge on this thought; one of them is that a range of visual illusions appear not to affect motor performance. Andy Clark suggests that there is a challenge here to the picture of vision generally favoured by non-conceptualists.[25] The non-conceptualists argue that there is a fundamental distinction between the contents of beliefs and the contents of visual perception; the rich and finely grained representations of visual perception are capable of guiding motor action independently of the subject's capacity to conceptualize that content. The view of Milner and Goodale challenges this by suggesting that

[25] Clark (forthcoming), Clark's discussion makes clear how complex the neuropsychological picture is, and how tentative must be the philosophical conclusions we draw. Clark is also not committed to the version of conceptualism about visual content described slightly further on in the text. The view of Milner and Goodale is discussed again, briefly, in Sect. 8.5. For some thickening of the empirical plot, see the summary in Plodowski and Jackson (2001).

the contents of visual perceptions serve to inform belief, and not to govern motor control. As Clark puts it, perceptual content is 'poised for use in conceptual thought and reason' (Clark, forthcoming). Non-conceptualists about perceptual content have suggested that the content of a perception is a function of its aptness to drive action; the new picture suggests that it may have to take its content from its aptness to generate reflective thought. If we grant that visual experience is conceptual in this sense, it is clear that we should say the same thing about visual imagery. Visual imagery has as its counterpart visual experience; if vision does resolve into visual experience for thought and a distinct stream for action, imagery lines up with the first component and not with the second. And while imagery may be good for the reflective and thoughtful planning of action, we do not expect it to be of any use in driving skilful, on-line performance.

No doubt there are further senses of 'conceptual', and they would all have to be dealt with on a case-by-case basis. For now we leave it to the sceptic to offer a sense of 'conceptual' that distinguishes imagery and visual experience.

Part III

Development and Disorder

Chapter 6

IMPRACTICAL REASON

In this chapter we discuss the role of imaginative projections in cognitive development, and in particular in the development of children's play. Questions about human cognitive functioning are, of course, partly empirical questions, and psychologists are working hard to map the development of childhood pretence, and of children's understanding of beliefs, desires, and emotions. Great advances are being made in all these areas. But questions about the development of mental capacities and their interrelations, and about the concepts we have of these capacities, are to some extent philosophical. Indeed, the doctrines that divide psychologists in this area are often partly philosophical in nature, and are recognized as such by workers in the field. While most of us are content to admire interdisciplinary work from a distance, developmental psychologists are getting on with it in good order.

While this chapter is, we hope, well informed by results and theories in psychology, its aim is a philosophical one: to bring conceptual clarity to questions about pretend play, imagination, and mind-reading, and about their development. It can be progress to see that there are more, or different, options than we originally thought there were, and expanding the horizons for theory is our main aim. Our one substantive assumption is that children's use of imagination is significant for the development of their competence in understanding beliefs and other mental states. Fortunately, that assumption is very widely shared by developmental psychologists. Throughout we shall bear in mind the distinction made in Chapter 2 between imagination and pretence, and see whether we can shed any further light on their ambiguous relationship.

6.1   PLAY

There are different kinds of pretend play; some (but only some) of them involve what we shall call 'role-taking'. Pretence that involves taking on a role can involve pretending to be someone else, as when a child pretends to be mummy. But there are cases of role-taking that do not seem to involve the pretence that one is someone else; they involve acting according to a scenario that is contrary to fact in some other way. This sort of role-taking occurs when a child pretends to be (herself) speaking on the telephone, though in fact she is merely speaking into a toy telephone. In fact, the distinction between role-taking that involves a pretended shift of identity and role-taking that does not seems, on reflection, rather problematic, because it depends on metaphysical theses about what constitutes an individual's essential properties. It is not a distinction that we feel any need to emphasize here, and we leave it as a matter for individual judgement as to which side of this divide particular cases fall. Of more importance will be the distinction between pretence that involves role-play of some kind, and pretence that does not, as when a child pretends to be a tree or a house. For us, a child's pretence will count as involving role-taking if it involves acting out the part of an intentional agent. Such a definition is going to make it hard to know how certain cases should be described; a child pretending to be a bear might in fact be pretending to be a creature who is like a bear in some ways but who also has some rather unbearish intentional states. And even pretending to be a house might be done in such a way that the house is presented as having beliefs and desires. These sorts of difficulties arise with any attempt to impose a coherent pattern on children's play; we all face this problem, whatever our theoretical perspectives. But it is important to note that we are *not* defining role-play in such a way that it follows, simply from the fact that a piece of pretence involves role-taking, that it involves imaginings. The question whether pretence involves role-play is answered by saying what is being pretended; the question whether pretence involves imaginings is answered by saying something about the mental states that underlie pretence. It is an aim of this chapter to provide a theory about the ways in which mental states that are imaginative can underlie acts of pretending.

Pretence used to be given a behavioural analysis. One feature of the overthrow of behaviourism and the current enthusiasm for cognitive approaches to psychological explanation is a tendency to explain pretence as the outcome of distinctive mental conditions. Alan Leslie, for example, described his own approach to pretence in this way: 'I shall try to explain the external symbolic activity of pretending in terms of properties of the internal mental representations that underlie it' (Leslie 1987: 414). Our own interest in pretence arises out of the conviction that pretence is often connected to inner mental acts of imagining, but in important ways our approach is different from Leslie's own. We shall argue that imagination is related to pretence, but we deny that there is a necessary connection here. We think there can be pretence without imagination, and that it is partly an empirical matter what kinds of pretence are actually connected with imagination. We also claim that there are complex and largely unrecognized conceptual issues concerning this relation that need to be sorted out.

Another question that interests all parties to this debate is whether the mental activity underlying pretence contributes in some way to the child's growing capacity to comprehend the mental states of others, and in particular to understand that people's beliefs vary according to the access they have to information. We turn to this question immediately.

6.2   PRETENDING AND MENTALIZING: THE EVIDENCE

One standard measure of a child's capacity to understand the mental is the unexpected transfer test, of which there are many variants. In the simplest version a puppet, Maxi, hides a sweet in box A before retiring from the scene. During Maxi's absence, the sweet is moved to box B. When Maxi returns, children are asked where she will look for her sweet. Three-year-olds tend to say that Maxi will look in box B; they seem unable to take account of the fact that Maxi's epistemic perspective on the situation differs from their own. By the age of 5, children are generally able to take account of this, saying that she will look in box A (Wimmer and Perner 1983).[1] Such tests are sometimes called false-belief tests.

[1] This experiment has been repeated many times in varying conditions. A very large-scale meta-analysis by Wellman *et al.* (2001) indicates that, despite some variation in results, most normally developing young 3-year-olds fail, with increasing rates of success as children get older.

It has been shown that younger children tend to do better on this kind of task if they are competent with pretend play, either alone or in a group; having an imaginary friend is also indicative of success with false belief (Chandler *et al.* 1991; Taylor and Carlson 1997).[2] One explanation of this is that experience with pretence alerts the child to the way in which agents can be motivated by distinct mental representations of the same objective reality (Schwebel *et al.* 1999). Later in this chapter we take up the question whether understanding pretence can lead to an understanding of false belief; we suggest that it can't. We shall also see that young children's competence with pretence goes along with a surprising ignorance of the mental conditions for pretending. The idea that pretence gives children lessons in the theory of mental representation may be on the wrong track. We suggest that pretence serves, not so much as a source of propositional knowledge about the mental, but as a means of acquiring (or perhaps merely exercising) certain imaginative skills.

The idea that pretence and mind-reading both involve the exercise of the imagination is not a new one. Paul Harris (2000: 41) advocates this view, suggesting that the difference between pretence and mind-reading concerns the output of the imaginative exercise: in pretence, imagination operates 'on-line' to generate pretend behaviour, while with mind-reading it operates 'off-line', and, by a process described in Chapter 3, to generate a prediction about the behaviour of another. As it stands, the theory does not tell us whether imagination is first recruited to pretence, turning up only later as an aid to mind-reading, or whether it is the other way round. Harris cites a study (Youngblade and Dunn 1995) which assessed pretend play in children under 3 years old, and found the results predictive of performance later on with mind-reading. Competent pretend play is manifested earlier than competence with false belief; the natural conclusion is that imagination facilitates pretend play before it helps with mind-reading.

One thing that is unclear from these studies is whether competence with pretence is predictive of competence on false belief because the first provides a training in rich and flexible imagining which is then put to good use in mind-reading, or whether competent pretending, since it happens to come

---

[2] We are grateful to Paul Harris for discussion of these issues.

before mind-reading, is merely the first indicator of an underlying imaginative skill that varies within the population. On the first model, high levels of performance on some aspects of pretence are causal factors in generating mind-reading capacity; on the second they are merely advanced notice that a certain capacity for mind-reading will be manifest later on. Plausibly, the truth involves some combination of these views: a strong basic capacity for imagination *and* plenty of imaginative exercise via pretence make for good mind-reading skills.

We put this difficult empirical issue aside for the moment, and focus instead on a question which is partly conceptual and which is raised by Harris's description of pretence as the on-line use of imagination. Appealing to the idea of mental simulation, he suggests that the child who acts out a game of pirates is adopting, 'in pretend fashion', versions of piratical attitudes; these pretend attitudes then fall under the control of the child's own planning and decision-making system, 'and the output of this system can be translated into a pretend action or statement' (Harris 2000: 35). Here, pretend attitudes are imaginings, but pretend actions are not to be thought of as merely imagined actions; the pretend attitudes have real consequences in behaviour: real actions that constitute acts of pretence. We consider this idea in the next section.

6.3 DOES IMAGINATION MOTIVATE PRETENCE?

Harris's description of on-line imagining suggests a parallel between, on the one hand, imaginings and pretence and, on the other, real beliefs and desires and those actions that are motivated by those beliefs and desires. According to a theory which has come to be called the Humean theory of motivation (Smith 1994), we answer the question 'What motivating reason did the agent have for Ψing?' by citing a desire of his to Φ and a belief of his to the effect that by Ψing he could Φ. (The qualification 'motivating' is required because there is another, normative sense of reason according to which you can be said to have or lack a reason for doing something irrespective of whether you have the appropriately related beliefs and desires. Someone who trod on your foot simply because he wanted to cause you pain and thought that this was a good way of doing so is in possession of a motivating reason, but lacks a normative reason.)

A good way to approach the question of whether imaginings can play a role in the explanation of pretence is to see whether they can ever play the role of motivating reasons for pretence. Given our account so far of motivating reasons, this idea cannot be accommodated, because motivating reasons just are beliefs and desires of certain kinds. The question ought to be put in this way: 'Can we extend our concept of a motivating reason so as to accommodate the idea that imaginings, as well as beliefs and desires, can be motivating reasons?' In particular, we can ask whether a motivating reason to pretend to Ψ might be that the agent has the desire-like imagining to Φ and the belief-like imagining that she can Φ by Ψing. If this is so, the right explanation of Smith's pretending to perform a magical ritual might be that he had the desire-like imagining that he conjure up a monster, and the belief-like imagining that the best way to conjure up a monster is to perform the magical ritual. Call this the 'imagination-as-motivation' view.

Shaun Nichols and Steve Stich (2000) deny that imaginings can motivate. Their argument begins from the uncontroversial thought that motivation involves desire. Suppose we seek to explain a piece of pretence, such as pretending to eat a (mud) pie; how can imagining that the glob of mud is a pie explain this? Imagining that *P* is a state that is like belief in various ways. But it is not desire-like: not enough like desire to provide an account of the motivation behind pretence. And there may be no real desire for the belief-like imagining to combine with so as to motivate; the child who pretends to eat may not really want to eat anything. Anyway, wanting to eat would not normally explain *pretending* to eat.

This objection depends on the identification of imagination with what we have called belief-like imagining. We have already given grounds, independent of the present problem, for thinking that there are also desire-like imaginings. Nichols and Stich note the suggestion that there might be a kind of imagination that is genuinely desire-like. They reject this idea for two reasons. The first is that if imaginary desires and real desires with the same content have the same causal powers, having the imaginary desire to eat some pie along with an imaginary belief that the glob of mud is a pie would result in really eating the mud pies—something pretenders don't normally do. But why should we assume that the motivating powers of desire-like imaginings and the motivating powers of desires with the same contents are the same? When we introduced the idea of belief-like and desire-like imaginings, we said they share the internal, but not the external, functional roles of the corresponding beliefs and desires. Indeed, we spoke as if imaginings have no external functional roles, no motivating powers. In fact, the choice is not between assuming that they have the same motivating powers as the corresponding beliefs and desires, and assuming they have no motivating powers at all. Imaginings may be type-individuated partly by their distinctive motivating powers. In particular, where the desire to P is apt to motivate one to Φ, the imaginary desire to P may motivate one to pretend to Φ.

The second objection Nichols and Stich offer is that some cases of pretence, such as pretending to be a dead cat, cannot plausibly be thought of as the product of any imaginary desire; there is no such thing as imagining yourself in the position of the dead cat, taking on in imagination the desires that would motivate the dead cat. We don't see why we should assume that all pretence has the same kind of mental cause; perhaps there is pretending that is caused by imagining and pretending that isn't. This would be an ad hoc response if we were not able to give an independent characterization of the kind of pretence to which the thesis of imagination-as-motivation is supposed to apply. But we can: it is supposed to apply to pretend play that involves role-taking, as we defined it earlier. This is sufficiently distinctive a kind of pretence for it plausibly to be thought of as having a distinctive kind of explanation.

Another objection to the imagination-as-motivation theory is that there are plenty of cases where imaginings seem *not* to have any motivating power. Take someone who passively imagines taking part in a battle while she is in fact sitting in an armchair. This is just daydream or fantasy. Compare this with someone who is actively engaged in a game that enacts the battle. There is certainly a difference in behaviour between these two cases, but we can suppose that there is no difference of imagining. How can imagining cause the behaviour in the one case, and the very same imagining not do so in the other? If they can be having the same imaginings, and if imaginings are motives for action, why is one of these people motivated and the other not?

One thing to be said in response to this is that imaginings in the context of pretence will almost certainly have contents not possessed by imaginings from the armchair; we shall see why this is so in the next section. Still, it may be possible to construct a case where the passive imaginer and the pretender have the very same imaginings. So we answer the objection in another way, by appealing to the holism of motivation. We all accept that beliefs and desires motivate only in the context of other beliefs and desires that the agent has. Two people may share a belief and a desire, while the belief–desire pair motivates only one of them, because of differences elsewhere in their cognitive systems. Note also that when belief-like imaginings are involved in practical and theoretical reasoning, they are not isolated from the agent's real beliefs; recall the example of young children who bring their real-world knowledge to the task of inferring the imagined condition of a toy elephant which has had water poured over it.[3] Even if we think that imaginings can motivate, we must remember that they never do so in isolation from the subject's other mental states. So while the passive daydreamer and the active war game player may not differ in their imaginings, they will differ in their relevant mental backgrounds: the game player really desires to play a game, really believes that she is playing a game, and the passive imaginer does not have that belief or that desire. So there will be many potentially relevant differences between the game player and the passive imaginer, and we may be able to explain the behavioural differences between them by appeal to one or other of these differences.

We disputed the assumption of Nichols and Stich that, if imaginings have motivating powers, they have the same powers as their counterparts. David Velleman holds the same view, though, as we shall see, he argues in favour of the idea that imaginings motivate. He says that 'When a child imagines that he is a nurse, for example, he is disposed to behave as would be desirable if he were a nurse' (Velleman 2000: 256). This is surely wrong. Very little of the child's behaviour is likely to be genuinely nurse-appropriate, even leaving aside the mistaken beliefs about nursing he will have. Compare having your injuries attended to by a nurse and being attended by a nurse who merely pretends to help; the results are likely to be radically different. Velleman explains differences in actual behaviour between believers of P and imaginers of P as due to differences elsewhere in their mental states (2000: 272). We should not, on this view, expect the same behaviour from two agents who differ in that one believes that P and the other imagines P, even though the difference is one between equipotent states. The reason is that agents rarely differ *just* in this one respect; differing in this way they are likely

---

[3] See above, Ch. 1.

to differ in other mental ways. And differing in these other ways, we shall expect their behaviours to differ.

There is nothing intrinsically objectionable about arguments, like this one, that appeal to the explanatory holism of mental states; in fact we appealed to the holism of mental states ourselves two paragraphs back, in order to explain how it is that imaginings sometimes motivate pretence and sometimes do not. Still, our argument and Velleman's should not be reckoned to have the same force. Ours is the uncontroversial point that the behavioural consequences of a given mental state depend on what other mental states it is taken in conjunction with. Velleman's point is that we can defend the motivational equivalence of two distinct state-types by postulating further differences elsewhere in the mental economy. This argument generalizes rather alarmingly. Consider the following: believing P and desiring P are motivationally equivalent; the fact that people who differ in that one believes P while the other desires P tend also to differ in behaviour is due to the fact that such a difference generally goes along with other, motivationally relevant differences. Why try to defend the equipotence of belief and imagining when there is a much more plausible view: both states motivate, but do so in different ways?

6.4   THE OPTIONS

In order to assess the idea that imagination can motivate pretending, we ought to get a clearer view of what the options are. We need to see more precisely what the possibilities are for describing pretence, and the imaginings that might go with it. Consider Walter (and assume, for simplicity's sake, that he is a mature adult), playing a war game involving toy guns, paint pellets, stalking behaviour, etc. He is doing various things: hiding behind a tree, jumping out at someone, firing a pellet of paint at him, etc. There are different ways to continue this story about Walter.

(1) Assume first of all that Walter is not pretending at all. Rather, he treats this game as one with rules specifiable in terms of actual states of affairs, such as 'the winner is the person who at the end of the game has no paint on him'. Here, an explanation of his behaviour in terms of beliefs and desires, and which say nothing about pretending or

imagining, seems right. Walter is someone who wants to win the game, and believes that he can do so by getting paint over everybody else and none on himself. He does not think about what he is doing in terms of 'shooting to kill' for example, or, if he does, that is incidental to his playing. For him, the goal is not to pretend to do anything; the goal is really winning the game, and nothing more.

(2) On the other hand, Walter might conceptualize his own activity in terms of its relation to an activity he is not really engaged in— attempting to shoot others with deadly rounds and not be shot by them—and he might allow this conception to guide his behaviour. Then we can count him as a pretender: he pretends to kill and to avoid being killed. His practical reasoning can be reconstructed along the following lines: I desire to pretend to kill someone, the best way to do this would, in the present circumstances, be to hit the person with a paint pellet, so I will try to hit the person with a paint pellet.[4]

There is no pretending in (1), though what one observes in this case might be indistinguishable from (2), which does involve pretending. Level (2), while it involves pretending, does not involve imagination; here the agent intends to pretend, and does so, without his pretence being motivated by imagining, or being related in any other significant way to imagination. How would a case where imagining gets into the picture differ from (2)?

(3) Suppose Walter is someone who desires to pretend in accordance with what he imagines; he wishes to act out his imaginings. Walter's imaginings guide his pretence in two ways. First of all, he desires to pretend in a way that is in harmony with what he imagines up to that point in the game. When he imagines that he has someone in the sights of his gun, he is apt to pretend to shoot them; when he imagines that he has been shot, he pretends to be injured, and so on. Secondly, Walter's pretending is done partly to enhance further imaginings he wishes to have. Walter may, for example, wish to imagine that he kills someone. Of course, he is free to imagine that he kills someone any time; he does not have to engage in pretence in order to imagine it. But for some of us—and, we'll assume, for

---

[4] This description of pretence corresponds to the theory of pretence developed in Nichols and Stich (2000, sect. 4.3).

Walter—imagining this might be a more pleasurable and exciting experience when the imagining is made especially rich and vivid through its connection with perception and the experience of action.[5] Imaginings thus keyed to behaviour have an element of adventure to them. When we merely daydream, things will typically turn out as we want them to; when our imaginings are related to what actually happens, we cannot guarantee how things will turn out.[6] And their turning out as we wish them to may depend on our exercising certain skills; if they then do turn out that way, we may enhance our pleasure by recognizing that the desirable outcome was due to our own skilful performance. Here Walter is motivated by beliefs and desires, in the conventional way, but imagination plays a role in explaining his behaviour, for it explains why it is that he has the particular beliefs and desires that motivate him. Walter's imaginings function for him as items on the shelves function for a shopper. The shopper's behaviour is motivated by what he believes and desires; he wants this item, and believes he can get it by reaching for the can. But none of this makes much sense without appeal to the items on the shelves; it is their presence in his perceptual environment that make his having the beliefs and desires he does have explicable. In Walter's case, his having the beliefs and desires that motivate him is understood, once we understand the imaginings he is reaching for.

So there are at least three possibilities for describing the behaviour of Walter the war game player, all of which stop short of endorsing the imagining-as-motivation theory. We can describe his behaviour as that of someone not engaged in pretence at all; as the behaviour of someone engaged in role-taking pretence but whose motivation is not connected to states of imagining; as the behaviour of someone whose motivation is partly

[5] On 'props' and their capacity to enhance the vividness of imagining, see Walton (1990: 26–8). There is evidence from adult subjects that enactment can affect the vividness and realism of an imagining. When people are simply asked to predict the proportion of people who would go up to 450 volts in a Milgram-style obedience experiment, their answers are wildly incorrect. But subjects engaged in active role-play reproductions of the conditions of the experiment displayed the very high levels of obedience that Milgram had found. See Greenwood (1999) for references and discussion.

[6] 'Turn out as we want them to' does not mean that the story necessarily ends happily for us; it means that it ends as we determine that it should. On wanting stories to turn out badly, see Ch. 9.

a response to his imaginings and to the thought of imaginings he might have in the future.

There is a further description of Walter available to us.

(4) His game-playing behaviour is motivated by belief-like and desire-like imaginings; his firing a pellet is motivated by the desire-like imagining that he kill someone, and his belief-like imagining that the best way to do this would be to raise his gun and fire a deadly round at the man before him. He may have real desires such as the desire to pretend, and the desire to imagine various things. He may also believe that he is playing a game and that he is imagining various things. But these are not the states that motivate him in this instance, though they may constitute the background to motivation.

As we rise up the hierarchy from (1) to (2) we introduce the idea of pretence. As we move from (2) to (3) we introduce a role for imagining. And as we move from (3) to (4) we introduce the idea that imagining motivates pretence.

The difference between (3) and (4) can be put in terms of a distinction due to Michael Stocker (1981).[7] Stocker distinguishes between *acting for the sake of* and *acting out of*. For example, Mary might act towards Jane out of friendship to her. Being Jane's friend, she acts towards Jane in certain ways and with certain motives. Thus she might act on the basis of her desire that Jane avoid doing something that will not be in her, Jane's, interest to do. On the other hand, Mary might act for the sake of her friendship with Jane. For example, she might be motivated by the desire to preserve her friendship with Jane, and decide not to say anything that will cause a breach. Acting out of friendship does not require it to be the case that the concept of friendship is deployed in the content of one's motivating beliefs and desires; acting for the sake of friendship does require this. When Walter's actions exemplify level (3) we have a case of acting for the sake of imagining; when they exemplify level (4) we have a case of acting out of imagining.

We should not see the steps up the hierarchy as steps of increasing cognitive sophistication. If pretence on the model of (4) above occurs—and that is a question we shall investigate further—then the player at this level

---

[7] Stocker offers his distinction as part of an argument against the Humean theory of motivation. We do not take it in that way; see Smith (1998).

can be described as the most absorbed player, the player whose pretence is driven by imagining in just the way ordinary behaviour is driven by beliefs and desire. But this player need not deploy the concept of pretence, or the concept of imagining, in his pretence. It is true of this player that he is pretending, and this is true in virtue of the fact that his behaviour is being driven, not by beliefs and desires, but by imaginings. It is not true in virtue of his wanting or intending to pretend, or in virtue of his believing that he pretends. And while it is true that this player has various imaginings that motivate his pretence, he need not deploy the concept of imagining.

Our account of the varieties of pretending suggests that pretence is only loosely connected to imagination. There are cases where someone is pretending by acting out of imagination, where the agent may not even understand what pretence is; cases where the person is acting for the sake of imagination, but out of belief and desire; and cases where the person's pretence is not connected with imagining at all, as in our (2). And cases like our (1) indicate that there is 'fool's pretence'; activity that is easily misidentified as pretending to do something.

It might be hard, in practice, for someone to pretend without recourse to imagining of any kind. Plausibly, the imagination plays an *executive* role in pretence; when one pretends, one has to plan one's actions, and planning actions involves imagining.[8] But to grant this is not to grant much; if imagination plays a role in the planning of pretence, it probably plays a role in the planning of actions of all kinds. There is no special connection here between pretending and imagining, but merely a general connection between action and imagining.

Should we conclude, then, that imagination can be motivation? David Velleman thinks so. To suppose, he says, that the child's pretence is always motivated by belief and desire

denies that the child ever enters into the fiction of being something other than he is. In order to enter *into* the fiction, the child would have to act it *out*; and in order to act it out, I think, he would have to act *out of* imagining it, not out of a desire to represent it in action. A child who was motivated by such a desire would remain securely outside the fiction, thinking about it as such—that is, as a fiction to be enacted. (Velleman 2000: 257)

---

[8] For more on the idea of the executive, see Ch. 7.

We reject this argument. Refusing to countenance (4) as an adequate description of Walter's behaviour does not mean we have to say that Walter remains 'securely outside the fiction'. (3) allows that, while imagination is not what motivates the pretence, it is, at one further remove, what drives the pretence. The motivation makes sense, for Walter and for us, in terms of how Walter responds imaginatively—in a presumably spontaneous and unreflective way—to the story. And we need not think, as Velleman's description encourages us to think, of someone who is motivated by beliefs and desires rather than by imaginings as a calculating and dispassionate agent. In all sorts of situations we act skilfully and creatively on the basis of beliefs and desires that make little or no conscious impact on us; the child's consciousness may be wholly absorbed by the imagining. Consistent with (3), the child's experience may be one of a rich and immediate connection between imagination and pretended action.

Perhaps Velleman does not have a phenomenological understanding of what it is to 'remain outside the game'; perhaps he means by this just that one's imaginings, whatever their other relations to one's behaviour, fail to make maximally close contact with behaviour because they don't motivate behaviour. If so, then we think his description of the case is question-begging. If imagination can motivate, then the child describable in terms drawn from (3) would be 'outside the fiction' in the sense that his imaginings are not maximally closely related to his pretending. If imagination cannot motivate, and (3)-type cases—where the force of imagination is mediated by beliefs and desires—present us with the best illustrations there can possibly be of behaviour under the control of imagination, then those cases ought to count as cases where the agent enters into the fiction.

None of this disproves the idea that imagination can motivate. One way to show that imagination can motivate is by elimination of the alternatives. We shall look at the pretence of young children—those between the ages of 2 and 5 years—asking whether their pretence *cannot* be explained in any ways corresponding to (1)–(3).

6.5   YOUNG CHILDREN'S PRETENCE

Should we say that young children, whose behaviour we naturally describe as pretence, conform to any of (1)–(3) above, or should we say that they are best described as engaging in pretence as motivated by imagining, on the model of (4)? With description (1), there is the appearance of pretence only. It is hard to believe that this is generally the correct account of children's play, given its often highly elaborated nature, and given the sorts of verbal accompaniments children produce. Children as young as 2 years old refer spontaneously to objects by means of expressions ('car', 'horse') which are applicable only in the context of that fiction; they seem to be in 'pretend mode', rather than simply working through behavioural routines (Harris and Kavanaugh 1993: 57).

Nor is (2) likely to be the appropriate level of description. In Chapter 1 we argued that we need not assume that fiction readers undertake 'mixed inferences', where only some of the premises involve the prefix 'In the fiction . . .'. Now consider children in a situation we have already described. In an experiment, a pretence is established: the experimenter pretends to fill a cup with water; the cup is then upended over one of a range of displayed soft toys. Children as young as 2 years clearly understand that it is this particular toy (the elephant, say) that is wet and that the cup is now empty, though it was not specified as part of the pretence that the elephant would be wet if the cup was tipped over it, nor that the cup would be empty after the tipping. For example, the children will 'dry' the elephant rather than any of the other creatures, and when asked to indicate the empty cup (though in fact all cups are empty), they indicate the one just tipped up (Leslie 1988; Harris and Kavanaugh 1993). Pretence like this, that effectively keeps track of how the game develops without explicit instructions or rules, we shall call *productive* pretence. Playing productively, the children end up pretending that this toy is wet, that this cup is empty. What gets the children to the point where they pretend these things, rather than something else? If we thought of their pretence as not related to imagining, we would have to assume that they undertook some such inference as this: it is pretence that the cup is full; the cup is upended; if a full cup is upended then it is empty; so, it is pretence that this cup is empty. Inferences of this form have a rather complex structure involving the selective application of the intentional operator *it is pretence that*, and it is not very plausible that such inferences are regularly undertaken by 3-year-olds. If we introduce the idea of belief-like imagining here, we can explain productive pretending without appeal to these peculiar inferences. But it is important to see that, in order to do this, we don't have to adopt the imagination-as-motivation theory as exemplified in (4); the model of (3) will do instead. The crucial step in the explanation is the idea that *imagination* is productive; our imaginings combine with our beliefs so as to give us new imaginings that correspond to the new state of the game. The productivity of imagining can explain the productivity of pretence if we assume that imagination serves to update pretence. But it can do that without having to motivate pretence. It can do it as long as the pretender wants to retain the right kind of conformity between what he imagines and what he pretends. He imagines the elephant is wet, and forms the desire to pretend in a way that is in conformity with that imagining. Believing that the best way to pretend in conformity with that imagining is to pretend to dry the elephant, he forms the desire to do that. Thinking that the best way to do this is to rub the toy elephant with a cloth, that is what he does. The other option is to say that when the child imagines the elephant is wet, he forms the imaginary desire to dry the elephant; this, together with the imaginary belief that he can dry the elephant by rubbing it with a towel, motivates the appropriate behaviour.

Before we try to decide between these options, we ought to ask whether we have to choose at all; might we have two legitimate ways of describing the same state of affairs, and no reason to reject one in favour of the other? In that case having the desire to pretend to dry the elephant *is just the same thing as* having the desire-like imagining to dry the elephant, and having the belief that I can pretend to dry the elephant by rubbing the toy elephant with a cloth is *one way of having* the belief-like imagining that I can dry the elephant by rubbing it with a towel.[9]

These proposed identifications cannot be right. Even if we confine ourselves to occurrent beliefs, surely I can desire to pretend to do something, or have beliefs about how I can pretend, without having any imaginings. Further, the beliefs and desires in question require different conceptual abilities from those required by the corresponding imaginings. Believing that I can pretend to Φ by Ψing requires that I have the concept of pretence; so does desiring to pretend to Φ. Imagining in a belief-like way that I can Φ by Ψing does not require me to possess that concept. And a state that requires me to possess a certain concept cannot be identical to a state that does not

---

[9] 'One way of having' because there are usually many ways you can pretend to do something.

require this. Perhaps we cannot ask for very much systematicity in belief and desire from 3-year-olds, but our crediting them with beliefs and desires concerning pretence surely requires some minimal facility with pretence. This is not required by our crediting them with the corresponding imaginings.[10]

We take it, then, that the alternatives are genuine rivals. One way to choose between them would be to take up the suggestion of the previous paragraph and ask whether one of the alternatives credits young children with implausible conceptual sophistication. If young children lack the concept of pretence, they can hardly be credited with the desire to pretend, in which case we ought to adopt the imagination-as-motivation theory. Some experimental results do suggest that young (and sometimes not so young) children are very confused about pretence. Josef Perner and colleagues showed children a character apparently feeding a rabbit in a hutch (Perner *et al.* 1994); in fact there was no rabbit there. In one case it was explained to the children that the character knew there was no rabbit inside. In the other case the character thought that there was a rabbit, and was acting on the basis of a false belief. Four-year-olds could reliably identify which cases were pretence and which were not; 3-year-olds could not do this. Most of the errors occurred when a child who was told that the character falsely believed there was a rabbit there nonetheless claimed that the character was pretending. Angeline Lillard found that young children are willing to describe a troll character Moe as 'pretending to hop like a kangaroo' even though Moe does not know anything about kangaroos (Lillard 1993, 1998; Rosen *et al.* 1997). Children persisted with the description even when they were given a plausible explanation for Moe's hopping behaviour in non-pretence terms: Moe was hopping because the pavement was hot. Even 4-year-old children often do not associate pretending with an intention to pretend. Some 3-year-olds and, depending on the conditions of the test, some 4-year-olds will attribute pretence to inanimate objects like vehicles, acknowledging at the same time that such objects cannot think

[10] Perhaps children of 3 lack the psychical complexity that could provide truth-makers for the sorts of fine-grained psychological attributions we are considering here. Indeed, the schema may be over-refined even for the description of adult minds. Given that we are trying to think of ways the imagination-as-motivation view *might* be tested, we should err on the side of generosity towards assumptions that enlarge the set of potential tests.

(Lillard *et al.* 2000). When children do deny that such objects can pretend, they don't always cite lack of thought as the reason; one child explained that aircraft cannot pretend because they lack the necessary clothes.

What would explain such a tendency to ascribe pretence in circumstances that seem evidently non-pretended to mature agents? Young children might start with what psychologists have called a *response category* concept (Bruner *et al.* 1956): they ascribe pretending to an activity just in case it prompts them to engage in imagining. Moe's antics and the activities of the confused rabbit-feeders are actions which, however described, are likely to prompt a young child to imagine a hopping rabbit, or someone feeding a rabbit. But if young children understand the pretence of others as that which leads those children themselves to imagine, they may understand their own pretence as that which is prompted by their own imaginings. We need not argue about whether this *really* constitutes an understanding of pretence; all that needs to be observed is that the child in this situation has the conceptual resources to act in a way that is prompted by her imaginings, and for this to be intentionally done.

In that case we have a choice between two ways of describing the productive pretence of children, where it is no longer so clear that either description goes beyond the child's conceptual competence. According to the first way, there is a very close connection between children's imaginings and their acts of pretence; imaginings can constitute the motivation for pretence. According to the second way, there is a close, but not such a close, connection; imaginings play a role in explaining pretence, but they do not constitute the motivation for pretence. Between the imaginings and the pretence stand beliefs and desires that motivate in the conventional way, aided by a conceptual grasp that may well not constitute a competent grasp of pretence, but which happens to be adequate for the job. Which view is correct?

Here is an argument for the view that pretence is motivated by beliefs and desires, and not by imaginings. We have found no convincing argument against the view that imaginings can motivate. But this theory and the view that it is always beliefs and desires that motivate do not start out on an equal footing; the theory that beliefs and desires motivate has proved so effective in so many areas that the presumption ought to be that it is universally true. If we had to admit that we *do not see how* the motivation of pretence could be explained exclusively in terms of beliefs and desires, then the temptation to adopt the imagination-as-motivation view would be strong. But we are not in that situation. Despite the claims of Velleman, the advocate of exclusively belief–desire motivation is able to offer a plausible explanation of how pretence is motivated. The claim is that beliefs and desires (not necessarily phenomenologically very salient ones) mediate between imagination and pretence. Velleman's remarks on the child whose pretence is motivated merely by beliefs and desires and not by imagination suggests a contrast: on the one hand there is the fluent, spontaneous pretence of the child motivated by imagining; on the other there is the hesitant, overly cerebral performance of the agent who pretends out of belief and desire. We have no reason to accept this picture. Beliefs and desires can lead to action quickly, fluently, and without the need for conscious deliberation. Imagination plays a role in all this. How beliefs and desires get to be deployed in the service of pretence is explained in terms of their sensitivity to what the agent imagines; it is because the child imagines the elephant to be wet that she forms the desire to pretend to dry the elephant. But with this idea in place, we do not need the idea that imagination motivates. Given that the theory of belief–desire motivation (i) is well supported in a vast range of cases outside the area of pretence, and (ii) can plausibly account for pretence, we should opt for the view that beliefs and desires motivate pretence.

This argument depends on the assumption that, outside the domain of pretence, the idea that action is motivated by beliefs and desires only is obviously true, or at least overwhelmingly probable. But is it? Following Adam Smith, Alvin Goldman has noted the widespread phenomenon of motor mimicry, whereby people conform their facial expressions and postures to those of others around them. Goldman suggests that this physical imitation is consequent on mental mimicry; we imagine ourselves in the situation of the other, and the mental adjustment produces a corresponding bodily change (1993: 196). It is unclear whether this is the correct explanation of motor imitation; it might instead simply be the direct imitation of posture. Smith himself notes our tendency, when we see a blow aimed at another, to move so as to defend our *own* bodies. If this is caused by our imagining ourselves in the victim's position, it might not be an example of motivation-by-imagination. For such protective behaviours may not fully be actions; perhaps they are more like reflexes, and hence not capable of being rationalized. But note that imaginings do have the capacity to rationalize emotional responses; my feeling sad about Desdemona is made to seem appropriate by what I imagine about her situation. This is not a claim to the effect that imaginings motivate anything, but, together with the evidence from cowering behaviour, isn't it rather suggestive? After all, cowering from a blow aimed at another suggests that imaginings have the capacity to generate behaviour, if not to rationalize it, and the emotions case suggests that imagination has the capacity to rationalize if not to generate behaviour. Put the two together and we have imagination as motivation.

Other kinds of cases point strongly in the same direction. Velleman describes a rich variety of intentional behaviours that are not easily explained as the product of belief and desires: yelling at another driver while sitting in your effectively soundproof car; talking to yourself; acting out 'corporeal images of your own thinking' (Velleman 2000: 270) by scratching your head while in thought, or striking your head in recognition of a silly error. Then there are more bizarre activities out of Freud: Young Goethe throwing crockery out of the window as a fantasy of throwing out his baby brother; the Rat Man removing a stone from the road, thinking it a danger to his beloved's carriage, and then—deciding this is absurd—carefully returning it to the same place. What about checking behind the furniture after watching a gripping horror movie: are you doing that because you believe there might be a vampire there? Some of these cases might be explicable as pretence; you yell in the confines of your car as part of a pretence that you are yelling in the face of the other driver. But did you check behind the furniture because you were pretending there are vampires around?

If the only candidates for actions motivated by imaginings were acts of pretence, there would, as we have emphasized, be ready and plausible alternative explanations in terms of beliefs and desires. By unsettling our conviction that action is uniformly motivated by belief and desire, examples like those from Freud create a space for thinking that pretence might, sometimes, be motivated by imagination. Do they shift the balance of probability sufficiently in the direction of the imagination-as-motivation theory? We think the position is more like a stand-off. Further arguments might decide the matter, but for now making a choice seems more a rhetorical move than a rationally dictated one. Nor do we have to make a choice. As we shall see further in this chapter and elsewhere, we can base our claims on a disjunction: either imagination motivates pretence, or the beliefs and desires that motivate pretence are guided by imaginings.

6.6 IMAGINATION, PRETENCE, AND MIND-READING

How then do we account for the relation between pretence and mind-reading? Remember, we have agreed that pretence is predictive of mind-reading, but we did not try to decide whether pretence facilitates mind-reading through providing practice for the imagination, whether pretence is merely indicative of pre-established imaginative skills, or whether some combination of these two factors is at work.

The question to be asked now is this: 'What are the relations between the two causal hypotheses just mentioned and the two rival accounts of the relations between imagination and pretence we tried, unsuccessfully, to decide between in the previous section?' Ignoring, for the moment, any combination of the two causal hypotheses, we have four potential combinations. Call the two causal hypotheses 'pretence as practice (with imagination)' and 'pretence as indicator (of imagination)'; call the two accounts from the previous section 'imagination as motivation' and 'imagination as guide'. Nothing is settled: if pretence serves as imaginative practice for mind-reading, the practice can come about either through imagination providing the motivation for pretence, or through it guiding pretenders to have just the motivating desires they do have; if pretence is merely an indicator of imaginative skill, it can serve as such an indicator either because rich and flexible imaginings are required to motivate pretence, or because without them the agent would not have the appropriate guides to motivating desire. And if neither causal hypothesis favours one theory of pretence over the other, it is unlikely that any blending of the causal hypotheses will do so either.

This sounds disappointing. We would like to know more about the precise role of imagination in pretence, and about the way that imagination as manifested in pretence relates to imagination as manifested in mind-reading. But our current empirical and conceptual understanding suggests at least the following: imagination makes a substantial contribution to pretence and to mind-reading. In the next chapter we shall see how a deficiency of imagination affects both these skills.

It is one thing to suppose that the capacity for pretence and the later-emerging ability to mind-read are causally connected in some way, if only by way of some common causal factor. It is another thing to say that pretence provides an opportunity to acquire the concepts necessary for mind-reading. According to our account so far, the child who imagines, and acknowledges what she imagines as pretence, is someone who uses reality as a guide to imagining; it is on the basis of seeing this particular cup tipped up by someone that the child imagines that this cup is empty. For the child who is fully competent with the notion of false belief, the connection also goes the other way: imagining is a guide to reality; imagining being in the other's shoes helps me get a grip on those troublesome bits of reality, beliefs. Several times in this book, and particularly in opposition to the views of Robert Gordon, we have stressed that imaginative capacity *alone* will never get one to a prediction about anyone's mental states or behaviour. One has, in addition, to use the results of the imaginative project in order to draw a conclusion about the mental state or the behaviour. And if one is to draw a conclusion about a mental state, one has to have some concept of the mental state concerned.

Might a proper grasp of belief itself emerge from the child's experience with imagination and pretending? The mark of a proper understanding of belief is the recognition that beliefs can be action-guiding and yet not reflect reality; that is what makes false-belief tests an important instrument for detecting conceptual development. Pretence seems a good model for this, since the child recognizes something as pretence at the same time as recognizing that it is not true. Suppose the child is able to distinguish, at this stage, between imagination and what we call proto-belief; imagination is the attitude appropriate to what is pretence, while proto-belief is the attitude appropriate to what is real (note that proto-belief is not belief, since it does not accommodate false belief). If she can recognize within herself this contrast of attitudes, perhaps it is not far from here to a recognition that one proto-belief (presumably hers) can be true while another is false. But the imagination–proto-belief contrast, if the child is able to recognize it, is the wrong model for false belief. The imagination–proto-belief distinction is essentially one of perspective only. As David Wiggins remarks, it is of the essence of a difference of perspective that there is no contradiction between their different deliverances; where opinions do contradict one another, that must be due to something other than perspectival differences (Wiggins 1998: 108). There is no contradiction between things really being one way and it being pretence that they are another way, or, as we saw in Chapter 1, between believing things to be one way and imagining them to be another. For this reason we are sceptical about the idea that there is enough in, on the one hand, the contrast between pretence and reality and, on the other, the contrast between the mental attitudes appropriate to that contrast, to supply us with an understanding of the contrast between beliefs that are true and beliefs that are not. There is no plausible developmental path all the way from imagination to *false* belief.

If engaging in imaginative projections that involve setting aside some or other aspect of one's own mental state is an essential part of the capacity to detect false belief, then it is easy to see why early facility as a pretender would be predictive of subsequent success with false belief—just so long as the child can be assumed to get the concept of belief from some other source.

Chapter 7

AUTISM: SOME PIECES OF THE PUZZLE

We have seen that there can be selective damage to perceptual imagination: deficits of vision often go with deficits of visual imagery, and deficits of movement control often go with deficits of motor imagery. It is not clear, however, that these are cases of disorders of imagination. Shouldn't my imagery be recreative of my *actual* capacities for perception and motor control? The person with problems of motor control who wants to plan an action needs a planning system that mirrors her actual capacities for motor control; we don't call a model bridge deficient because it mirrors the battered state of the bridge of which it is a model.

In this chapter and the next we examine disorders of systems that are proprietary to the imagination itself. We are interested primarily in damage to imaginative capacities that affect belief-like and desire-like imagining, though questions about perceptual imagination will come up from time to time.

It sounds odd to speak of *pathologies* of the imagination. Common-sense psychology recognizes that imagination is a capacity requiring balance; people are frequently described as having too little or too much of it. But this goes with the idea that imaginative balance is mental fine-tuning. People with too little or too much imagination can be tiresome, or unsuited to certain occupations; it is unlikely on this account alone that they will suffer the crippling incapacities we associate with psychopathology. In this chapter and the next we want to suggest that the consequences of imaginative imbalance can be catastrophic. We look first at a condition where imagination seems to be impoverished, then at a condition where there is failure to monitor and control imagination. These two conditions are, respectively, autism and schizophrenia.

Theorizing about the nature and causes of disease is not usually regarded as the province of the philosopher. We do not aim to add to the body of evidence available; our role is purely interpretative. Also, philosophy and psychiatry are enjoying closer and better relations than they have experienced for some time. Philosophers are interested in understanding the malfunctions of the mind, and psychiatrists are keen to take philosophical ideas and use them to structure their explanations. One philosophical idea that has been very influential in shaping recent theories of autism and schizophrenia is that these conditions result from difficulties people have conceptualizing mental states. In some expositions this is described as a difficulty with metarepresentation. It will be a consequence of what we say in this chapter and the next that this last idea is not very promising.

However, our aim here is not to insist on a dichotomy between our approach and all the proposals that have been advertised as based on metarepresentation. That label is often not used in any very precise sense, and relying on it can mask underlying similarities between different approaches. Accordingly, we shall try to show that imagination-based approaches to psychopathology and metarepresentation-based approaches are not always divided on questions they seem to be divided on, and in the next chapter we shall highlight ideas about schizophrenia that, despite their metarepresentational packaging, converge with our own.

7.1   AUTISTIC SPECTRUM DISORDER

In the mid-1940s two Viennese psychiatrists independently gave remarkably similar accounts of a hitherto unrecognized condition of childhood. Leo Kanner, by then working in the United States, called this 'autistic disturbance of affective contact' and described what came to be regarded as the classic symptoms of autism: social isolation, impaired language development, and rigid, uncreative behaviour that rarely involved the pretend role-play that young children normally take to so readily (Kanner 1943). The children described by Hans Asperger were a little different; their language development and general intelligence were better and their physical coordination worse than that of Kanner's group (Asperger 1991). But like Kanner's group they showed, in Asperger's words, 'severe and characteristic difficulties of social integration' (Asperger 1991: 37). Asperger labelled the condition he identified as 'autistic psychopathy'; following Lorna Wing (1991), we will speak of *Asperger's syndrome*. What we now call 'autism' is very much a refinement of Kanner's description. Perhaps because Kanner published in English, his work was originally more influential than Asperger's.[1]

Both Kanner and Asperger took the term 'autism' from Bleuler, the Swiss psychiatrist who had also introduced the term 'schizophrenia'. Bleuler described people with schizophrenia as autistic in the sense that their condition involved a loss of contact with the real world. As we shall see, autism and schizophrenia are in many ways unalike. Bleuler also spoke of autistic thinking, by which he seems to have meant over-imaginative thinking—something quite unlike the thought of people we would now call autistic. Recall: our claim is that schizophrenia is characterized by an unmonitored imagination, while autism involves imaginative poverty.

While it is clear that Asperger's and Kanner's descriptions are similar, there is little agreement on the relation between the disorders they described. In the view of some, Asperger's syndrome is merely the extreme, 'high-functioning' end of the autism scale; according to others, it is a distinct condition.[2] But the similarities between the two, at least at the phenotypic level, are acknowledged: lack of imagination, difficulty understanding the ideas and feelings of others, problems with language. More refined descriptions of at least these last two reveal some differences: while both groups find it difficult to get along with other people, those with Asperger's syndrome seem more aware of others than do people with autism; Van Krevelen (1971) said that, while the child with autism lives in a world of his own, the child with Asperger's syndrome lives in our world in his own way. And while both groups have trouble with conversational speech, the language of people with Asperger's syndrome is often remarkably and inappropriately elaborate, while those with autism are less in command of vocabulary and

[1] Asperger's paper remained untranslated until it appeared in U. Frith (1991), which is an excellent source of information on Asperger's syndrome and its relation to autism. Asperger's syndrome was not included in the *International Classification of Diseases* until 1990.

[2] See Wing (1991) for review. See also Happé (1994b, ch. 8).

grammar.[3] Some autistic people have no speech at all. In what follows we will generally not make a distinction between autism and Asperger's syndrome, unless we are relying on work where the distinction is sharply drawn.

7.2   TWO KINDS OF THEORIES

There are currently a variety of theories about the nature and causes of autism. It is useful to make a distinction between two kinds of theory in this area. Theories of the first kind are 'domain-specific'. They claim that there is some specific aspect of the world, or domain of things in the world, that people with autism have particular difficulty comprehending or responding to in appropriate ways. Kanner himself said that autism was a disorder of 'affective contact', meaning that it involved a failure to recognize and respond to the emotional lives of others. Autistic children are said to treat their care-givers as mere instruments to the attainment of their goals, rather than as fellow humans with whom to interact emotionally. Although they are capable of emotion, and sometimes display extreme emotional disturbance, autistic children do not seem to react sympathetically to the emotions of others. This idea has been pursued more recently by Peter Hobson.[4] He has suggested that autistic children are unable to conceive of others as persons, and hence as subjects capable of expressing and sharing emotions. In some of his work he has claimed that autistic children are impaired in their capacity to recognize the facial expression of emotion, and has argued that children blind from birth and hence unable to learn much about faces often possess symptoms within the autistic range (Brown *et al.* 1997).

To some extent in opposition to the Kanner–Hobson programme, a 'cognitive' theory of autism emerged in the mid-1980s as a result of studies which indicated that autistic children had difficulty understanding false belief, as measured by the sorts of tests we described in the previous chapter. In reporting their first examination of autistic performance on false-belief tests, Simon Baron-Cohen and colleagues suggested that autistic subjects lacked a 'theory of mind'; like other writers at this time, they took this

---

[3] Baron-Cohen and Botton (1993: 48).
[4] See e.g. Hobson (1989, 1993).

phrase to mean something like 'whatever enables us to grasp the mental states of others and ourselves', leaving open whether it really involved a theory or not (Baron-Cohen *et al.* 1985).[5] The next substantial development of this idea was Alan Leslie's (1987) essay on pretence, which postulated an incapacity with metarepresentations, supposedly explanatory of difficulties both with false belief and pretence. Metarepresentations are conceived by Leslie as linguistically encoded representations of another's thought; Smith's thought that it is raining is a representation of a state of the world; my thought that Smith thinks it is raining is a metarepresentation: a representation of Smith's representation. As Leslie's view has developed, it has become clear that the issue for him is one of concept possession, not theory possession. Leslie (2000) argues that one can have metarepresentational concepts without possessing a theory that embeds those concepts. We discuss metarepresentation in the following section.[6]

While affective theories of autism and the theory of mind approach differ in various ways, they share the basic assumption that autism is centrally a difficulty with the mental–social world. They are thus both domain-specific theories.

At precisely the time that Baron-Cohen and his colleagues were developing the theory of mind approach, Judith Rumsey was beginning to examine autism systematically from the point of view of cognitive neuropsychology, focusing on what is called *executive function*.[7] Through her work, and more recently through the work of Pennington and colleagues, there has emerged a substantial body of evidence according to which deficits of executive function are central to autism.[8]

This approach to autism is at odds with the domain-specific theories we have described, because the executive system is supposed to be domain-

---

[5] See also U. Frith and Happé (1999: 2).

[6] Leslie now uses 'theory-theory' to refer to the view that we acquire a theory of mind through general learning. But the issue whether concepts are prior to theories is orthogonal to the issue of how theory develops. One can be a theory-theorist in the sense that one believes mental concepts to be of a piece with theory and believe that the development of theory is a matter of maturation rather than of learning.

[7] Rumsey (1985); Rumsey and Hamburger (1988, 1990). The two most commonly used tests of executive function are the Wisconsin Card Sorting test, and the Tower of Hanoi. For accounts of these tests, see Mitchell (1996: 175–6).

[8] For reviews, see Pennington and Ozonoff (1996); Russell (1997b).

general. It is a system designed to help us plan and perform actions, disengage from unsuccessful strategies, and inhibit prepotent but inappropriate responses, particularly in situations where there are competing options subject to complex constraints. Such situations arise very commonly in our social interactions with others, but they can arise in just about any kind of interaction with the world. Advocates of the idea that autism is an executive disorder say that the heavy demands placed on the executive system by problems in the social domain give the misleading impression that the key to autism is to be found within a mental system dedicated to the social domain. Sometimes the claim that autism is an executive disorder is understood as offering an elimination of the idea that autism involves problems with mentalizing; people with autism understand other minds, but their understanding is masked by inappropriate responses they cannot inhibit. Alternatively, we might think that poor executive function itself affects the development of mentalizing. To the extent that we are sympathetic to the executive function hypothesis, it is this latter version of it that we have in mind.

Like the executive system hypothesis, our approach is largely a domain-general one. We propose that autism be regarded as a disorder of imagination, and we think of the imagination as a device which assists us in understanding and solving problems across a range of different domains.[9] One of these domains is likely to be the mental: the recreative imagination is heavily employed in helping us understand and respond to the thoughts and feelings of other people. It is an additional advantage of our approach that there are other domains where it is antecedently plausible that recreative imagination is heavily used—domains where people with autism show poor performance. These domains are pretence and planning.

Apart from the fact that our theory and the executive function hypothesis are both domain-general theories, there are complex connections between the two. Indeed, one can think of the recreative imagination as an executive device. The basic function of the executive is to supplement learned or pre-programmed responses to environmental cues with thoughtful strategies that are sensitive to consequences. The recreative imagination gives us ways of planning action, enabling us to work through a proposed course of action in advance of carrying it out. Executive theorists

---

[9] See Harris (1993); Gordon and Barker (1994).

have started to develop accounts of the different aspects of autism, and Chris Jarrold has suggested that 'children with autism have problems in generating the pretend schemes necessary for flexible and creative pretend play' (Jarrold 1997: 117).[10] Another way to put this might be to say, with the imagination theorists, that the child has problems accessing and controlling inputs—the relevant pretend beliefs and desires—to the acts of imaginative projection that underpin pretence.

There is another reason why someone who believes that autism is an executive disorder ought to be interested in the question whether it is also an imaginative disorder. There is a standard battery of tests of executive function, and it is widely accepted that people with autism do poorly on a number of these tests. It is also true that people with schizophrenia do badly on executive tests. However, the standard tests of executive function have not succeeded in discriminating very decisively between autism and schizophrenia, even though these conditions are in other ways so very different.[11] To the extent that the imagination hypothesis points to very different imaginative defects in these two disorders, it can be seen as suggesting ways for the executive function hypothesis to be developed, so as to account for the differences between autism and schizophrenia.

7.3   AUTISM, PRETENCE, AND METAREPRESENTATION

Metarepresentationalism begins from the thought that mind-reading depends on the possession of mentalistic concepts, such as thinks, wants, and imagines. We have seen that Alan Leslie holds this to be a separate matter from the possession of a theory of mind; others assume that possession of such concepts depends on, and is constitutive of, a theory of mind. Our argument below will be independent of the issue of priority.[12]

---

[10] See also Harris (1993).

[11] The most substantial difference is on the Stroop test, which is thought to measure inhibition: inhibition seems to be a 'spared' component of executive function in autism but not in schizophrenia (see Ozonoff 1998). Baron-Cohen and Robertson (1995) examined one subject with autism and one with Tourette syndrome, and found that they were not distinguished by executive function measures.

[12] Leslie himself suggests that visual sensitivity to colour is a good model for concept possession without theory (2000: 216). Such a model will be regarded as unpersuasive by those who think that perceptual states are non-conceptual.

There is an obvious plausibility in the idea that mentalizing deficits in autism are due to problems with metarepresentation. But autism involves other deficits. Advocates of the metarepresentational approach have tried to explain autistic difficulties outside the domain of that which is self-evidently the mental; their strategy has been to argue that such domains have, despite appearances to the contrary, a strongly mental component in the problems they present. Alan Leslie has suggested that children with autism have impaired pretend play because pretence taps the same metarepresentational capacity that is deployed when we figure out people's mental states.[13]

Why should pretending depend on metarepresentation? Leslie himself suggests that pretence depends on the capacity to understand pretence in others, which in turn depends on an ability to understand another's mental state. But Howes and Matheson (1992) showed that communication about pretence was very rare prior to age 3, by which time normally developing children are experienced pretenders.[14] Certainly, children who are well able to pretend themselves show a remarkable insensitivity to the mental states of those they judge to be pretending. Recall some results discussed in the previous chapter; Lillard found that young children attributed pretence to a character without attributing any intention to pretend, even when told that the character did not have the necessary knowledge, and even when there was a plausible non-pretence-based explanation of the behaviour to hand.

If these results are well founded, we think it unlikely that the capacity for pretence depends on a sensitivity to the mental states of others. But our previous chapter does contain the seeds of an argument for metarepresentationalism. We said there was merit in the idea that the agent who pretends in a fluent and productive way is acting out of beliefs and desires that refer to his own imaginings. A metarepresentational deficit that meant that an agent could not represent his imaginings as well as other mental states might then be able to explain autistic incapacity with pretence, as well as the difficulty that people with autism have in understanding the minds of others.

We happen not to think that this is the right explanation. We will argue that problems with pretend play in autism are caused, not by difficulties

---

[13] 'underlying... play and mental states... there is a common form of internal representation' (Leslie 1988: 27).

[14] See Currie (1998); see also the discussion in Jarrold et al. (1994), to which we are much indebted.

representing your own imaginings when you have them, but by difficulties having the imaginings themselves. But we stress here our agreement with the idea that competent mind-reading depends on metarepresentation. One of the peculiarities of the debate over autism is that there has been a tendency to suppose that imagination-based accounts of mentalizing must stand in opposition to accounts that appeal to metarepresentation; Leslie and others have suggested that it would be a damaging concession for the imagination-based approach to have to admit that the capacity to attribute mental states requires metarepresentation (Leslie and German 1995: 127). But the idea of metarepresentation is neutral as between an imagination-based account of mind-reading and a theory-based account. Both approaches require the subject to have a metarepresentational capacity; if you lacked concepts of such mental states as beliefs, how could you form beliefs about beliefs? The most that can be at issue concerning metarepresentation is its place in the order of explanation. Are deficits in mind-reading and pretend play in autism to be explained in terms of a lack of metarepresentational capacity? Leslie's answer is yes. One can quarrel with this without denying that mind-reading depends on metarepresentation.

The difficulty for Leslie's view is that all studies indicate that a substantial minority of autistic subjects pass the various false-belief tests, such as the unexpected transfer test. A number of studies have failed to identify any significant differences on these tests between the performance of children with autism and those in various control groups.[15] One response to the evidence for autistic success on false-belief tests has been to say that this involves people with relatively high levels of ability who are able to formulate general rules of thumb by which to work out answers to problems about mental states (U. Frith *et al.* 1991: 436). This is an adequate response only if the relevant rules of thumb can be formulated without using mentalistic concepts; there cannot be recourse to rules like 'By and large, people who look for beer in the fridge think there is beer there and want to get beer'. It is hard to see how rules of any practical use could be formulated that would avoid such concepts. We know that small numbers of people with autism

[15] See Yirmiya *et al.* (1996); Tager-Flusberg and Sullivan (1994); Dahlgren and Trillingsgaard (1996). Ozonoff *et al.* (1991*a*) found that a group of people with Asperger's syndrome and high IQs did as well as normal controls on first-order false-belief tasks and nearly as well on higher-order false-belief tasks.

pass quite complex false-belief tests: tests that probe understanding of one person's thought about another person's thought. In such cases it is particularly difficult to come up with metarepresentationally innocent rules that would explain performance. Uta Frith and colleagues looked at the extent to which performance on false-belief tests correlates with social competence in the real-world; they found quite a close connection between performance on the tests and those aspects of interpersonal life that seem to depend on understanding the mental states of others. They concluded that some people with autism do genuinely possess the capacity to mentalize (Frith *et al.* 1994). This is not consistent with the idea that metarepresentational incapacity is central to autism. What the data seems to support is the idea that people with autism find it unusually difficult to get the right answers to questions about mental states. Some of the time they are able to get it right, and even when they don't get it right, they are often attempting to find an appropriate answer in mentalistic terms. We should not forget that the performance of normal adults on mind-reading tests is sometimes influenced by irrelevant factors. Mitchell *et al.* (1996) told a story in which character *A* sees juice in a jug but is subsequently told by character *B* that it was milk. When asked, subjects were inclined to say that the character thought, later on, that the jug had contained juice. However, when it was additionally said that *B* had, unknown to *A*, replaced the juice with milk, subjects were much more inclined to say that *A* thought there was milk in the jug. This result coheres well with the idea that imaginative projections are capable of being derailed in certain conditions, and that what marks out people with autism is an unusual fragility in their imaginative capacity. Absence of metarepresentation does not provide us with a way of explaining the broader picture of human performance on such tests.

George Botterill and Peter Carruthers offer a different version of the metarepresentational hypothesis. They argue that play is enjoyable only when one is able to represent one's own agency. A child who pretends, they say, has a representation something like 'My goal is to move the object like a car'. Otherwise, 'it is hard to see how pretend-actions could be differentially rewarding' (1999: 101). Botterill and Carruthers do not offer this as an explanation of why children find play pleasurable; they agree that this is something of a mystery. They say only that, without the accompanying representation of agency, children could not find pretence enjoyable. One might respond by pointing out that many things are enjoyed that surely do not depend on metarepresentation: food and sex, for example. Their point is that the pleasures of pretence are unlike those of food or sex; whatever is pleasurable about pretence cannot be intrinsic to the activity, since the movements one undertakes in pushing a block around the floor as if it were a car are not necessarily different from movement which, out of the context of pretence, would not be experienced as pleasurable. Because people with autism lack metarepresentational capacity, and therefore lack the capacity to represent their own agency, the pleasures of pretence are unavailable to them.

Here we have one explanation of why pretence is pleasurable. Other explanations could be based on our own earlier account of how pretence is motivated. Recall that we offered a definite maybe: either imagination motivates pretence, or imaginings guide the selection of the beliefs and desires that motivate pretence. Suppose the first disjunct is right; then children may find the behaviours undertaken in pretence pleasurable because they are caused by imaginings. Suppose the second disjunct is right; perhaps children find pretence pleasurable when they experience a certain kind of harmony between their pretend actions and the imagining which, though they do not motivate, do, at one further remove, guide the pretence. Either way, we can explain why behaviours in pretence are pleasurable even though equivalent behaviours outside pretence might not be. This does not tell us why children, or anyone, should find this experience pleasurable. But Botterill and Carruthers admit that their own explanation is incomplete in the same way. The sensible aim is to show that there is some difference between the experience of movements undertaken in pretence and the experience of equivalent movements undertaken in a non-pretend context. Judged by this criterion, our explanation does about as well as that of Botterill and Carruthers.

Are Botterill and Carruthers vulnerable to the objection that many children with autism seem to possess a capacity to represent mental states? Their claim is that the child with autism is unable to represent his own agency, not that he is unable to represent beliefs and desires. But it is surely not very plausible that a being who is unable to detect so fundamental an aspect of his own being as agency would grasp mentalistic concepts like belief and desire. As we shall see in the next chapter, Chris Frith and others

have argued that aspects of schizophrenia are explicable on the hypothesis
that the subject is unable to monitor her own goals and actions. But people
with autism do not generally exhibit the symptoms that make this a
plausible explanation for schizophrenia. People with schizophrenia often
have experiences of 'alien control', the feeling that their movements are
prompted by external forces; this becomes understandable if we think of the
subject as unable to detect her own agency. We will argue that a similar
incapacity leads, in schizophrenia, to a confusion between imaginings and
beliefs and hence to delusional states. Experiences of alien control and
delusions are not symptomatic of autism, nor is there independent evidence
that people with autism lack a sense of agency. All this must surely count
against the hypothesis that impoverished pretend play in autism is due to a
failure to detect one's own agency.

7.4   AUTISM AND IMAGINATION

Our own proposal is that autistic difficulty with pretending is due to
difficulty with recreative imaginations, and that the imaginative defect
also explains other important aspects of the condition. Difficulties with
pretence or imagination, social competence, and communication have
come to be known as 'Wing's triad' of autistic disabilities (Wing and Gould
1979). We discuss each of the three below before turning to other aspects of
autism. We start with social competence and communication, taken together.

Social Competence and Communication

Few of us always manage our social relations with ease, but for most people
with autism social relations are impossibly difficult. Even for those able
people with autism who are capable of some independence, making friends,
holding down a job, and even managing casual interactions with strangers
are formidable tasks. We take it that these tasks depend on mind-reading
skills, and that the autistic person's difficulty with social interaction is really
a difficulty with mind-reading. People with autism find it much harder than
the rest of us do to know what people think and want. And they find this
hard because they find it hard to put themselves imaginatively into other
people's shoes. We suggest that this is also the source of much of the

communicative difficulty that people with autism face, since understanding what people say often involves mentalizing. People do not always speak literally, and conversational skill is partly a matter of detecting a difference between what the speaker intends to get across and what his or her words mean. People with autism have particular difficulty with this, and take people literally even when it seems inconceivable to the rest of us that the speaker would have *meant* her words literally. It is this contextual or pragmatic aspect of language, rather than difficulty with vocabulary and grammar themselves, that most often creates communicative difficulties for those people with autism who possess language.[16]

Understanding a speaker's meaning where it differs from the meaning of what is said is a plausible candidate for something one would do by imaginative projection—in conjunction with some theory to scaffold it. It has been suggested that speakers know a set of principles that govern rational conversational exchange (for example, 'be relevant'), and detect disparities between literal and speaker's meaning by noting when the principles seem to have been violated.[17] But it is one thing to detect an apparent violation, and hence to know or suspect that the speaker's meaning is not the literal meaning of what is said, and quite another to determine what the speaker really meant. Putting yourself in the speaker's shoes and asking 'What would I have meant by that?' would be a good way to solve the problem.

Taking someone literally can sometimes involve spectacular misunderstanding of desire. Uta Frith (1989: 154) describes an autistic child who was upset at being told to 'Give me your hand'.[18] Patricia Howlin (1997: 33) describes a young autistic woman who took literally the request in an art class to paint the flowers. And the judgements and actions of people with

---

[16] See Happé (1994a). Misunderstanding non-literal speech is one aspect of this, but there are others: people with autism sometimes repeat phrases in irritating ways, or use inappropriately flowery language. They also have difficulty maintaining conversational relevance, presumably because they find it difficult to judge, or have no interest in, the knowledge and interest of their conversational partners. See Howlin (1997, ch. 3) for examples, and Loveland and Tunali (1994) for a review of investigations into the skills of high-functioning autistic children in conveying information through explanation and narrative. Difficulties with language in autism are almost certainly related to problems of joint attending that become evident much earlier than mentalizing difficulties do. See Tomasello (1995), and also later in this chapter.

[17] Grice (1989); but Sperber and Wilson (1986) deny that their Principle of Relevance is known; see (1986: 162).

[18] See Goldman (1992: 199) for discussion.

autism indicate poor perception of desire in situations where the rest of us would need no verbal indication one way or the other. Margaret Dewey (1991) devised a series of stories involving odd behaviour: asking a stranger if you could borrow his comb, following closely behind a female shopper, checking a baby's nappy without asking the mother, etc. She then sought the opinions of a group of high-functioning autistic adolescents. Sometimes they proffered rules like 'you should not follow closely behind someone', but they often made strange judgements about what was inappropriate. Many had no sense that people don't like to share combs, and one seized instead on the fact that the possessor of the comb had said 'It's a nice day' in a lift—where you can't see what the weather is like outside.

If problems like this are the product of a faulty imagination, what exactly has gone wrong? Placing yourself, in imagination, in another's position requires the capacity to make use of appropriate imaginative states; temporarily, one puts aside some aspect of one's own mental economy—some belief or desire, say—and substitutes for it a thought content you actually don't believe, or don't want. One might simply lack the capacity to do this altogether, or lack any motivation to do it. We have suggested that the imaginative deficit in autism is not generally as catastrophic as this. We can think instead in terms of an evolved aversion to effort; adjustments to one's mental set are costly and not to be undertaken lightly, so we tend to favour minimal adjustments when projecting into another's situation.[19] As in other areas, capacity and enthusiasm for imaginative adjustment vary in the normal population, and show abnormal deficits in special populations. People with autism might have particular difficulty making the correct adjustments, and increasing severity of autism may go with more substantial difficulty. Exactly where the difficulty in making the adjustment lies is not clear. Two hypotheses are plausible; we do not know which, if either, is right; perhaps the truth is a combination of both. The first hypothesis is that the difficulty is finding the right input. On this account, normal young 3-year-olds and older autistic children have difficulty *accessing* an alternative to their own belief about, say, where Maxi's sweet is. Performance improves with increasing verbal mental age, but is substantially delayed in the autistic

---

[19]   Robert Gordon (1992) has suggested that the default position is what he calls 'total projection': I project myself into your situation without any adjustment whatsoever.

population. The second hypothesis is that the difficulty is with integrating the inputs into the subject's mental economy. We consider the accessing hypothesis first.

Differences of accessibility explain some of the empirical data. Henry Wellman and Jacqueline Woolley (1990) set out to compare young children's understanding of false belief with their understanding of discrepant desire— desire different from the subject's own; they found the children generally better at taking account of discrepant desire than at taking account of false belief. But in their study the two situations do not seem to be equated for accessibility. False-belief tasks ask the child to set aside his or her own belief in favour of something the child definitely does not believe. In the discrepant desire task the children were asked whether they would like to play or swim. The ones who said they wanted to swim were told about a character who wanted to play, and they correctly predicted the character's behaviour. Here it is plausible that the relevant content is easy to access; the child has expressed a preference for swimming, but playing is nice too. Indeed, it is not clear that the children, in expressing a preference for swimming, were doing anything more than preferring it *for the sake of the argument*. In other words, they may simply have accessed a desire-like imagining. Predicting the story character's behaviour could then be done simply by substituting one imaginative state for another. When experiments of this kind are done in such a way as to increase the perceived distance between the relevant desires—as with the desire for a very exciting-looking badge and the desire for a very dull-looking one—young children do find it much more difficult to predict the story character's choice when it differs from their own (Moore *et al.* 1995). Similarly, young children find it hard to predict that a character will be happy as a result of satisfying a wicked desire, such as the desire to hit another (Yuille *et al.* 1996).

The accessibility of an imagined mental state need not always be measurable in terms of distance between the child's own mental state and that of the target. Caroline Rieffe (1998) found that children's ability to predict action on the basis of a desire for a food variety depended heavily on how different the desire was from the child's own desire.[20] In the case of choice of

---

[20] But there might be evolutionary reasons why a sensitivity to another person's food choice should be on a trajectory for early maturation. Repacholi and Gopnik (1997) found that even toddlers were able to predict the preference of an adult who very dramatically indicated a distaste for the crackers preferred by the child.

a toy, this was not always so. The difference seems to be that in the case of toys, but not in the case of food, the child's prediction is influenced by prior beliefs about certain toys being gender-specific. A boy, told that a girl likes trucks, will have difficulty predicting that she will choose a truck, even though he would choose a truck himself. In that context, the boy's own desire turns out to be difficult to access, given his beliefs about the subject of the projection. Here imagination, the executive, and theory come together. The child has an imaginative task; executive limitations restrict the range of accessible mental states; one factor that makes a mental state less accessible is prior beliefs about its plausibility.

Measuring the accessibility of an alternative to one's mental set is clearly a difficult matter; the danger is that it will provide an excuse for parameter-fixing strategies designed merely to save our theory. We cannot always respond to evidence that normal or autistic people perform well on some imaginative task by saying that this merely establishes the ease of accessibility of the relevant inputs. On the other hand, we cannot develop a theory of accessibility a priori; as more and more evidence comes in, we may find that a coherent and plausible picture of imaginative performance based on the idea of substitutes for one's current mental set emerges—or that it doesn't. We are a long way from that at the moment. To underline the difficulty, we note the puzzling evidence from autistic savants.

Very often people with autism are mentally retarded; however, some people with autism exhibit a remarkable talent in a single domain. Usually the talent is striking only relative to the poor development of the subject's other skills; occasionally savants exhibit a talent which is remarkable relative to the level of development found in normal populations. There are, for example, autistic visual artists and musicians whose skills vastly exceed those of the average person of normal development.[21] Baron-Cohen and colleagues have described three people with Asperger's syndrome who are enormously skilled in the areas of mathematics, physics, and computer science.[22] Mathematics is a crucial case here because it is scarcely arguable that mathematical creativity depends on the capacity to make assumptions and draw conse-

[21] For descriptions of such cases and a general introduction to savantism, see Howe (1989).

[22] See Baron-Cohen et al. (1999). The mathematician won the Field Medal, often described as 'the Nobel Prize of mathematics'. Thanks to Simon Daniels for drawing our attention to these important cases.

quences from them. In Chapter 2 we argued that this is, precisely, a use of the recreative imagination, because assumptions are simply belief-like imaginings. It looks as if at least some people with autism or autism-like disorders are good at setting aside elements of their current mental state, making assumptions about mathematical structures contrary to what they believe about those structures—since in mathematics one often makes an assumption with the aim of proving that it reduces to absurdity.

What might be said in our defence? One thing that seems distinctive about reasoning in mathematics is that it calls for very selective assumption-making. Proof in mathematics proceeds by logical argument and not by counterfactual reasoning, where the assumption has to be integrated with one's background beliefs (recall the Ramsey test). The difference is brought out nicely in the observation that deductive reasoning is, while counter-factual reasoning is not, monotonic. If Q follows logically from P, then Q follows logically from P together with any other premises. But counter-factual reasoning is sensitive to the addition of information. The answer to the question 'Would the play have been better if the last line had been cut?' might be yes, while the answer to the question 'Would the play have been better if the last line and the rest of the text had been cut?' is no. Decision-making—and hence the simulation of decision-making—is like counter-factual reasoning in this regard; it makes a difference to my decision whether I acquire the belief that P, or the belief that P and Q. So the suggestion is that mathematical talent can coexist with poor mentalizing in the case where the subject has difficulty integrating assumptions but has no difficulty in employing those assumptions that can be used without the need for integration, of which mathematical propositions are excellent examples.

Savant abilities in autism are rare, and are unlikely to be much of a guide to what is an extremely heterogeneous condition. Is there evidence that logical reasoning from disbelieved premises is generally preserved in autism? A study by Fiona Scott and colleagues (1999) suggested that children with autism might actually have special ability in this area. Children were given the premises 'All fish live in trees' and 'Tot is a fish'. They were then asked: 'Does Tot live in a tree?' Scott and colleagues found that children with autism did as well as normally developing children and those with moderate learning disabilities (MLD). Indeed, when the test was carried out without any encouragement to form a mental image of a fish in a tree, they did better than these two groups, and better than they themselves had done when encouraged to use imagery. Leevers and Harris (1999) did not find the same pattern of results. They found that the autistic group had a tendency simply to answer 'yes'; this went a long way to explain good autistic performance on the tests of Scott and colleagues. But Leevers and Harris did not conclude that the children with autism had special difficulty with logical reasoning. In their study the normal and MLD groups had a tendency to do better if they were instructed in the use of imagery, and to retain the better performance on a second and later session, even if at that time they received no such instruction; the autistic group did not. Leevers and Harris concluded that the effect of imagery prompting was to clarify the instructor's intention that the subjects should take the false premiss as a basis for reasoning. The autistic children, who could reasonably be assumed to have special difficulty understanding intentions, were not less able logically; they were simply less able to take the instruction to form an image as a clue to intention.[23]

We have said that counterfactual—as opposed to deductive—reasoning and simulation-based reasoning about false beliefs both depend on a capacity to integrate premises into one's mental economy. Is there evidence for an association between performance on these tasks? Kevin Riggs and colleagues (1998) found a close association between the performance of normal 3- and 4-year olds on false-belief tasks and on questions like 'If the fire had not started, where would Peter be?' Examining a group of autistic children, Donald Peterson and Dermot Bowler found that the children passed a false-belief test only if they passed a counterfactual-reasoning test. But the children in this study performed better on the counterfactual task than on the false-belief task. In fact they did not do significantly worse than normal controls on the counterfactual task. So the evidence for a strong connection between false-belief tasks and counterfactual tasks is not as good as it might be.

The hypothesis that integration of premises has a major role to play in the explanation of autistic reasoning must be treated with caution. But it does suggest an approach to some other symptoms, such as circumscribed interests and resistance to change. If people with autism have difficulty integrating

[23] Leevers and Harris describe deductive reasoning from false premisses as 'counterfactual' and do not distinguish between reasoning which is deductive, and hence non-integrative, and integrative reasoning such as we find in judgements about the truth values of subjunctives (1999: 81).

their imaginings into their belief systems, we would expect that they would have a comparable problem integrating new beliefs, which cannot always be accommodated without substantial revision to present beliefs. People with autism often take an interest in such apparently dull topics as the addresses of police stations or the details of the railway timetable; perhaps such interests are favoured because they call for very modest belief revision as one learns; there is not likely to be much you currently believe that learning the address of a police station will overturn. And one advantage of settled routines is that they minimize the impact of unanticipated information, which might pose special problems of integration.

The accessing hypothesis needs to be distinguished from the view, some-times expressed by advocates of the executive theory, that the difficulty for autistic children lies in not being able to 'set aside' current reality. On this view, the difficulty is the replacement of the subject's belief that P by an imagining that contradicts P. According to the accessing hypothesis, the difficulty is more complex. One does not integrate not-P into one's mental economy simply by suspending P; there will be other elements in what I believe that will contradict not-P or be in strong probabilistic tension with it. This suggests a broad spectrum of integrative difficulty, ordered by the amount of mental reorganization required. And difficulty is not experi-enced exclusively by those in special populations; the novels of Ivy Compton Burnett are difficult partly because we are required to integrate some rather alien assumptions into our folk psychology. We return briefly to the idea that difficulties with imaginative projection are difficulties of integration in our discussion of pretending below.

In Chapter 2 we argued that assuming is a kind of imagining. We are happy to continue with this view, regarding the making of assumptions for the purposes of logical proof as a limiting case. But someone might argue that this is not really imagining at all, and that assumptions count as imaginings only when integrated into one's mental economy. We grant the point to anyone who wants to make it. All we insist on is that it is wrong to say, quite generally, that assuming is not imagining.

It has been said that children with Williams syndrome, a rare genetic disorder, create a difficulty for any view of mind-reading skill that invokes imagination or the executive. While children with this syndrome perform poorly on tasks indicative of executive and imaginative skills, they are said to be remarkably good on tests of social intelligence. Peter Carruthers has said that the 'social and communication skills [of these children] are precocious' (Carruthers 1996a: 272), and Gabriel Segal has said that these children display 'an intact psychology faculty' (Segal 1996: 154).

It may be that Williams syndrome presents an anomaly for the imagination–executive alliance. However, it seems to us that the preservation of mentalizing in Williams syndrome has not been adequately demonstrated. Tager-Flusberg and colleagues looked in detail at false-belief performance of children with Williams syndrome; in a group with a mean mental age of 5 years 5 months, 43 per cent passed a simple false-belief test (Tager-Flusberg *et al.* 1997). Results not very different from this have been found in children with autism. Other studies indicate that these children, and the adults they become, do in fact have considerable difficulty in social understanding. In one survey of relatives of adults with Williams syndrome, subjects 'were reported to have high rates of behavioural and emotional difficulties, particularly in terms of poor social relationships, over-friendliness and social disinhibition, preoccupation and obsession'. Care-givers were said to have expressed concern about adults with Williams syndrome being too trusting of others and hence vulnerable to exploitation; many such adults were prone to make socially inappropriate statements; and high levels of anxiety were evident as a result of even minor changes to the routine or daily environment—descriptions reminiscent of typical cases of autism (Davies *et al.* 1998). Another study found 'very low levels of social competence' in Williams syndrome (Howlin *et al.* 1998).

Pretending and Imagining

People with autism of all ages display few of the signs we normally associate with imagination:

Autistic children show a striking absence of spontaneous pretend or 'symbolic' play . . . while the normal 2-year-old will pretend that a toy brick is a car, and happily drive, park and even crash the pretend car, an autistic child (even of a much higher mental age) will simply mouth, throw or spin the block. Pretend play seems to be replaced in autism by repetitive activities, which may become obsessional; the child may line up objects in a certain arrangement that must not be interfered with, or may spin all objects which he can get his hands on. In adults with autism the same lack of imagination may be shown in a rather different way. For example, adults with autism, even those of higher IQ, show little interest in fiction in the form of TV soap operas, novels or films. In general there is a great preference for facts, and the obsessive functional play of the young autistic child may give way to obsessional interests in, for example, railway timetables, dates of birth, bus routes, and so on. (Happé 1994b: 37)

Francesca Happé says that it is 'spontaneous' pretence that is absent in autism; there is evidence of a limited capacity for, and understanding of, pretence in autism. Children with autism can answer simple questions about pretence quite well, and they can even engage in what is called 'instructed' pretence, where there is careful prompting. But they do seem to play much less often, producing fewer pretend acts, in particular fewer novel acts, and at a slower rate than other children.[24] In one area their imaginative capacity seems particularly good. Paul Harris and Hilary Leevers asked children with autism to complete a largely intact drawing—a man without a head, for example. The children were to complete the pictures in two ways: to produce a real or possible object, and to produce an impossible one. Thus the child might complete the man's body by giving it one head (a real object) or two heads (an impossible one). Children with autism performed as well on this task as normal children of the same mental age (Leevers and Harris 1998), and produced some solutions that seem, intuitively, quite imaginative.

In the previous chapter we distinguished various ways that pretence and imagination can be related. We argued that, whether or not imagination ever actually motivates pretence, it plays a role in guiding fluent and productive pretending. But pretence is not necessarily connected with imagination and our analysis allows for limited forms of pretence even among children notably deficient in imagination, which is what we find with autism. It may even be that some children with autism have a limited capacity for imagining, in which case we might find occasional occurrences of richer, imagination-guided pretence among this group. The distinct advantage of our theory is that it can explain poverty of play in autism in terms of an imaginative deficit, without predicting total absence of play. How should we explain the Leevers and Harris (1998) finding that children with autism performed as well as normal children on a test of visual

---

[24] Charman et al. (1997); Jarrold et al. (1996).

imagination? Leevers and Harris appeal to the low executive demands of the test, which required the children merely to complete a drawing rather than to begin one from scratch. They also point to some, admittedly limited, evidence that the primary mode of thinking among people with autism is visual or imagistic (Harris and Leevers 2000). It may be that children with autism are relatively competent in setting aside aspects of the visual environment and replacing them with imagined alternatives, whereas they are less able to access alternative propositional states. This would be consistent with their impoverished pretend play, since the imaginings that go with pretence are not exclusively or even primarily imagistic; imagining, of one's act of sitting in a cardboard box, that it is the act of driving a car is not a matter of having mental images in any modality.

This suggestion bears comparison with one we made earlier on about the explanation of extraordinary mathematical skills. We suggested there, rather tentatively, that mathematical assumptions might be easy to make (assuming the propositions are understood) because they pose no problem of integration with the rest of the mental economy. Something similar can be said for perceptual imaginings. It is of the nature of propositional states to bear logical and evidential relations to one another. So when I suppose that Napoleon won the battle of Waterloo and try to work out what the consequences are, I have to integrate the supposition with my current belief state, and that means making some complex adjustments. But a purely perceptual piece of imagining, because it has non-conceptual content, does not require this sort of integration; recall the argument of Chapter 5.

Let us be clear: we are not explaining the facility of autistic people with mathematical assumptions and with mental imagery (in so far as they exist) in exactly the same way. The explanation we offered for facility with mathematical assumptions is that such assumptions don't require integration with the rest of one's mental economy because of the nature of mathematical inference. The explanation we now—again, rather tentatively—offer for facility with mental images is that such images don't require integration with the rest of one's mental economy because of their non-conceptual nature. What is common to the two explanations is the plausible but admittedly untested assumption that integration is a difficult task.

7.5   JOINT ATTENTION, PROTODECLARATIVE POINTING, AND EMOTIONAL RESPONSES

Poor performance by children with autism on false-belief tasks indicates that these children have difficulty forming reliable beliefs about beliefs; that much is scarcely in dispute. But we should not suppose that the first contact that normally developing children have with the minds of others is the formation of beliefs about them. If there is truth in the idea that the explosive growth in hominid mental capacity was driven by competition for access to the mental states of conspecifics, it is probable that mind-reading skills would be supported by much earlier developing capacities.

In fact there is evidence to support the idea that contact with minds does begin much earlier. It has been suggested that acts of facial imitation by infants—acts which are said to be elicitable within moments of birth—provide the earliest insight into the mindedness of others (Meltzoff and Gopnik 1993). In later infancy *joint attending* develops: a child is able to bring about a situation in which she and a care-giver attend to the same object. In situations of joint attention the child follows the direction of the care-giver's gaze until she finds the likely object of attention; in protodeclarative pointing she points at something she herself is already attending to, with the aim of getting the care-giver to attend to it also. In both cases the joint attention is pursued for its own sake rather than because of any practical benefit that will follow, such as getting the carer to retrieve a toy. For normally developing children, joint attending is probably a source of affective contact with others. Indeed, such occasions are likely to produce complex, multi-layered emotional experiences. The child may experience an emotion that has as its object the thing attended to, but may also register the emotion of the other who is also attending, responding emotionally herself to the care-giver's emotion. Finally, the child may experience emotion as a result of her knowledge that joint attending is taking place. It is easy to see how the emotions involved here can, depending on circumstances, be in some considerable tension: mild unease about the object of attention, a deeper disturbance consequent on recognition that the care-giver herself is troubled by it, together with pleasure taken in the joint attending itself. Such occasions are thus potentially very rich and instructive sources of emotional experience.

Young children with autism engage in very little joint attending, and seem to have a reduced capacity to perceive and share emotions.[25] There is other evidence that autistic children do not respond normally to the emotional expressions of others. They are not good at recognizing the emotion expressed in another's face,[26] or in body posture,[27] and seem to go about the task of detecting emotion in ways different from those of normal subjects (Hobson *et al.* 1988). Moreover, they do not attend much to adult expressions of negative emotion, like anger, fear, and pain (Sigman *et al.* 1992). It looks as if such early behaviours as joint attention are precursors to the later, more sophisticated acts of mentalizing probed by false-belief tests, and that difficulties with joint attending may be causally linked to the impoverished mentalizing we see in older children with autism.

How should we think about the relation between these precursor states and full-blown beliefs about beliefs? We suggest that perception offers a useful model here—and one that we shall draw on again in the final chapter. Before they form beliefs about objects, children are able to perceive them, and their perceptual experiences are essential to the formation of many kinds of beliefs. Can we think of very young children as perceiving mental states before they are able to form beliefs about them? We won't

---

[25] Baron-Cohen (1989) has argued that autistic children rarely engage in protodeclarative pointing, but have normal levels of 'protoimperative pointing' the aim of which is to have someone perform an action. Poor empathic response in autistic children as young as 20 months is reported in Charman *et al.* (1998); see also Charman *et al.* (1997). Children with autism do not show reduced levels of emotional expression themselves, though there are certain elements of incongruity in that expression, and they are not well coordinated with the emotional expressions of those with whom they are interacting (see Kasari and Sigman 1996 for discussion). They are less likely than normal or retarded children to show pleasure at being praised (Kasari *et al.* 1993). They do, however, show a normal capacity to give examples of common emotions like happiness and anger (Jaedicke *et al.* 1994).

[26] See Ozonoff *et al.* (1991b); Mundy *et al.* (1993).

[27] Psychologists have studied people's responses to filmed point-light displays, produced by having people in a darkened setting wear reflective patches on their joints and at other places on their bodies. Normal adults can recognize the resulting display as indicative of a human figure, even with very brief display times, and infants only 3 months old respond selectively to them. Peter Hobson and colleagues studied the responses of autistic subjects to such patterns. While the autistic subjects in Hobson's experiment had no difficulty recognizing human figures as well as various objects from such displays, they were much less apt than controls to describe what the human figures were doing in emotional terms (whereas normal subjects readily described a figure as, for example, 'sad'), and were poor at judging the emotional states of the figures when specifically asked to do so (Moore *et al.* 1997).

argue that such children literally perceive mental states. We argue instead that they have a preconceptual capacity for mental-state detection that is in significant ways like perception. Nor is this a transient phase: we suggest that the same capacity is evident in normal adults.

In what ways is this capacity like perception? It is, as we have said, preconceptual; at this stage children can be credited with ways of representing the mental states of others without possessing the concepts necessary to form beliefs about them. We argued in Chapter 5 that we represent things in perception non-conceptually. Early modes of mental-state detection are perception-like also in respect of encapsulation and what we call *evidential primacy*. Encapsulation, said to be the most significant feature of modular systems, is the resistance perception shows to change in belief. The lines in the diagram that illustrates the Müller-Lyer illusion look different in length even after we come to know that they are actually the same length. On the other hand, perception makes a distinctive contribution to belief fixation: when something looks red, we do not normally weigh up the various possibilities concerning the effects of drugs, unusual lighting, etc.; we simply form the belief that it is red. Perception leads quickly and automatically to belief, except where some other salient belief serves to block it, as with the Müller-Lyer case.

It is the same with our capacity for the recognition of emotion in faces. The man's face continues to look sad even after we realize that it is an actor's performance, and emotional expressions push us quickly towards belief in the reality of the emotion, unless there is some countervailing belief, like the belief that this is a play I'm watching. Some people have concluded that there is a mind-reading module: a module that fixes beliefs about mental states. We reject this idea, and say that belief is not at issue here, any more than it is in the case of visual illusions. The Müller-Lyer illusion is evidence for the modularity of visual perception, not for the modularity of beliefs about length. Similarly, the illusion of there being a rich mental life behind the statue's troubled expression is evidence for the modularity of a preconceptualized, perception-like capacity for the recognition of emotions that is prior to belief; it is not evidence for the modularity of beliefs about mental states.[28]

We suggest that this quasi-perceptual capacity for emotion recognition develops very early—it may be present even at birth—and that this capacity

---

[28] See the much more detailed discussion in Currie and Sterelny (2000).

is exercised through such behaviours as early infant imitation and joint attending. Further, we suggest that imitation and joint attending subserve this capacity by providing opportunities for what we will call proto-projections. In fully developed imaginative projections we set aside some aspect of our current mental state in favour of an imagination-based substitute that helps us model the mental state of our target. At this stage the performance constitutes an action; imaginative projections are things that we do, though we are not always fully aware of them, and are not always able to exert as much control over them as we would like. With proto-projections, the adjustment to one's mental economy is automatically triggered by another activity, such as imitating the facial expression of another, checking the other's expression for signs of unease, or bringing about a situation of joint attending. We suggest, finally, that the exercise of this capacity for proto-projection is crucial to the later development of imaginative projections that involve such complex conceptualized states as belief-like imaginings. It is not surprising then that we see, in children with autism, abnormalities in the activities that trigger proto-projections.

We have focused in this discussion of early mental-state detection on primitive ways of detecting *emotions*, though we mean the term in a broad sense that covers responses of contentment or mild unease. Partly this is because the evidence we have suggests that the earliest detection of mental states is confined to the emotions. There is another reason. In the final chapter we will argue that emotions are peculiar states in that they are, so to speak, their own counterparts. In imagination we do not take on another's belief or desire; we take on a belief-like or a desire-like imagining that corresponds to those beliefs and desires. But when I put myself imaginatively in the position of someone being threatened, it is genuine fear I come to experience, not an imagination-based substitute for fear: so we shall argue. This makes emotions good candidates for the material on which to base a simple and automatic proto-projection system; the system does not require one kind of mental state (a belief, say) to be set aside and replaced by a state of another kind (a belief-like imagining); it can operate simply by replacing one emotion with another. So the proto-projection system is simple in various ways: it is automatic, it delivers preconceptual contact with mental states, and it does not need to trade one kind of state for another.

Our developmental story goes like this. Early imitation, gaze-following, and joint attending feed the proto-projection system, the operation of which eventually triggers the capacity for imaginative projections. This capacity shows itself first in acts of imagination-driven pretence, and later in the capacity to make predictions about and give explanations of increasingly complex behaviours in terms of mental states. If those earliest socially oriented behaviours do not flourish, the proto-projection system will not develop properly, and nor will its successor, the capacity for imaginative projections. The result will be impoverished pretend play and poor mentalizing.[29]

---

[29] It might be objected that children with autism show a relatively preserved capacity for taking on the visual perspective of another, as indicated by their good performance on tasks that require them to answer questions about what another person can see (Baron-Cohen 1989). It is unlikely, however, that their performance on such tasks genuinely requires imaginative perspective-taking rather than, say, solving the problem of who can see what geometrically. As Sue Leekham and colleagues put it, 'children with autism approach eye direction detection solely as a geometric problem' (Leekham et al. 1997).

Chapter 8

SCHIZOPHRENIA: THE MONITORING OF THOUGHT AND ACTION

Wittgenstein thought it was a great error to say that images are distinguishable from perceptions primarily by their lesser vivacity. He held that they were distinguished by their being subject to the will. While I can choose where to look, I cannot choose what to see in the direction of my looking. Seeing something is in one respect like having a pain; it is something that merely happens to you. Having a mental image is not at all like having a pain; no part of it is something that merely happens. At various points Wittgenstein seems to be saying that I cannot be mistaken about whether I am seeing something or having an image of it; Perky's experiment refutes this idea. In Perky's experiment people thought they were forming mental images when in fact they were perceiving a physical image.[1] But Wittgenstein's view might really be this: that I cannot be wrong about whether I am having an image unless I am trying to have an image—which is what the subjects in Perky's experiment were doing (Budd 1989: 112). What about the converse mistake: forming an image and thinking that one is really seeing something? Wittgenstein's view seems to rule out this possibility. What matters in the Perky-type case is that one knows, or at least has a sense, that one is trying to form an image; it is this sense of trying that makes it

---

[1] See above, Ch. 4. Wittgenstein's observations on this are mostly in his (1980). Budd (1989) is an excellent guide.

possible for one to be deceived into thinking that one's trying has succeeded. So if I do form an image, and so do try to form an image, and do know that I try, then I can't think that I am actually seeing something.[2]

Do we always have this sense that we do something, or try to do it? People suffering from schizophrenia sometimes say that their movements and even their thoughts are not under their control. They also sometimes experience hallucinations. Might this be because they, unusually, are not able to monitor their own acts, including their acts of will? In this chapter we examine the idea that the imagination, normally recognized as such by its subjection to the will, might fail to be so recognized in schizophrenia. Here we focus mostly on propositional imaginings. We say something about perceptual imaginings at the end.

In addition, we want to display some connections between the idea that schizophrenia is a disorder of imagination and a hypothesis about schizophrenia developed by Chris Frith.[3] Frith's hypothesis is interpretable in two ways; in fact it would be better to say that what we have here is two different theories. One of them provides a natural underpinning to our own proposal. The other theory, which takes up the idea of metarepresentation discussed in the previous chapter, seems to us not very promising. So we will take some trouble to distinguish these two theories. We start by saying something about the kind of explanatory hypothesis we are offering.

8.1 METHOD

Ideas about fantastical conspiracies, bizarre causality, and supernatural creatures are standard in schizophrenia; it difficult for the rest of us even to imagine a perspective from which these ideas could seem persuasive.[4] For people with schizophrenia, they can seem compelling even when the mind is long used to applying very high standards of argument and proof. John Nash is a mathematician who did work on game theory in the late 1940s, for which

[2] But see Wittgenstein's puzzling remarks about fancy not obeying the will: (1980, paras. 100–1).
[3] There are many papers on this topic by Frith and his co-workers; see e.g. Cahill and Frith (1996); Frith (1987, 1989, 1994, 1996, 1997); Frith and Corcoran (1996); Frith and Done (1989a,b); Frith et al. (1988). See also Frith's accessible (1992).
[4] As Freud acknowledged: 'I had to confess to myself that I do not care for these patients, that they annoy me, and that I find them alien to me and to everything human' (Buckley 1988: 143).

he was awarded the Nobel Prize for economics in 1994. For much of the time in between his life was devastated by schizophrenia. He turned down a university post on the grounds that he was about to be made emperor of Antarctica, became fascinated by numerology, and tried to renounce his American citizenship, fearing that he was the object of attentions from the FBI. Asked by a colleague how he, 'a man devoted to reason and logical proof', could believe in messages from extraterrestrials, Nash said, 'the ideas I had about supernatural beings came to me in the same way that my mathematical ideas did. So I took them seriously' (Nasar 1998: 11).

The psychiatrist and philosopher Karl Jaspers said that the ideas of the person with schizophrenia are intrinsically non-understandable: they are simply the by-products of a biological disorder, lacking rational structure (Jaspers 1993: 577).[5] One way to defend rationality in the face of this strangeness is to argue that beliefs in schizophrenia are rational responses to strange experiences (Maher 1999). There are limits to the plausibility of this idea; rational folk would surely question the veracity of their experiences rather than believe in a hypothesis inconsistent with their whole prior world-view.[6] Our approach will be rather different, and we do not claim wholly to preserve the rationality of schizophrenic ideas. We locate irrationality in another place. On our view schizophrenic delusions are not beliefs. At least, they do not start out as such. We say that the problem is a loss of the distinction between what is believed and what is merely imagined: a distinction essential for the maintenance of rational thought.

We do not say, with Jaspers, that there is complete loss of rationality here. We need not think of rationality as a seamless whole; it may possess a complex inner structure not generally available to introspection or to a priori reflection. This complex inner structure may be vulnerable to damage which, depending on its extent and location, can result in selective failures of rationality.[7] So it may be possible to understand the peculiarities of schizophrenic thought as resulting from specific, functionally localizable

---

[5] But Jaspers did not deny that these were thoughts with intentional contents. On the difficulties involved in holding both of these views, see Eilan (1999). See also below, Sect. 8.8.

[6] See Bermudez (forthcoming); Davies et al. (forthcoming).

[7] On the relations between reason and subpersonal cognitive structures, see the concluding remarks in Campbell (1999a). Richard Bentall (1994) argues that schizophrenia must involve biases rather than deficits in reasoning because people with schizophrenia are not wholly incapable of

damage to a system, a proper function of which is to support reason. In other disorders reason may be damaged in other ways, with other consequences for behaviour and for the phenomenology of thought.

8.2   IS METAREPRESENTATION USEFUL FOR UNDERSTANDING SCHIZOPHRENIA?

One of Frith's theories—the one we are going to reject—takes its inspiration from a theory about autism: that autism is centrally a deficiency in the capacity for metarepresentation. Frith suggests that while autistic children never develop a metarepresentational capacity, people with schizophrenia suffer damage to a previously intact and normally developed capacity. And the hypothesis that we shall be arguing for here—the hypothesis that delusions and hallucinations in schizophrenia are due to a failure to identify imaginings—is itself closely related to a hypothesis about the causes of autism—the hypothesis, discussed in the previous chapter, that autism involves a lack of imagination.

Frith's theory and the one offered here differ in how they deal with the obvious and pressing fact that autism and schizophrenia are very different conditions. Schizophrenia is much more common than autism; it typically appears during a person's early twenties, whereas autism is usually identified in early childhood. While the prognosis for schizophrenia is generally poor, many people do make at least a partial recovery from it; autism, on the other hand, is a lifelong condition. Delusions and hallucinations, which are collectively described as 'reality distortions', are very common in schizophrenia but are not found in autism. On Frith's view, the underlying cause is the same in both disorders and the differences between them are due to prior personal history and in particular to the age of onset. On our view, autism and schizophrenia both involve disorders of the imagination, but these are different disorders.

reasoning. But, as Coltheart and Davies (2000) point out, there are many cognitive disabilities which we are happy to explain as deficits because we think that the system in question is susceptible to selective damage. They mention surface dyslexia as an example. For much more extensive discussion of the relations between rationality and subpersonal systems (with intriguing examples of the subversion of rationality such as the tendency to give implausible justifications for compulsive imitation), see Hurley (1998, esp. ch. 10).

In his book *The Cognitive Neuropsychology of Schizophrenia*, Frith (1992) argues that various symptoms of schizophrenia are the result of an underlying deficit of metarepresentation, the capacity to formulate thoughts about thoughts (1992: 115).[8] One important feature of schizophrenia is 'poverty of action': those suffering from schizophrenia are often listless and inactive. Frith suggests that poverty of action is due to an inability to produce self-willed (as opposed to stimulus-elicited) action, that this is in turn due to an inability to access one's goals, and that it is failure of metarepresentation that is responsible for this lack of access. For the same reason, delusions of persecution and of reference are due to a faulty awareness of other people's intentions, and delusions of control and thought insertion are due to faulty awareness of one's own intentions. Third-person hallucinations—the experience of hearing voices discussing one's actions—arise when what begins as a thought of the form '*S* thinks that *P*' turns, because of a metarepresentational incapacity, into the 'free-floating' thought *P*.[9] So metarepresentational incompetence is supposed to lead to (i) inability to access one's goals, and hence to poverty of action; (ii) inability to access one's intentions, and hence to the impression that one's actions, including one's acts of thinking, are not under one's own control; (iii) inability to access the thoughts of others and hence to mistakes about what those thoughts are; and (iv) inability to identify a thought as one's own, and hence to third-person hallucinations.

Take first the explanation of third-person (auditory) hallucinations (iv). Frith says that when a schizophrenic subject *S* infers that *T* thinks that

(1) *S* is boring,

S ends up having *that* thought, (1), rather than the thought she should have, namely,

(2) *T* thinks that *S* is boring.

This is because *S* has lost her capacity to metarepresent: she can represent a thought like (1), but not a thought about a thought, like (2). Frith's

---

[8] The taxonomy of symptoms given in Frith (1992) is superseded by that in Johnstone and Frith (1996), where hallucinations and delusions are treated as constituting a single dimension. We discuss hallucinations and delusions below.

[9] See Frith (1992: 126). Frith's metarepresentational theory is affirmed and elaborated in Cosmides and Tooby (2000).

suggestion here does not cohere well with the idea that metarepresentational capacity is *lost* in schizophrenia. The proposal assumes, on the one hand, a metarepresentational deficit, and on the other, a capacity to formulate thoughts about others; the schizophrenic subject is supposed to formulate the thought that '*T* thinks *P*', but to experience merely the thought that *P*. But if the subject genuinely lacked a metarepresentational capacity, she would not be able to formulate the thought that someone was thinking *P* in the first place. Anyway, one of the most striking aspects of schizophrenia is that the patient's delusional beliefs (a characterization we are accepting just for the moment) are very often metarepresentational, being concerned with the intentions of others, about which people with schizophrenia may have elaborate theories. These ideas are defective in many ways, but they do not exhibit a poverty of metarepresentation. It would be better, from Frith's point of view, to suppose that schizophrenia is characterized by a *fragility* of metarepresentational capacity. If we suppose that the subject has a capacity to metarepresent which is unreliable, then we can suppose that she formulates the thought (2), but that the intentional operator 'thinks that' sometimes becomes detached, leaving her with the thought (1). How, on Frith's view, does (1) come to be experienced as the thought (or even the speech) of another? It will not do to say that defective metarepresentation attaches (1) to another operator, leaving the thought, say, that '*F* thinks that *S* is boring'. For this is just another thought, and we have been given no explanation why it should be interpreted by the subject as the thought or speech *of someone else*. Appeal to fragile metarepresentation alone cannot explain these experiences of thought ownership.

Another difficulty for the metarepresentational hypothesis is that the thoughts that schizophrenic patients experience as third-person hallucinations tend to have peculiar content, referring to bizarre events and conspiracies. Recall: Frith's explanation for these hallucinations is that *S*'s thoughts about other people's thoughts become 'disattributed'—the thought that '*T* thinks that *P*' becomes the thought that *P*. Then we must attribute to the patient not merely a difficulty with maintaining thought attribution, but a tendency to attribute to others bizarre or threatening thoughts. Such a tendency does not seem to be explicable solely in terms of a metarepresentational deficit, since the generation of the bizarre content must take place at a point prior to that at which the metarepresentational deficit takes effect.

At one point Frith presents what purports to be an explanation of the strangeness of thoughts present in schizophrenia, suggesting that what starts as a perfectly reasonable thought ('I must go to work') becomes, through what he calls an 'impairment of content', a different and inappropriately grandiose thought, say, 'I must become the boss' (Frith 1992: 127). Impairment of content, whatever it is, cannot be explained in metarepresentational terms; deficient metarepresentation might turn the thought '*T* thinks I should go to work' into the thought 'I should go to work', but it cannot explain how the thought 'I should go to work' gets turned into the thought that 'I should become the boss'.

It is also doubtful whether metarepresentation is the right notion in terms of which to account for our normal ability to monitor our goals and intentions. Frith's view seems to be that we monitor goals and intentions by having thoughts of the form 'Such and such is my goal' and 'So and so is my intention'. It is implausible that every time I perform an action on the basis of an intention, I formulate a thought which identifies that intention as mine, and that if I omitted to do so that action would seem to me to be something over which I had no control. And there is a suspicion of a regress threatening: to identify the intention as mine I have to formulate the thought that it is mine, but what enables me to identify the thought that it is mine as my thought? Our sense that our actions are our own must be constituted by the operation of more primitive, subpersonal mechanisms than those that are supposed to be operative in metarepresentation.

8.3   AGENCY

This brings us to the second of Frith's two theories, and it is a theory on which we shall draw heavily in what follows. While Frith sometimes treats metarepresentation as his central theoretical concept, there are places where he gives more emphasis to the notion of efference-copying. In a remarkable example of the simultaneous formulation of ideas, Roger Sperry (1950) and von Holst and Mittelstaedt (1950) suggested an explanation of how animals distinguish changes in the appearance of things due to their own movement from changes due to external causes. The idea was that when a motor instruction is created preparatory to movement, a copy of the instruction (what von Holst and Mittelstaedt called an 'efference copy' and what Sperry called a 'corollary discharge') is created and then compared to the reafference, or information about the actual movement. Von Holst likened the efference copy and the reafference to positive and negative photographs, which nullify each other by superposition. This cancellation serves as a signal that it is the agent rather than the world that has moved. Fish whose eyes had been surgically rotated through 180 degrees were known to circle endlessly. This was now explicable as the result of a reafference that failed to cancel the efference copy.

Frith proposes that there is impairment of action-monitoring in schizophrenia due to impairment in the copy-and-compare process and that there is comparably based impairment to intention-monitoring.[10] This makes it difficult for the schizophrenic person to detect her own actions, and also her own acts of will.[11] We have here the postulation of a failure in a subpersonal mechanism to explain schizophrenia, rather than the postulation of a difficulty with the personal-level mechanism of metarepresentation. Thinking that someone believes that today is market day is something I do. Comparing efference copy with reafference is something that happens within me. Indeed, efference-copying is assumed to take place in creatures that probably lack personal-level psychological states altogether.[12]

There is evidence to support Frith's idea. It is common for people with schizophrenia to say that their movements are controlled by another agent. This is called the *delusion of control*. Frith and colleagues have argued that this occurs when the subject performs an action but has no sense of having acted. They have also shown that people with schizophrenia do badly on tasks that require one to monitor one's own actions (Mlakar *et al.* 1994). There is, on the other hand, evidence that people with schizophrenia sometimes over-attribute actions to themselves. Is that consistent with the hypothesized loss of a sense of agency? Often these claims of control are not

---

[10]   Frith (1992: 81). See also Cahill and Frith (1996); Frith (1987); Mlakar *et al.* (1994). Feinberg (1978) suggested that we could explain certain aspects of schizophrenia on the assumption that thinking is a motor process where efference-copying is faulty.

[11]   Philosophers sometimes assume that if something is done by an act of will, then the agent will be able to know that it is. See e.g. Williams (1973*b*: 148): 'if I can acquire beliefs at will, I must know that I am able to do this'.

[12]   There are connections here with an approach to psychopathology due to Jim Russell (1997; see also Pacherie 1997). Frith goes beyond Russell in supposing that we can apply the idea of reafference-copying to explain the monitoring of intention as well as of action.

based on anything like the ordinary experience of agency. One patient believed that he could release bombs over England by urinating. But he is reported as describing this as a God-like ability which was exercised 'without his willing it' (Bovet and Parnas 1993: 590). Such claims seem to exemplify delusional ideas about the mysterious connectedness of things rather than misleading experiences of agency.

Failures to monitor action correctly are unusual, but they can be induced in normal subjects under special conditions. In one experiment subjects carried out a simple movement of fingers or wrist as they watched a moving hand displayed on a TV screen; in some cases the hand was their own, in other cases it was the hand of another. When the hand on the screen was observed to move in a way different from the way the subject's hand was moving, subjects had little difficulty telling that it was the hand of another. If the hand's movement was the same as their own, it was more difficult, and even normal subjects were wrong about 30 per cent of the time—indicating that even at the best of times our mechanisms for distinguishing our own actions from those of another 'operates with a relatively narrow safety margin' (Daprati *et al.* 1997: 84). Interestingly, subjects with schizophrenia did significantly worse, with delusional patients doing worst of all; their error rate was 80 per cent. Daprati and colleagues offer an intriguing explanation. There is evidence from studies in monkeys and in humans that parts of the motor system are activated in response to the observation of action by conspecifics. These authors suggest that, in schizophrenic patients, there is reduced ability to distinguish between these empathic signals and signals produced by one's own motor intentions. But they say that 'At present there is no direct evidence as to the nature of the mechanism, the alteration of which would create these problems in schizophrenic patients' (Daprati *et al.* 1997: 84). See also Georgieff and Jeannerod (1998, esp. 474).

Let us assume that Frith's theory of damage to the subpersonal systems that monitor intention and action is on the right lines. Can we bring Frith's two theories together by supposing that the subpersonal-level theory which appeals to efference-copying is a theory about how the person-level meta-representational deficit is realized? That is unlikely. The two theories seem to differ in important ways about what they predict about schizophrenia.[13]

---

[13] Frith himself seems to regard the reafference copy theory as a special case of the metar-epresentational theory. See Frith (1992: 84).

Thus the fragility of metarepresentation theory suggests that people will start by formulating the thought that '*T* thinks that *P*' but end up with the thought that *P*, while the fragility of efference-copying theory suggests that people will formulate the thought that '*T* thinks that *P*' but end up by not recognizing this as a thought of their own. The second theory is in much better accord with the data.

From now on we are going to ignore Frith's metarepresentational theory, but we shall make use of his idea that schizophrenia involves damage to subpersonal mechanisms that result in a loss of the sense of agency. We propose that delusions are unrecognized imaginings, and we shall use Frith's hypothesis as a means of explaining how, in schizophrenia, a subject who imagines *P* can fail to recognize that the source of this thought is his own imaginative construction, can think of *P* as a fact about the world, and regard his thought that *P* as imposed on him by the world, or at least by some external agency. We next introduce the idea that delusions are imaginings, and we give it some intuitive motivation. We then return to Frith's hypothesis.

8.4   IMAGINATION AND DELUSION

We call our proposal the *disorder of imagination theory*. According to this theory, the schizophrenic patient does not have a problem formulating thoughts of the form '*S* thinks that *P*', nor of distinguishing this thought from the thought that *P*. Rather, she finds it difficult to recognize that what she imagines is merely that—something imagined. There is certainly nothing original about this idea. Here, for example, is the psychiatrist Harold Searles describing what he calls *dedifferentiation* in schizophrenia: 'the patient has little or no realm of *fantasy* experienced as such; whenever he experiences a new combination of thoughts or mental images he immediately assumes it to be, instead, a representation of outer reality' (Searles 1988: 103). Note that Searles does not say that the patient lacks fantasy (what we are calling 'imagination'); he says that the patient lacks fantasy *which he recognizes as such*.

How would such a disability affect one's mental life? Normally, a great deal of what we imagine has a fleeting, inconsequential character that means it is not much attended to, even when its content is bizarre or potentially threatening; we recognize that these thoughts are merely imagined. And when we attend to our imaginings because they are useful to us, we are usually able to disengage from them when they have served their purpose. When a person with schizophrenia fails to register a thought as an imagining, it is likely to become a focus of attention, to absorb mental resources, and lead to the elaborate constructions we see in schizophrenia.

This would not be a plausible line of thought if imaginings lacked the intrinsically attention-grabbing powers of belief. Recall from Chapter 1 that imaginings can have emotional effects very much like those of beliefs and desires. It is commonly acknowledged that imagining dangerous or frightening situations can make one feel afraid. And fictions hold us, primarily, by their capacity to generate emotions in response to the characters and their situations. These emotions can themselves be hard to distinguish from our responses to what we believe is really happening in the world. Keith Oatley describes some work on emotional responses to fiction done by his students:

adults and adolescents reading short stories by James Joyce, Alice Munro and Carson McCullers, could readily mark the margins of texts where emotions occurred while reading a story, and could later describe these emotions, say what caused them, and rate their intensities. Emotions occurring while reading were similar to those of ordinary life. During reading they were typically experienced around the midpoint of a scale of intensity, ranging from 0 = barely noticeable to 10 = the most intense ever experienced, and sometimes towards the top of this range. (Oatley 1994: 54)

And Paul Harris (2000: 71) summarizes other work:

The imagery-based reactions of individual readers mirror the reactions that they would produce when confronted by an actual situation equivalent to the one being imagined. For example, if readers are given a text that prompts them to imagine an encounter with a snake, an increase in heart rate is especially marked among snake phobics—people who would display a similar pattern of cardiac acceleration when shown a live snake—as compared to social phobics who are especially fearful of public speaking rather than snakes.

While imaginings have these emotional powers, the fictional scenarios that provoke them rarely come to dominate our thought as a result. Presumably this is connected with our recognition that these are, after all, imaginings, and their sources are indeed fictions. Once the source of the imaginative stimulus is switched off—we leave the theatre, put down the book, or turn aside from our fantasy construction—belief-based concerns and interests will tend to crowd out the imaginings and their emotional reverberations cease. If, on the other hand, the imaginings were not recognized as such, one's attention might be held by them, and their emotional impact would continue, encouraging further attention to and elaboration of the imagined scenario. Thus the mental economy of the person with schizophrenia is prone to be taken over by thoughts that most of us are well able to keep under control.

One question that might be raised here concerns the level of emotion typically experienced by schizophrenic subjects, since an important feature of the condition is said to be 'flat affect'—a much reduced capacity for emotional expression. If schizophrenic patients experience significantly lower general levels of emotion than normal subjects, then the imagination's capacity to mirror the affective component of belief may not be significant in causing imaginings to hold attention inappropriately. Recently some attention has been paid to the question of whether a lack of emotional expression in schizophrenia goes with correspondingly reduced emotional experience. Preliminary studies are somewhat inconclusive, but there is evidence that reduced emotional expression coexists in schizophrenia with levels of emotional sensitivity that are higher than normal.[14] In that case a person with schizophrenia, robbed of her normal capacity to identify imaginings as imaginings, might well be captured by their emotional power.

What is it, then, that the person with schizophrenia has lost and which allows the rest of us to distinguish our imaginings from our beliefs? Might one distinguish an imagining from a belief by tracking the role of the thought in inference? What we have said about the role of imaginings in inference makes this unlikely. In Chapter 1 we pointed out that imaginings tend to mirror the inferential liaisons of beliefs, though in a somewhat restricted way. It would take considerable attention to one's own inferential processes in order to distinguish imaginings from beliefs. Ordinarily, we distinguish them easily and immediately, without, it seems, appealing to considerations of inferential role at all.

[14] See Neale et al. (1998). Stressful emotions also seem to be a significant cause of relapse in schizophrenia (see Kavanagh 1992). Naomi Eilan suggests that schizophrenic experiences generate powerful negative emotions, and that this is one reason it is so hard for us to identify imaginatively with the schizophrenic person (Eilan 1999). See below, Sect. 8.8.

A better suggestion is that imaginings and beliefs are generated in very different ways, and that we are normally able to keep track of thoughts according to how they are generated. Our beliefs are formed in response to perceptual information, or by inference from other beliefs we already have. Imaginings can be generated quite independently of these things; what we imagine usually contradicts what we believe and what we perceive. What is distinctive about imaginings is that they are autonomously generated, and it is our capacity to identify this form of generation that enables us to identify our imaginings. Of course it would not do to say that we look inward at our mental processes and form the belief 'this one was internally generated'. For one thing, this would open up a regress: identifying imaginings would depend on having thoughts like 'this one is internally generated' which could *already* be identified as beliefs rather than imaginings. We take it that the situation here is very much like that of the subject to whom it seems that the world has moved because processes of efference-copying and -comparing are going on at a subpersonal level; such a person does not form any beliefs about efference-copying, and would normally not have even the concept of an efference. We suggest that, because of some breakdown at the subpersonal level, the person with schizophrenia is failing to monitor the autonomous generation of her imaginings, and in consequence it seems to her that these thoughts are not imaginings at all.

The question now is this: 'How can we explain, by appeal to subpersonal mechanisms and processes, the schizophrenic subject's failure to detect autonomous generation of thought?' We might simply refuse to answer the question, citing the reasonable principle that the explanation of A by appeal to B is not undermined by our having no explanation for B; rejection of this principle would mean that no explanation of anything could ever be satisfactory. So we might feel free to explain delusions by appeal to the loss of a capacity to identify imaginings, without offering any explanation of that loss. However, there is a reason why, in the present case, we ought to have some interest in the subpersonal underpinnings to the disruption of thought-monitoring that takes place in schizophrenia. For we have seen evidence that people with schizophrenia have trouble with the monitoring of action. It seems unlikely that these two kinds of monitoring difficulties would be entirely unrelated. And it would certainly add strength to the disorder of imagination hypothesis if we could find a subpersonal mechanism, damage to which is a plausible candidate for being the cause of both kinds of monitoring difficulties. The suggestion of Frith is that, in the case of the monitoring of action, the relevant subpersonal mechanism is efference copying-and-comparison. Could this also be the mechanism responsible for keeping track of the ways that thoughts are generated? Could it be that 'thinking is a motor process', as John Campbell, following Irwin Feinberg, has recently argued?[15] The problem, as Campbell remarks, is that we think of thought as underlying motor processes, and not as dependent on them. Here is a suggestion, somewhat different from Campbell's own, about how thought could be dependent on motor processes. As it stands it is certainly incomplete, but it seems to us worth pursuing.

Higher cognition is of recent evolutionary origin. But creatures without cognitive capacities of any kind are capable of sometimes sophisticated behaviours. It is not implausible, therefore, that cognition has developed by seizing hold of parts of the brain already connected with behaviour generation—perceptual and motor systems being the obvious candidates—and putting them to new uses. How might this have happened? Andy Clark and Rick Grush (Clark and Grush 1999) have a hypothesis about how internal representation got a 'foot in the door' of mental processing. The first step was the use of a mechanism that we described in Chapter 4: the emulator. This was selected for initially as a way of providing internally based feedback in situations where signals from the periphery take so long to arrive that they are useless for the on-line correction of errors. According to Clark and Grush, the emulator was then recruited for use as a planning tool. At this stage the emulator is free to operate in ways that need not reflect actual bodily movements. It can model, and provides information about, a planned or otherwise hypothetical movement. The information is channelled through the sensory system that helps us monitor bodily movement, so it has the phenomenal character of motor perception; it is what we call motor imagery. In that way a device designed to support motor performance ends up driving a system that mimics motor perception, and is able to operate in the service of reflection.

---

[15] See Campbell (1999*b*) and Feinberg (1978). The idea is an old one; Hughlings Jackson remarked that 'It being quite certain that the lower centres are sensori-motor, it is surely a legitimate hypothesis that the highest are so too' (Feinberg 1978: 636).

So our tentative suggestion is that the recreative imagination draws extensively on systems designed for motor control. Thinking may not be a motor process, but it may still use systems that otherwise would contribute to motor control. If that were so, we could see how, at least in principle, a breakdown in the monitoring of the motor system could lead to corresponding difficulties in the monitoring of imagination-based thought.

8.5   TWO KINDS OF BELIEF?

The study of cognitive deficits is showing us surprising ways in which mental processes can resolve into relatively autonomous parts. It is natural to think that the pathways from sensory transducers to action are routed through perceptual experience; but Milner and Goodale (1995) argue that the pathways for perceptual experience and action are distinct.[16] And a plausible explanation of Capgras delusion depends on assuming that face recognition resolves into a pathway for overt recognition, and a distinct pathway for affective response.[17] Might something as cognitively fundamental as belief go the same way? We said that delusions need not be beliefs. We also said that delusions, even when they are not beliefs, can be subjectively compelling for the patient. It is usual to think of beliefs both as the source of action *and* as thoughts which carry a certain kind of conviction for the subject. Our proposal has it that these two features can come apart to this extent: when imaginings masquerade as beliefs, you can have conviction without action guidance. Assuming there are unconscious beliefs, and hence beliefs that are action-guiding yet lacking conviction for the subject, this gives us a double dissociation.

If action guidance alone is sufficient for belief, as is suggested by the phenomenon of unconscious belief, is the sense of conviction alone sufficient also? If the answer is yes, then there are (at least) two kinds of beliefs, and there are consequences for our theory of the imagination. For imaginings that are unrecognized as such and which are compelling to the subject

---

[16] See above, Sect. 5.2.

[17] Ellis *et al.* (1997). In Capgras delusion patients claim that close relatives have been replaced by impostors of similar appearance. The idea that autonomic and conscious recognition involve different pathways is due to Bauer (1984).

would then be beliefs, perhaps in one of several distinct senses of 'belief'. And we argued in Chapter 1 that imaginings are never beliefs.

We said that imaginings are never beliefs because beliefs are subject to consistency constraints that do not control imaginings. One way to resolve the problem would be to say that the constraints control only action-guiding beliefs, and that there is therefore no reason why imaginings could not be beliefs of other kinds. That would amount to the complete abandonment of our position in Chapter 1. Fortunately, we feel no pressure to take that path, for we take the consistency constraint to be a minimal constraint on belief of any kind. If someone says that he has discovered a kind of belief which is peculiar in that there is no obligation to resolve or even to be concerned about inconsistencies between these beliefs and beliefs of any other kind, then the correct response to him is to say that he is talking about something other than belief. Suppose we now characterize a kind of state in just this way, that people with states of this kind possess a feeling of subjective conviction about those states. Are states of this kind governed by the obligation to try to resolve or at least be concerned about inconsistencies between them? The answer is no; if all that characterizes states of this kind is a subjective feeling, there can be no reason why states of that kind should, even ideally, satisfy a consistency constraint. So states thus characterized are not beliefs, though of course it may be and probably is true that many states which are characterized by feelings of conviction *and which satisfy other conditions as well*, are beliefs and so are subject to the consistency condition. Under normal conditions, P's being a state that carries conviction for its subject can be an almost infallible sign that P is a belief of the subject.

8.6   SOME ADVANTAGES OF THIS ACCOUNT

Our claim, however, is not that delusions are never beliefs. Our claim is that delusions start life as imaginings and not as beliefs. It may well be that over time certain delusions come to take on the action-guiding character of beliefs, and we know that people with schizophrenia and other kinds of delusions do sometimes act on the basis of their delusions. But it is an important consequence of our view that delusions need not be beliefs. It is often supposed that delusions are beliefs. Thus the *DSM*-IV definition runs: 'Delusion: A false belief based on incorrect inference about external reality that is firmly sustained despite what almost everyone else believes and despite what constitutes incontrovertible and obvious proof or evidence to the contrary' (*DSM-IV* 1994: 765). So our view seems to be contrary to informed medical opinion. Is there any independent reason to support our view? There is. It is frequently noted that people with schizophrenia do not always act on, or even attempt to act on, the strange ideas that they appear to believe. Bovet and Parnas describe a patient, 'a 50-year-old female with paranoid schizophrenia and delusional ideas, which she in no way enacted, [who] lived peacefully with her mother in a small Swiss town ... She expressed her paranoid ideas about her sister, which she maintained for years quietly and without anger' (Bovet and Parnas 1993: 588). And Bleuler wrote of his own patients: 'None of our generals has ever attempted to act in accordance with his imaginary rank and station' (Sass 1994: 3).[18] The psychiatrist Louis Sass (1994) has argued at length that belief is the wrong category for delusions, or at least for a large proportion of them.[19]

Another point in favour of our proposal is that much of what exemplifies the strange and disordered thought of people with schizophrenia would not be remarkable if it were treated as the flow of imagination. We often imagine things having a significance or a connectedness that we know they do not really have; we imagine connections between events, and we imagine those events as connected to ourselves. The psychiatrist Klaus Conrad noted an incident that followed a soldier's being taken to hospital because he was behaving oddly: 'He noticed that there were some cows lowing outside the building, and he suddenly was convinced that he was to be exterminated, that he had to be slaughtered like cattle.' Later the patient was overwhelmed by the thought that 'he would be converted into an animal through hypnosis' (Bovet and Parnas 1993: 587).[20] Many of us, especially in a situation

---

[18] See also Berrios (1991).

[19] We are in agreement with Sass in emphasizing that belief is often not the right category within which to place the thoughts of the person with schizophrenia. He also argues that, far from delusions constituting beliefs, the patient's experience of the world becomes wholly that of an imaginary realm (Sass 1994: 44). However, as a reaction to popular representations of people with schizophrenia as a major source of disruption and violence, responsible investigators may have underestimated this phenomenon. See Buchanan and Wessely (1997: 260), where it is argued that 'actions based on delusional beliefs are more common than had previously been recognized'. For action based on the delusions of Capgras syndrome, see the discussion in Young (2000).

[20] Jaspers (1993) describes many examples of this kind. See esp. (1993: 99–103).

we could not fully account for and which we found worrying, might see cows and be prompted to imagine ourselves being 'slaughtered like cattle', or even imagine becoming a cow. If we could not identify these thoughts as imagining, we might respond to them as we would to our beliefs, or at least attend to them and give them consideration that we would not give to what we knew to be imagination.

A third reason for thinking that delusions might be imaginings is this. If they were, it would be intelligible how it is that people with delusions often do not follow out the consequences of their delusions very far, or try to resolve tensions between their delusions and their other beliefs. And, as the *DSM*-IV definition notes, delusions are rarely revised or eliminated in response to appeals to reason and argument.[21] All this is often taken as evidence of the irrationality of schizophrenic thinking. But this assumes that delusions *are beliefs*—beliefs that do not match up, in terms of sensitivity to reason and evidence, to what we expect from beliefs. Recall our discussion in Chapter 1 of the way in which imaginings mesh with beliefs. When someone acquires a new belief, a potentially wholesale process of belief revision will take place; the person ceases to believe things she previously believed, because they are inconsistent with the new belief. And failures to resolve clashes between older beliefs and the new belief will, if made evident to the subject, seem problematic to her. When we imagine something, on the other hand, we do not cease to believe things that are inconsistent with what we imagine, and we do not regard clashes between what we believe and what we imagine as in need of resolution. Rather, beliefs inconsistent with the imagining move temporarily into the background; they are not available as premises in inferences that involve the imagining, but are available as premises in inferences that do not. Finally, imaginings are not apt to be revised in the light of evidence; the whole point of imagining is to enable us

---

[21] This is also the case with delusions outside schizophrenia. Here is a patient with what is called reduplicative paramnesia, following a right parietal stroke, in conversation with a psychologist (Breen *et al.* 2000: 92):

EXAMINER. How can your husband be in this hospital if he is dead?

PATIENT. That's what a lot of people say, 'don't you get worried about it?', and I said I'm not religious fortunately or I might be worried about it, you know.

EXAMINER. It strikes me as odd. If he was cremated, how could he still be here?

PATIENT. Death is final isn't it, as a rule.

to engage with scenarios we know to be non-actual. Thus imaginings seem just the right things to play the role of delusional thoughts; it is of their nature to coexist with the beliefs they contradict, to leave their possessors undisturbed by such inconsistency, and to be immune to conventional appeals to reason and evidence.

It is one thing to say that delusions carry subjective conviction for the subject, another to say that the subject finds it easy to defend these delusions, or even, on reflection, to see how, given what he or she believes, the delusion could be true. The subject who can no longer tell an imagining from a belief may yet retain the capacity to see that some particular delusional item is wildly inconsistent with the rest of her epistemic corpus. A feature of delusional states of various kinds is often an acknowledgement on the subject's part that the claim is implausible, inexplicable, and unlikely to be believed by anyone else.[22] This is exactly what one would expect on the hypothesis that the patient's mental economy is being invaded by states which masquerade as beliefs but which fail, sometimes spectacularly, to be integrated with what the subject really does believe.

8.7   THOUGHT INSERTION AND WITHDRAWAL

One of the most puzzling symptoms of schizophrenia is called 'thought insertion', where a patient claims that the thoughts of another are inserted into his mind. John Campbell comments:

The thought inserted into the subject's mind is indeed in some sense his, just because it has been successfully inserted into his mind; it has some special relation to him. He has, for example, some especially direct knowledge of it. On the other hand, there is, the patient insists, a sense in which the thought is not his, a sense in which the thought is someone else's, and not just in that someone else originated the thought and communicated it to the subject; there is a sense in which the thought, as it were, remains the property of someone else. It is not really enough to say that we can make no sense of them; these are compelling reports of experience which many people agree in giving; at the very least we should want to understand why it is so natural, so compelling, to describe experience in this way. (Campbell 1999*b*: 610)

---

[22] Insight in schizophrenia is correlated, unsurprisingly, with depression (see Schwartz 2000).

We agree with Campbell that we should take these reports seriously—not as literal and veridical reports of thought insertion, but as reports prompted by experiences which either seem to be experiences of thought insertion, or are experiences which seem, to the subject, to make some sense in the light of the hypothesis that they are experiences of thought insertion. We have seen how someone with an impaired capacity to monitor action might fail to recognize her imaginings *as* imaginings. What needs to be explained is how this failure of recognition might lead the subject to believe that she is subject to thought insertion.

When we come to believe something, we normally do so on the basis of perception or on the basis of what we already believe; we do not choose what to believe, though it may be true that what we believe is influenced by what we want to be the case. But imaginings are internally generated. To fail to recognize an imagining as such is to fail to recognize its internal generation, for it is this feature which most saliently distinguishes imagination from belief. If one fails to recognize the thought's internal source, it may seem to one that the thought comes from without. In many cases it will seem to the patient that the source of the thought is an external one of a kind that we commonly acknowledge; the patient may claim that the thought 'this person is plotting against me' has its source in experiences which make that thought a well-founded one, or that the thought 'I am evil' is conveyed by a voice that speaks (whereas in fact the patient is subject to an auditory hallucination). Another possible strategy would be to ascribe the thought to the actions of another; to describe it as a thought 'inserted by another'.[23]

A phenomenon which is, if anything, stranger than thought insertion is 'thought withdrawal'. This sense of having a thought removed from one's mind is certainly difficult to make sense of—does one continue to know

[23] But note aspects of the experience of thought insertion that are not accounted for here. Cahill and Frith (1996) report a patient who claims to be able to identify the exact point of entry into his head of the inserted thought. We need here to emphasize that, in speaking of imaginings as 'internally generated' and thus distinct from beliefs, we mean 'internally generated' in a specific sense. In a broad sense, all our thoughts are internally generated; they depend on processes going on in us as well as on processes that impinge on us from the outside. And beliefs that arise by inference from other beliefs can certainly be thought of as internally generated, since the inferential processes are internal. See Peacocke (1999: 243–4) for a discussion of thought insertion which employs a notion of self-generation somewhat broader than ours; Peacocke is considering the conditions necessary for the rational self-ascription of belief.

which thought was removed? Suppose the subject engages in a piece of otherwise perfectly ordinary imagining which, through loss of a sense of agency, she does not recognize as such. This involves the imagined thought being allowed to play a role, along with genuine beliefs and desires, in inference and possibly also in the generation of emotional response. Once an episode of imagining has run its course, the imaginative thought content ceases to play a role in the agent's inferences and in her emotional experience. This does not mean that the subject is thereafter unable to access the propositional content of that thought; that content is thinkable by the subject just as any other is. It is just that the thought has ceased to play a belief-like role in the subject's mental economy. This might be experienced as the removal of a thought.

8.8 DELUSION AND EMPATHY

In declaring that delusions cannot be understood, Jaspers seems to have meant that we cannot empathize with them. Certainly, a common reaction to descriptions of delusions is 'I cannot imagine thinking that'. This is quite different from not being able to understand the contents of the delusions, which certainly can be a problem given the incoherence of some schizophrenic discourse. The problem of empathy is that, assuming that the delusions have the contents they are said to have, one cannot place oneself imaginatively in the position of someone who believes *those* things.[24]

Given what we have said here about the nature of delusions in schizophrenia, is there any light we can shed on the issue of barriers to empathy with delusion? An obvious point to make is that since, on our account, delusions are not necessarily beliefs, the project of empathizing with a deluded subject is not, at least primarily, the project of empathizing with someone who has beliefs that correspond to the delusional contents. What

---

[24] We take empathy to involve sharing another's mental state, or possessing an imaginative surrogate for that state. As Sober and Wilson (1999: 234) point out, it must involve something more than this: a recognition, perhaps, of the other's emotional state via the experience of the surrogate state. In this respect empathy is like joint attending, to which, as we saw in Ch. 7, it seems to be ontogenetically related. But we do not agree with Sober and Wilson that empathizing with O's emotion *E* involves feeling *E* for O. One can empathize with someone's jealousy without feeling jealous *for* them.

you need to do is to place yourself, in imagination, in the position of someone who has lost the capacity to distinguish beliefs from imaginings. There is no more reason to think that we can do that than to suppose that we can place ourselves imaginatively in the position of a person who has suffered any of a whole range of subpersonal catastrophes resulting in disordered cognition. Those of us who have not experienced these conditions are not able to empathize with people who suffer from unilateral neglect, or who have lost the ability to recognize people by their faces, or who can no longer negotiate their way through space.[25]

It might be objected that, when people have remarked on the difficulty of empathizing with schizophrenic delusions, they have had in mind the problem of empathizing with people who have come to believe the strange things that people with schizophrenia are said to believe. Putting to one side the question of whether this problem is aptly called 'the problem of empathizing with delusion', we can ask 'Why is it difficult to take on in imagination beliefs with these strange contents?' Since we have argued that imagined belief is simply what is otherwise called 'assumption', why should it be difficult to take on, in imagination, beliefs with delusional contents? Surely we can assume just about anything we like.[26]

In response we point out that imaginative projects can have very limited, or very ambitious, scope. One can aim to take on, in imagination, a single belief, or a whole body of beliefs; one can imaginatively recreate a moment of thought, or a substantial period of thinking, or even a connected sequence of such periods; one can try to see how a thought might affect a certain specific decision, or how it might affect one's response to a broad class of problems, or one's whole approach to life. The project of empathizing with delusional beliefs is presumably a project that is ambitious in at least some of these ways; one wants to imagine how a whole range of very alien beliefs

---

[25] This is of some relevance to Jaspers's thesis because he illustrates the impenetrability of schizophrenic delusion by reference to thought insertion and withdrawal (Jaspers 1993: 578–9). We have suggested that these may be explicable as the result of a loss of the capacity to monitor one's own creative generation of imaginative thoughts. Here the problem is not so much with the thoughts and their contents as with the experience as of one's thoughts being under the control of another. The barrier to empathy here is presumably our inability to imagine what such an experience is like.

[26] Here we are grateful to Martin Davies.

would affect the course of one's life. And ambitious projects of identification are generally regarded as difficult. It is difficult to place oneself, in imagination, in the position of the Azande as described by Evans-Pritchard, or of a medieval peasant. Such imaginings, though perhaps not impossible, require sustained and disciplined mental control, as well as a deep knowledge of the sorts of things that these people actually believe, since there does not seem to be any way to infer the rest of their beliefs from a small core. The same difficulties face someone who wishes to empathize with an agent whose beliefs have the contents of the delusions we find in schizophrenia. And to the extent that the beliefs in this system are even less predictable than those of the Azande or the medieval peasant, it may be even more difficult. This sort of response will probably not satisfy Jaspers, who seems to have thought that delusional states are uniquely resistant to empathy. If this is Jaspers's claim, he has certainly not made it out.

8.9 HALLUCINATION AND AGENCY

Other positive symptoms of schizophrenia are predictable on the assumption that the disease involves misidentification of imaginings. So far we have been discussing the kind of imagining where I imagine that such and such is the case: propositional imagining, as we have called it. There are other kinds of imaginings, and like propositional imaginings they are recreative in form. Thus the various modes of perceptual imaginings such as visual and auditory imagery share important features in common with the corresponding kinds of perception. As we saw in Chapter 4, the subjective experience of visual imagery is strikingly similar to that of vision, and our ordinary ways of identifying both imagery and perceptual experience are similar enough for us sometimes to mistake perception for imagery.

It is estimated that 50 per cent of people with schizophrenia suffer auditory hallucinations, which often involve the experience of someone speaking to or about the subject, while 15 per cent have visual hallucinations and 5 per cent tactile hallucinations (Cutting 1995). To explain hallucinations in terms of the misidentification of imagining, we may assume that a loss of a sense of agency robs the subject of the capacity to distinguish between genuinely perceptual experience and mental imagery in its various modes. Just as with belief-like imaginings, imaginings that have visual, auditory, or other modes of imagery as their counterparts would be apt to be confused with experiences in those modes, were it not for our sense that they are willed experiences.

That there might be a connection between hallucinations and imagery has occurred to people before, but research in this area has tended to concentrate on the question of whether hallucinations are correlated with vividness of imagery—a question concerning which the evidence is equivocal.[27] If the suggestion above about the reason why imagery and perception are confused is correct, there would be no reason to expect such a correlation.

[27] Bentall (1990); Nayani and David (1996).

Part IV

Emotions in Imagination

Chapter 9

EMOTION AND THE FICTIONAL

Until now we have emphasized the integration of imaginings with the subject's beliefs and desires. Now we look at situations where there are tensions between imaginings and desires. We will argue that some of the most valued and complex human artefacts are designed to bring about and sustain these tensions—tensions we value because of their capacity to generate rewarding emotions.

9.1   CHILDREN AND GROWN-UPS

Novels, plays, and films are fictions; so are stories improvised in the imagination. Even small children construct elaborate fictions, sometimes involving imaginary characters. These fictions display some surprising continuities with the mature, canonical works that prompted Hume to wonder why we seek representations of misery.[1] Children's fantasies often develop in ways the children themselves find distressing:

children express anger at various misdemeanors allegedly carried out by imaginary companions, or they engage in arguments with them. . . . When a 3-year-old with an imaginary pony as a companion was taken to an actual horse show, the child's day was ruined because he 'discovered' on arriving at the show that the imaginary pony had made other plans and was not there. . . . The child was unable to solve the problem by simply pretending that the pony was there. (Harris 2000: 58)

[1] We return to Hume's question in Sect. 9.5.

Marjorie Taylor reports that perhaps a third of children with imaginary companions are sometimes angry about their behaviour, and notes one stormy relationship between a child and the chest of drawers in his room (Taylor 1998: 9). Perhaps children in such situations as these, as well as those who complain of being frightened of imaginary ghosts and monsters, confuse what they imagine with reality. If that was so, their responses would have little connection with those of mature theatre audiences who, despite their obvious involvement with the plot, do not think that Lear and Cordelia are real. The idea that there is a systematic confusion here ought to be taken seriously, especially in the light of our suggestion in the previous chapter that this is exactly what is involved in schizophrenia. But the evidence does not support the view that young children mistake fantasy for reality. Four- and 5-year-olds are well able to distinguish between real and imaginary things, and their discrimination is not affected by the imaginary things being presented in frightening or otherwise emotionally involving ways (Harris *et al.* 1991). Also, children with long-term imaginary companions—a group sometimes thought to have lost touch with reality in some way—show when pressed that they also are able to distinguish between real and imaginary things, including real and imaginary friends (Taylor 1998: 115). On the whole it is better to assume that children become absorbed in fictions of their own devising that are sometimes distressing to them, but which they do not confuse with reality. In that case children as well as adults respond to fictions primarily through imagination and not through belief. We can acquire beliefs from fictions; we learn facts from a historical novel and acquire evaluative beliefs from didactic ones. But when it comes to the characters and events of the plot, we imagine that these things happen to those people. Some of these imaginings are belief-like. For the reasons given in Chapter 1, they are not beliefs.

We said that imagining is often the goal of pretence, that children, and sometimes adults as well, pretend in order to have vivid imaginings. Fictions, especially when they are well structured and richly described, presumably offer the same opportunities.[2] But it would be wrong to suppose that we

---

[2] We cannot define fictions simply as works that appeal to the imagination, for non-fictional works do that also. Indeed, the intended effect of a non-fictional work is sometimes achieved *primarily* through imagination. Southey intended his *Life of Nelson* as a vividly imagined example for the young sailor, who would treasure its example 'in his memory and in his heart' (Southey 1894; see also Walton 1990: 27).

generally find satisfaction in the mere having of a belief-like imagining to the effect that a character did this or that. The primary rewards of fiction are emotional ones, though the emotions involved don't always *appear* rewarding: recall the child's disappointment at the non-arrival of his imaginary horse, and your anguish at the fate of Cordelia.[3] We need to understand the relations between emotion and the imagination if we are to understand the rewards of fiction.

9.2   IMAGINATION AND TRANSPARENCY

Proust's narrator, Marcel, spends a great deal of time reflecting on his affair with Albertine, wondering in particular what the affair had meant to her. For Marcel now knows that Albertine was not exclusively or even primarily interested in him. Drawing on his own substantial experience in this area, Marcel imagines her 'voluptuous excitement' awaiting a lover's arrival compared with which 'serious conversations with me about Stendahl and Victor Hugo must have counted for very little' (Proust 1992: v. 622–3).[4] The unwelcome insights that Marcel gains from this imaginative projection concern not so much Albertine's beliefs and desires as her emotions: excitement at the prospect of a new lover; boredom and irritation with Marcel.

Marcel's imaginative project involves him in recreating, as best he can, Albertine's emotions. Does this mean that there is a category of recreative imagining the elements of which have as their counterparts the various emotions? Are there states which are not emotions but which are emotion-like? Beliefs and desires possess imaginative counterparts, but we should not assume that every mental state-type does. Amusement does not have an imaginative counterpart. You might experience amusement as part of an imaginative project, being amused by something you merely imagine. But in that case you are genuinely amused, though what amuses you in imagination might not amuse you if it really happened. You can, of course, imagine that you are amused and really not be amused, but this is belief-like imagining, where being amused appears as part of the content of the imagining. There is no imagining that has an amusement-like character; there is only being really amused.[5]

The case of amusement shows that a state that has no counterpart in imagination can sometimes itself occur in imagination. As part of an imaginative project, one is often actually amused by some aspect of what is imagined, and here one's amusement is caused by what one imagines, as well as having the imagined event as its intentional object. In that case we can say that imagination is transparent to amusement. Contrast the case with that of pain. You can be really amused by imagined events, but you cannot be really hurt by imaginary blows. A masochist might so arrange things that he suffers pain caused by real blows, and this might go along with various imaginings. But here the pain is not, properly speaking, internal to the imaginative project. It is caused by events from outside, and in this respect is unlike the real amusement which is causally integrated into the imagining.

Do pains have imaginative counterparts? The phenomenology of imagining suggests that they do. Imagining painful occurrences generates unpleasant bodily states that seem to act as imagined substitutes for pains, though they are not themselves real pains. If that is right, amusement and pain are different in two ways: amusement, but not pain, can be causally integrated into an imaginative project; pain has an imaginative counterpart, but amusement does not.

Amusement might not count as an emotion, but it is not far from amusement to disgust, anger, and other paradigmatically emotional states. Is imagination transparent to the emotions, or are they states like beliefs, desires, and perceptions that merely have counterparts that appear in imagination? Two arguments naturally come to mind that support the conclusion that imagination is not transparent to emotion. One is that real emotions are related to actions, but that whatever is emotion-like in imagination is not related to action in the same way; we do not, as a result of fear-like experiences in imagination, flee the theatre. The second is that if real emotions occurred in imagination they would be a source of almost limitless emotional conflict. I might admire someone in real life but then read a fictional story about them in which they do something despicable, and as a result come to despise them. If this is really a case of despising, I am landed

---

[5] The case of amusement was suggested to us by remarks in Walton (1994).

with an emotional conflict: admiring and despising the same person. Emotional conflict does occur, when a person's character calls forth an ambivalent response. But it would be absurd to say that I feel ambivalent about someone just because I read a story in which they did something they did not do, and which I know, or at least believe, they would not do in real life.

These two arguments fail for essentially the same reason. We have already granted that imagination is not transparent to perception, to belief, and to desire. And the phenomena appealed to in the arguments above, action-relatedness and ambivalence, have to be understood as dependent on, exactly, perception, beliefs, and desires. Emotions have the relations to actions that they do have only in the context of what we perceive, or believe, or desire. So we can coherently think of two people having the same emotions and only one of them acting on the basis of the emotions, when there is some difference between them which consists in, say, one of them believing P while the other merely imagines in a belief-like way that P. And when I say that I have conflicting emotions about another, it is readily understood that the conflicting emotions are thought of as arising as a result of what I believe and desire about that person; it doesn't automatically count as ambivalence if one of the conflicting emotions is the result of what I merely imagine about them.[6]

None of this *proves* that imagination is transparent to emotion. Seeking to economize on the postulation of kinds of mental states, our presumption is in favour of transparency for emotions; we will say that a given state S itself occurs in imagination if (i) there is phenomenological or other evidence that something at least like S occurs in imagination and (ii) there is no strong reason for denying that S itself occurs in imagination. So our first, tentative, conclusion is that imagination is transparent to emotion. Later we will offer an evolutionary argument to support this conclusion.

9.3   PERCEPTION-LIKE EMOTIONS

If imagination is transparent to emotion, an account of imagination must be partly an account of emotion itself. So we need to say something about what

---

[6] Although imaginings don't always create conflicts in our emotions and other mental states, they can do so. The fact that I find it all too easy to imagine Smith doing something despicable may make me genuinely ambivalent about him.

emotions are. One approach to emotions that has been popular with philosophers over the last quarter-century is to think of them as very closely related to—and in extreme formulations as identical with—highly conceptualized states such as beliefs and evaluations. It seems to us that beliefs are not at all the sorts of things on which to model the emotions. Emotions can be conceptually and cognitively sophisticated, and there are emotion-kinds we can't identify and distinguish without invoking beliefs: envy and jealousy are sometimes given as examples of emotions that differ in respect of little more than the belief one has about the object of the emotion. But this is the top end of the emotion spectrum; there are a great many items lower down. Infants and the members of various non-human species experience emotions, though it is doubtful whether they have beliefs.

Looking around for an alternative model, perceptual states are an obvious choice; they seem to be suitably undemanding conceptually. In fact, we take as our model a class of states that includes paradigmatically perceptual states like seeing and hearing, but also includes states that are less obviously perceptual: we are thinking of bodily sensations, such as pains, sensations of heat and cold, satiation, etc. These states differ, in various ways, from perceptual states such as those we enjoy when we see or hear things. First of all, what we see or hear is not intrinsically valenced; we may see something dangerous and act on what we see, but what we see might well be neutral with respect to our interests; similarly with what we hear. The various bodily sensations seem to be much more closely connected with our interests; we might call them primitive indicators of well-being. Also, sight and hearing are only minimally egocentric; what we see or hear we locate in relation to our own bodies, but, nonetheless, what we see and hear is seen and heard as part of a world that exists independently of our bodies. By contrast, bodily sensations are essentially and exclusively of our bodies. It is remarked that we can have bodily sensations where no part of our body is, as with phantom limb experience, so-called extra-somatic experience, and, via futuristic prostheses, pain experiences caused by damage in someone else's body. But in all these cases, one feels that a part of one's body is located where, in fact, no part of one's body is located (Martin 1993, 1995). Some people take the view that bodily sensations are not perceptual states because they are exclusively of our own bodies, so they do not present us with ways to distinguish one thing from another, as sight certainly does. These may be reasons for saying that bodily sensations are not perceptions. But whether or not bodily sensations really are perceptions, they certainly are like perceptions. In particular, both perceptions and bodily sensations provide us with a phenomenologically rich form of awareness of things. I may know, without hearing it, that there is a mouse in the room, and I may know, without feeling pain, that my body is damaged; I may know these things because, for example, someone told them to me. Contrasted with this kind of knowing, the forms of awareness through perception and through bodily sensation seem rather similar. Further, bodily sensations, we have just seen, are subject to misidentification through hallucination, as perceptions are. A pain may represent my body as damaged in some way, when in fact it is not damaged in that way.

Emotions, like perceptions and bodily sensations, are also phenomenologically rich forms of awareness. What are they forms of awareness of? We said that sight and vision make us aware of an independent world, while bodily sensation makes us aware, exactly, of our bodies. Emotions, we suggest, lie somewhere between the two; to have an emotion is to be made aware, via a certain kind of sensitivity, of a relation between one self and the world. The qualification 'via a certain kind of sensitivity' is essential here because you can be aware of these relations in a way that does not involve emotion, just as you can be aware that there is damage to your body without feeling any pain, or that there is a tree in front of you without seeing or otherwise sensing it. And the sensitivity that is involved in emotion is in some ways akin to forms of perception and bodily sensation. Emotions are like pains and perceptions in having an associated phenomenology; pains, perceptions, and emotions are states about which it is sensible to ask 'What is it like to be in that state?' We also take it that emotions, like pains and perceptions, are in a certain sense preconceptual states: you can be in pain and yet not believe that there is anything wrong with your body; you can be in a perceptual state the content of which is that one line is shorter than another yet not believe that they are of different lengths; and you can feel anxious without believing that there is anything to be anxious about.

Emotional forms of awareness, like those exhibited in bodily sensation, are essentially valenced; our emotions tell us that some aspect of our relation to the world is well or ill. Emotions are perception-like sensitivities to what we might call, generally, *degrees of congruence*. There is a high degree of congruence between the world, or some aspect of it, and myself when the world is, roughly speaking, the way I want it to be.[7] Usually the world is in some respects the way I want it to be and in some respects not. Particular emotions are sensitive to different aspects of this relation, as different parts of the eye are sensitive to different wavelengths of light, and different parts of the visual cortex sensitive to differently oriented lines. Certain incongruences are indicated to us by feelings of fearfulness, others by feelings of envy or jealousy. When a fear-inducing incongruence is significantly reduced, we feel relief, and so on. As the last example indicates, the emotions are particularly sensitive to *changes* in degree of congruence; they are poor indicators of the absolute level of incongruence. You can be delighted by an improvement in fortune to a level which, a week earlier, you would have been horrified to contemplate. Perceptions and bodily sensations also seem particularly good at informing us about changes in the states they monitor.

Thinking about emotions as at least rather like perceptual states has some advantages. First of all, it is a noted feature of the emotions that they tend to generate 'patterns of salience and tendencies of interpretation ... An emotion suggests a particular line of inquiry and makes some beliefs seem compelling and others not, on account of the way the emotion gets us to focus on a particular field of evidence' (Jones 1996: 11).[8] Similarly, our perceptual states have the effect of getting us to attend preferentially to those bits of the environment they represent to us. This is usually for good reason, though the effect can produce unwanted biases; people are said to become irrationally prejudiced against a particularly safe make of car if they recently saw a car of that make involved in an accident. And while emotions typically help us attend to urgent aspects of our predicament, they sometimes foreground one aspect of it at the expense of another that is equally or more important.

We have said that emotions are perception-like sensitivities. In one way emotions are strikingly different from ordinary perceptual states. In perception we are sensitive to the world, whereas emotion provides us with

[7] For reasons that will soon be obvious, 'want' here cannot mean the same as 'desire'. It is intended to cover desires but also more primitive drives possessed by preconceptual creatures as well as by ourselves.

[8] Jones is summarizing a view she finds in the work of Amelie Oksenberg Rorty, Cheshire Calhoun, and Ronald de Sousa. She says that these patterns and tendencies are partly constitutive of emotions.

sensitivity to a relation between the world and something else, namely how we want the world to be. The question then arises as to whether emotions might be sensitive to even more complex states, for example states which involve relations between the world and desires we have concerning the satisfaction of our desires. At the end of this chapter we will suggest that they are.

One other way the emotions differ from perceptions and bodily sensations is that the last two kinds of states have, as it were, their own independent access to the objects they make us aware of. Perceptual systems and systems that support bodily sensation take information directly from the relevant part of the world, or the relevant part or aspect of the body. But the emotions rely on other systems, including perception and bodily sensation, to track the relations that are their business. Thus emotion depends on perception, bodily sensation, and belief for information about the relevant bits of the world, and on desire, on more primitive drives, as well perhaps as on bodily sensation once again, for information about how we want the world to be.[9] This explains why there is such a spectrum of emotions. Fear tends to be indicative of incongruences that threaten a creature's safety, but it can arise in various ways. It can arise in a creature where the source of information about the relevant incongruence is simply perception and primitive drives; it can be the fear of a man who believes that the bank will fail next week and who desires that it should not.

On our account, emotions carry information. The information they carry is egocentric in this respect: they tell us how the world is relative to how we want it to be. It is important to see that this does not amount to an endorsement of emotional egoism. Not all our desires need be selfish desires, and egoism is not established by observing that we act on our strongest desire, because our strongest non-instrumental desire may be an unselfish one (Sober and Wilson 1999, ch. 6). Selfish emotions (of which there are no doubt many) are those which indicate relations of congruence or disparity between the world and our selfish desires (however we define 'selfish'). Being pleased because someone has gained, where their gain was at your expense, and where you treated their success as an end in itself and not as a

---

[9] Bodily sensations are, we take it, unusual in that they do not respect the factive–connative divide. Beliefs and perceptions are purely factive states, whereas desires and primitive drives are purely connative.

means towards some selfish end of your own, is a case of a non-egoistic emotion.

As a first attempt at a theory of the emotions this may have something to recommend it. But it cannot be right as its stands, because it does not explain what urgently needs explaining: our emotional responses to the merely imagined. We discuss this problem in the next section.

9.4 RESPONDING EMOTIONALLY TO THE IMAGINED

If emotions were sensitive exclusively to actual congruences, we could not explain how there could be emotions directed at fictional characters and imaginary situations. We need to say instead that emotions are sensitive to degrees of congruence, real or imagined. We said just now that emotions are unlike paradigmatically perceptual systems and bodily sensations in not having direct access to the bits of the world they monitor. This is crucial to their capacity to be sensitive to imagined situations. Sight takes its inputs from the environment and there is no seeing (no genuine seeing) of what is merely imagined to be there. There is no imaginative counterpart of the environment itself. There can be emotional responses to what is merely imagined because imagination takes its input from things that do have counterparts: perception, belief, and desire. Taking its inputs from these things, it is possible for it to take input also from their counterparts.

Can we give a naturalistically acceptable account of how we acquired such emotional sensitivities to imagined events? Surely what matters to me is how the world is. Fictional characters and events are not part of my world, however generously we might judge its boundaries; Iago's schemes and Captain Hook's treachery are things that will never affect me and of which I need take no account as I go through life. Fictions like *Othello* and *Peter Pan* are, of course, real things of which I may need to take account in assessing my predicament. I can be upset at the prospect of missing *Othello* and glad that *Peter Pan* ends the way it does. But for reasons we made plain in Chapter 1, our responses to fictions cannot be accounted for solely in such terms; one is glad that *Othello* ends the way it does—but desperately sorry about the death of Desdemona. It's that latter kind of being sorry of which we have yet to give an account.

One plausible story about how emotions can be sensitive to imagined relations between how the world is and how we want it to be concerns planning. Go back to Damasio's patients with frontal damage that seems to leave their reasoning and factual knowledge remarkably intact. These people find it difficult to make sensible real-life decisions and suffer various set-backs in business and in their personal lives as a result. What seems to be lacking with them is an appropriate emotional response to imagined circumstance. It is not enough, it seems, to conclude that R is a risky option; one needs also to imagine the occurrence of R and to experience fear or another negative emotion in response to it.[10] And of course at this point R is a merely imagined circumstance, not a real one; the imagining and one's emotional response to it are designed to ensure that R stays merely imaginary. Damasio's theory can help us give a naturalistically respectable account of emotional reactions to fictions—respectable in that it involves no postulation of special mental capacities for dealing with fictions, which would certainly be implausible from the point of view of natural selection. Damasio's suggestion shows how an emotional sensitivity to merely imagined circumstances can help me manage my affairs: in order to affect my predicament I must act; to act effectively, I must plan; to plan, I must imagine alternative scenarios and choose between them. Having a system of emotional responses poised to respond to what I imagine is a capacity we would expect to find in creatures able to choose between alternatives.

There may be other good, adaptive reasons for connecting the emotions to the imagination system. If imagination gives us a window into the minds of others by having us see and think about the world as another sees and thinks about it, it should also have us respond emotionally to the world thus seen and thought about as the other does. It is particularly important that we be able to model the affective components of those states that Strawson calls 'participant reactive attitudes', such as resentment and gratitude (see Strawson 1992). If we want to please or placate others, we need to know how they feel about us, as well as what they see and think. Examples of this kind can sound as if they are fundamentally different from those that fuelled the preceding argument about planning; after all, my contemplated course of

---

[10] See Damasio (1994, ch. 8). As Simon Blackburn notes, the problem in at least some cases seems to be inappropriate rather than absent emotional response (Blackburn 1998: 126).

action is merely possible, while your resentment is all too real. But while your resentment is real, my imaginative modelling of it *represents* it as mine, and I am not actually resentful, or if I am it is not my own resentment that I am seeking to model. Imaginatively modelling my own reaction to things that haven't occurred, and imaginatively modelling your reaction to things that have—these are both cases where emotion displays a sensitivity to the unreal.

We said that emotions are perception-like in various ways. We can now describe another way. In action we try to adjust the boundary between how the world is and how we want it to be; emotions give us a phenomenologically rich picture of how things are at various places on that boundary. What happens if we lose reliable access to that rich and detailed picture? Think how it is when the lights suddenly go out; you know quite well where you are in the room and what things lie in your path to the door. Still, progress is painfully slow without the rich and vivid awareness of the room's layout given in perception, and attempts to speed it up lead to unpleasant encounters with the furniture. Or imagine an orthopaedic surgeon with a broken toe and no pain sensations. He might have as good a knowledge as anyone of the nature of the damage, the likely effect of certain movements, the best way to move. Compared with the pain, that knowledge is a poor guide to action; unless he stays immobile, he is likely to make the damage worse, despite his expert knowledge. These situations are relevant analogues of those Damasio's patients find themselves in. Those patients don't lack for knowledge or a capacity to reason; they lack our rich and detailed emotional picture of the boundary between the world as it is and the world as they would like it to be.

Thinking about how emotional responses to imagined circumstances can have an evolutionary explanation helps to make plausible our claim that imagination is transparent to emotion. If one focuses on the contrast between fiction and reality, this can seem less plausible. Kendall Walton asks, 'What is pity or anger that is never to be acted on? What is love that cannot be expressed to its object . . . We cannot even try to rescue Robinson Crusoe from his island, no matter how deep our concern for him' (Walton 1990: 196).[11] Think instead of cases where the imagined events are of relevance to my situation. Take my fear of heights, as triggered by my imagining climbing out onto the window ledge to rescue the cat. The result of my

[11] This remark and the issues it raises are discussed in Matravers (1997: 85–6).

experiencing that episode of fear is that I very sensibly don't go out onto the windowsill. It does not seem particularly odd to say that this is genuinely an episode of fear, even though the situation to which it is a fear response is merely imagined; the connection between the fear and my real behaviour is clear enough. And it is simply an extension from this case to that of pitying Robinson Crusoe even though I can't go and rescue him. If we interpolate emotion-in-response-to-action-planning-via-imagining between emotion-in-response-to-my-real-predicament and emotion-in-response-to-fiction, it starts to look much more as though we have a single psychological kind than a gerrymandered union of kinds.

9.5   NEGATIVE EMOTIONS

Fictions often provoke negative emotions like sadness, disappointment, and pity. Sometimes, we value them for doing so. Hume said that spectators are, on such occasions, 'pleased in proportion as they are afflicted' (Hume 1987: 217). How do people get satisfaction from experiencing negative emotions in imagination? Hume's own explanation seems to be that, in general, a stronger emotion overpowers a weaker one of opposite valence and gives it the valence of the stronger. So when our pleasure at the representational artistry of the playwright is greater than our sadness at the events represented, that sadness becomes pleasurable and adds to the pleasure of the artistic experience. But both Hume's general principle and his application of it to the case of tragic emotion are simply wrong. We can experience, say, a stronger positive emotion and a weaker negative one at the same time without the weaker losing its negative affect. And our experience of tragedy and other forms of mimesis suggests that this is just how it is in those cases. Indeed, Hume's own description of the audience at the tragedy, as pleased in proportion as they are afflicted, would be a misdescription if the theory he offers were correct; there would be no affliction. Hume has misdescribed what we experience when we are moved by tragedy.[12]

One thing that might be wrong with Hume's account is noted by Kendall Walton. Hume assumes that emotions such as sorrow, pity, and fear are intrinsically disagreeable. This, says Walton, is wrong: 'What is clearly

---

[12] On Hume's solution to his problem and its shortcomings, see Budd (1991).

disagreeable, what we regret, are the things we are sorrowful about . . . not the feeling or experience of sorrow itself' (Walton 1990: 257).[13] And if our sorrow is not intrinsically disagreeable, we need not invoke Hume's dubious theory that our pleasure in Shakespeare's artistry converts the intrinsically negative feeling of sorrow at Desdemona's death into something experienced as pleasure. How far does Walton disagree with Hume? Hume says that an emotion normally experienced as negative is experienced as positive in the context of the fiction. Walton also says that it is experienced as positive in this context, though it is unclear whether he thinks it is normally experienced as negative. The difference between them is that Walton has no need of Hume's theory according to which the valence of an emotion is changed to that of a stronger emotion with which it combines; Walton might say simply that whether an emotion is experienced as positive or negative depends on a number of factors, and one of them is whether the object of the emotion is fictional. So Walton agrees with one part of Hume's theory and disagrees with another. He agrees with Hume's claim that, in the context of a fiction, negative emotion is experienced as positive; he disagrees with Hume's explanation of why that is so.

We disagree with both Hume and Walton, because we hold that the negative emotion is, in the context of tragedy, generally experienced as something negative. There is every reason to suppose that what is unpleasant about sorrow is not merely the sorrowful object, but the experience of sorrow itself. It is very common for people to have negative experiences of emotions in response to imagined situations; try imagining something terrible happening to your loved ones. The object of the experience is imaginary, yet the distress caused is real enough. And we have suggested that there are good evolutionary reasons why people would be so constructed as to have unpleasant emotional experiences when considering merely hypothetical or imagined situations. An account of tragedy ought to allow, therefore, that there is an irreducibly and intrinsically unpleasant aspect to one's emotional response to the work (Feagin 1983). But we deny that this negative aspect

---

[13] Walton's own view is that we do not really experience sorrow for fictional characters; instead it is fictional that we do. But that need not be relevant here. For, as Walton notes, his claim that sorrow is not in itself unpleasant would dissolve Hume's problem even if, contrary to his own view, we did really feel sorrow for fictional characters. Also, Walton agrees that we do feel something—he calls it 'quasi-sorrow'—for fictional characters, and if that were the case our claim would be that quasi-sorrow is experienced as unpleasant.

detracts from the work's overall positive impact; on the contrary, it contributes essentially to it. If this sounds paradoxical, that is because emotions are
being treated as if they were numbers. Adding a negative number to a positive
one always reduces the count. But positive and negative emotions are not
related in the way that positive and negative numbers are.

Consider a competitive rower. The rower forces herself to the limit of her
physical capacities, producing painful sensations and a feeling of exhaustion
that brings her near to collapse at the end of the race. Does this detract from
an experience it is fair to assume is on balance a positive one for the rower?
We think this unlikely. It is much more likely that the rower would report
substantially reduced levels of satisfaction with the experience of the race if,
for some reason, she did not feel painfully exhausted by it. Nor should we
deny that the pain and the exhaustion were, in themselves, unpleasant. The
pain the rower feels need not be qualitatively different from a pain which, if
experienced in a different context, would be judged distinctly unpleasant;
had the rower suddenly felt like that when sitting quietly reading, she would
sincerely have judged the experience a thoroughly unpleasant one. We say it
is just like that with tragic emotions: a desired, positive, and indeed valued
experience has as a constituent something that is intrinsically unpleasant,
where the unpleasantness of the constituent makes an essential contribution to the desirability, value, and positive valence of the whole.[14]

In what way does a negative experience of sorrow and other negative
emotions contribute to the positive experience of the play? Our answer is
that there is an experienced tension between this emotion and other aspects
of our imaginative engagement with the work, and this tension is something
we experience as valuable and even pleasurable. We feel not only an anxiety
about Desdemona's fate, but a tension between this and other aspects of our
involvement with the work. This tension is not an ambivalence about
Desdemona's fate. Her fate seems irredeemably bad to us as audience, and

---

[14] Although this does not seem to be the solution Walton opts for, some of what he says seems
to favour it. Thus he notes that our contemporary view of human psychology allows for 'mixed
and conflicting feelings' and for welcoming opportunities for suffering (Walton 1990: 256–7). Flint
Schier argues that we value tragedy because tragedy yields knowledge of painful truths. 'As we
know that the really valuable revelations are going to be painful, their painfulness is a criterion of
their authenticity' (Schier 1989: 22). On this view, the painful aspect of the experience of tragedy is
valued, not for itself, but as an index of truth. On our view, the pain itself makes a positive
contribution. See text following.

we do not respond to it with a mixture of grief and pleasure.[15] Yet there is, somehow, a mixture in what we feel; the problem is properly to locate it.

Recall our earlier talk of the thoughts that we have concerning the narrative itself: a real thing and unproblematically the subject of our beliefs and desires. We may desire that the narrative turn out a certain way and, as a result of exposure to it, we may come to believe that it does turn out that way. In that case we emotionally perceive a congruence between how things are and how we want them to be, and feel gratified as a result.[16] This gratification is consequent on the satisfaction of a desire: our desire concerning the narrative. Our *narrative* desire is that the story end the way that it does end, and that means that it should end with Desdemona's death. But part of our imaginative stance towards Desdemona is a desire-like imagining that she should be saved. Our attitudes to the narrative and to the character are at odds; the negative emotion that we feel as a result of our attitudes towards Desdemona's death is at odds with our wanting, and presumably being positively affected by, the outcome of the play.[17] For if the play is to end the way we want it to, it must end with Desdemona's death. So we are bound to imagine that she dies, and our desire-like imagining that she live cannot be satisfied.

In more detail, we suggest that a paradigmatic response to *Othello* has the following structure. The play brings me, at a certain point, to imagine that Desdemona dies; this frustrates my desire-in-imagination that she live, and a negative emotion results. But there is a positive emotion also—a response to the satisfaction of my desire (my real desire) that the play turn out the way it does. So far we simply have a case of conflicting emotions; we do not have what we have promised to give: a positive emotion which depends for its positive character essentially on the presence of a negative one. A standard response to

---

[15] One might respond in an ambivalent way, or in any other way for that matter. Our focus here is on the sort of response that is encouraged by the work and which, as a matter of fact, typically occurs.

[16] We note a complication in all this: that there may be an element of imagining in this process, because we can feel tense about the outcome of a narrative when we in fact know how it will turn out. But for the sake of simplicity we ignore this here. It's a complication we could factor in easily enough.

[17] The distinction between a narrative desire and a character desire is a special case of the distinction made by Peter Lamarque between external and internal perspectives (see Lamarque 1996: 146). Lamarque says, 'When Othello kills Desdemona, viewers are appalled by the senselessness and injustice of it, internally and imaginatively. Yet externally, reflecting on the remorseless logic of the drama, they accept that there can be no other outcome' (1996: 163).

Othello also involves the desire that the play generate this conflict of emotions. When the play does this, we have a case of congruence between the world and my (higher-order) desire. A tragic emotion is, exactly, a quasi-perceptual sensitivity to this congruence—a positive emotion that depends essentially on the presence of a negative one. The relevant parts of the world—the parts that determine the satisfaction of our desire—are the work itself, which has to end a certain way, and my own psychology, which has to respond in a certain way to the play. A tragic response is thus as much a response to our own responses as a response to the work itself. Perhaps this is why cultivated responses to tragedy never entirely evade the suspicion of self-congratulation.

9.6 NARRATIVE DESIRES OUTSIDE FICTION

Emotions are the only states we have encountered capable of crossing the boundary between imagination and reality. Still, there seems to be this much difference between the pity we feel for real people and the pity we feel for characters of fiction. The latter kind of pity is capable, we have suggested, of playing a peculiar role: although experienced as something negative, it is commonly desired as a part of a satisfying experience of fiction. Does that mean that we desire this negative emotion for itself? In one way yes, in another way no. If desiring it for itself means desiring it for its intrinsic (negative) qualities, the answer is yes; we reject theories according to which the fiction is enjoyed *despite* the negative qualitative character of the emotion. If desiring it for itself means desiring it irrespective of what is experienced alongside it, the answer is no. The emotion would not normally be desired except in conjunction with the positive emotion that results from the satisfaction of our narrative desire: the desire that the fiction turn out badly for the characters. It is just the same with the rower: the pain enhances the experience of the race, but would not be desired in other circumstances.

Hume thought that no account of tragedy could survive that was only an account of our responses to fictional stories, because we are capable of responding with tragic emotions to narratives we take to be exclusively and intentionally reports of fact. Cicero's audience was delighted by his account of the butchery of the Sicilian captains, though they were 'convinced of the reality of every circumstance' (Hume 1987: 219). It might be argued that such responses come from treating the stories as if they were fiction and hence as the objects of imaginings. This would not be plausible if believing and imagining *P* were incompatible states, for then we would somehow have to shed our belief in the reality of the events, and beliefs cannot be put off at will. But perhaps beliefs and imaginings with the same contents are not incompatible. Still, there is no reason to insist that tragic emotions in response to sober truth always work by fictionalizing the story. We have said that emotions cross the fiction–non-fiction divide, and an emotion which can be generated by imaginings ought to be able to be generated by belief and desire. So we could have the following situation. I believe in the reality of the story and its characters, and have perfectly respectable desires concerning the welfare of those characters; I certainly don't wish gratuitous suffering on them. Still, the narrator's art is such as to generate in me narrative desires such as the desire that this story turn out badly for the characters concerned. The result is an emotional tension much like one I would experience in response to *Othello* or some other evidently fictional story.

We now have tragic emotions in the realm of non-fiction. But the response is to the narration of the events, and not to the events themselves. And if the narrative is a report, the events reported on must precede the narration. So while a tragic response to the reporting of sober fact may be even more worryingly self-indulgent than a tragic response to *Othello* is, it stops short of being wicked.

Tragic emotions, and the desire to experience tragic emotions, might, however, be a cause of wickedness. Suppose, in accordance with a familiar idea, that events, episodes, and even lives can be narrativized; the events are lived as narrative, the narration concurrent with the events themselves, and making a contribution to the motivation of the people who take part in them. Suppose someone builds a narrative around his own life and the lives of others. The narrative has it that some of the characters will suffer in various ways. The agent need not desire suffering for them, any more than we desire it for Desdemona. But if his desire to see the narrative played out is strong, he may pursue a wicked course. The agent is motivated to do harm, not primarily because of malice towards the victims, but because of the satisfactions that derive from the conflict between a proper regard for others and his narrative desire.[18]

---

[18] Thanks here to Jon Jureidini.

References

ABELL, C., and CURRIE, G. (1999), 'Internal and External Pictures', *Philosophical Psychology*, 12: 429–45.

ACREDOLO, L., GOODWYN, S., and FULMER, A. (1995), 'Why Some Children Create Imaginary Companions: Clues from Infant and Toddler Play Preferences', paper presented at the Biennial Meeting of the Society for Research in Child Development, Indianapolis.

ANNETT, J. (1995), 'Motor Imagery: Perception or Action?', *Neuropsychologia*, 33: 1395–417.

ASPERGER, H. (1991), 'Autistic Psychopathy: Reprinted in Childhood', in U. Frith (ed.), *Autism and Asperger's Syndrome* (1944; Cambridge: Cambridge University Press, 1991).

BAHN, P. (1997), *Journey through the Ice Age* (London: Weidenfeld & Nicolson).

BARON-COHEN, S. (1989), 'Perceptual Role Taking and Protodeclarative Pointing in Autism', *British Journal of Developmental Psychology*, 7: 113–27.

—— (1995), *Mindblindness: An Essay on Autism and Theory of Mind* (Cambridge, Mass.: MIT Press).

—— (1999), 'The Evolution of a Theory of Mind', in M. Corballis and S. Lea (eds.), *The Descent of Mind* (Oxford: Oxford University Press).

—— and BOLTON, P. (1993), *Autism: The Facts* (Oxford: Oxford University Press).

—— and ROBERTSON, M. (1995), 'Children with Either Autism, Gilles de Tourette Syndrome or Both: Mapping Cognition to Specific Syndromes', *Neurocase*, 1: 101–4.

—— LESLIE, A., and FRITH, U. (1985), 'Does the Autistic Child have a "Theory of Mind"?', *Cognition*, 21: 37–46.

—— ALLEN, J., and GILLBERG, C. (1992), 'Can Autism be Detected at 18 Months? The Needle, the Haystack, and the CHAT', *British Journal of Psychiatry*, 161: 839–43.

—— BURT, L., SMITH-LAITTAN, F., HARRISON, J., and BOLTON, P. (1996), 'Synaesthesia: Prevalence and Familiality', *Perception*, 25: 1073–9.

—— WHEELWRIGHT, S., STONE, V., and RUTHERFORD, M. (1999), 'A Mathematician, a Physicist and a Computer Scientist with Asperger's Syndrome: Performance on Folk Psychology and Folk Physics Tests', *Neurocase*, 5: 475–83.

BARTOLOMEO, P., D'ERME, P., and GIANOTTI, G. (1995), 'The Relationship between Visuospatial and Representational Neglect', *Neurology*, 44: 1710–4.

BARTOLOMEO, P., BACHOUD-LEVI, A., and DENES, G. (1997), 'Preserved Imagery for Colours in a Patient with Cerebral Achromatopsia', *Cortex*, 33: 369–78.

BAUER, R. (1984), 'Autonomic Recognition of Names and Faces in Prosopagnosia', *Neuropsychologia*, 22: 457–69.

BEHRMANN, M., MOSCOVITCH, M., and WINOCUR, G. (1994), 'Intact Visual Imagery and Impaired Visual Perception in a Patient with Agnosia', *Journal of Experimental Psychology: Human Perception and Performance*, 20: 1068–87.

—— BLACK, S., and MURJI, S. (1995), 'Spatial Attention in the Mental Architecture: Evidence from Neuropsychology', *Journal of Clinical and Experimental Neuropsychology*, 17: 220–42.

BENTALL, R. (1990), 'The Illusion of Reality: A Review and Integration of Psychological Research on Hallucinations', *Psychological Bulletin*, 107: 82–95.

—— (1994), 'Cognitive Biases and Abnormal Beliefs: Towards a Model of Persecutory Delusion', in A. Davids and J. Cutting (eds.), *The Neuropsychology of Schizophrenia* (Hillsdale, NJ: Erlbaum).

BERMUDEZ, J.-L. (forthcoming), 'Normativity and Rationality in Delusional Psychiatric Disorders', *Mind and Language*.

BERRIOS, G. (1991), 'Delusions as "Wrong Beliefs": A Conceptual History', *British Journal of Psychiatry*, 159: 6–13.

BERTHOZ, A. (1996), 'Neural Basis of Decision in Perception and the Control of Movement', in A. Damasio (ed.), *Neurobiology of Decision-Making* (Berlin: Springer).

BISIACH, E., and LUZZATTI, C. (1978), 'Unilateral Neglect of Representational Space', *Cortex*, 14: 129–33.

—— and PERANI, D. (1979), 'Unilateral Neglect, Representational Schema and Consciousness', *Brain*, 102: 609–18.

BLACKBURN, S. (1992), 'Theory, Observation and Drama', *Mind and Language*, 7: 187–203; repr. in Davies and Stone (1995a).

—— (1998), *Ruling Passions: A Theory of Practical Reasoning* (Oxford: Oxford University Press).

BLAKEMORE, S., WOLPERT, D., and FRITH, C. (1998), 'Central Cancellation of Self-Produced Tickle Sensation', *Nature Neuroscience*, 1: 635–40.

BLOCK, N. (1981), 'Psychologism and Behaviorism', *Philosophical Review*, 90: 5–43.

—— (1990), 'Mental Pictures and Cognitive Science', in W. Lycan (ed.), *Mind and Cognition* (Oxford: Blackwell).

BODEN, M. (1992), *The Creative Mind* (London: Weidenfeld & Nicolson).

BOTTERILL, G., and CARRUTHERS, P. (1999), *The Philosophy of Psychology* (Cambridge: Cambridge University Press).

BOVET, P., and PARNAS, J. (1993), 'Schizophrenic Delusions: A Phenomenological Approach', *Schizophrenia Bulletin*, 19: 579–97.

BRATMAN, M. (1992), 'Belief and Acceptance in a Context', *Mind*, 101: 1–14.

BREEN, N., CAINE, D., COLTHEART, M., HENDY, J., and ROBERTS, C. (2000), 'Towards an Understanding of Delusions of Misidentification', *Mind and Language*, 15: 74–110.

BREWER, B. (1995), 'Compulsion by Reason', *Proceedings of the Aristotelian Society*, suppl. vol. 69: 237–53.

——(1999), *Perception and Reason* (Oxford: Oxford University Press).

BROOKS, L. (1968), 'Spatial and Verbal Components of the Act of Recall', *Canadian Journal of Psychology*, 22: 349–68.

BROWN, J., and DUNN, J. (1991), ' "You can Cry, Mum": The Social and Developmental Implications of Talk about Internal States', *British Journal of Developmental Psychology*, 9: 237–56.

——HOBSON, R. P., LEE, A., and STEVENSON, J. (1997), 'Are there "Autistic-Like" Features in Congenitally Blind Children?', *Journal of Child Psychology and Psychiatry and Allied Disciplines*, 38: 693–703.

BRUNER, J., and GOODNOW, J. (1956), *A Study of Thinking* (New York: Wiley).

BUCHANAN, A., and WESSELY, S. (1997), 'Delusions, Action, and Insight', in X. Amador and A. David (eds.), *Insight and Psychosis* (New York: Oxford University Press).

BUCKLEY, P. (ed.) (1988), *Essential Papers on Psychosis* (New York: New York University Press).

BUDD, M. (1989), *Wittgenstein's Philosophy of Psychology* (London: Routledge).

——(1991), 'Hume's Tragic Emotions', *Hume Studies*, 17: 93–106.

BUTTER, C., KOSSLYN, S., MIJOVIC-PRELEC, D., and RIFFLE, A. (1997), 'Field-Specific Deficits in Visual Imagery Following Hemianopia due to Unilateral Occipital Infarcts', *Brain*, 120: 217–28.

CAHILL, C., and FRITH, C. (1996), 'False Perceptions or False Beliefs? Hallucinations and Delusions in Schizophrenia', in P. Halligan and J. Marshall (eds.), *Method in Madness: Case Studies in Cognitive Neuropsychiatry*, (Hove: Psychology Press).

CAMPBELL, J. (1999a), 'Can Philosophical Accounts of Altruism Accommodate Experimental Data on Helping Behaviour?', *Australasian Journal of Philosophy*, 77: 26–45.

——(1999b), 'Schizophrenia, the Space of Reasons and Thinking as a Motor Process', *The Monist*, 82: 609–25.

CARROLL, N. (1997), 'Art, Narrative, and Emotion', in M. Hjort and S. Lavers (eds.), *Emotion and the Arts* (New York: Oxford University Press).

CARRUTHERS, P. (1996a), 'Autism as Mindblindness: An Elaboration and Partial Defence', in P. Carruthers and P. K. Smith (eds.), *Theories of Theories of Mind* (Cambridge: Cambridge University Press).

——(1996b), *Language, Thought and Consciousness*, (Cambridge: Cambridge University Press).

CAVE, K. et al. (1994), 'The Representation of Location in Visual Images', *Cognitive Psychology*, 26: 1–32.

CHAMBERS, D., and REISBERG, D. (1985), 'Can Mental Images be Ambiguous?', *Journal of Experimental Psychology: Human Perception and Performance*, 11: 317–28.

CHANDLER, M., LALONDE, C., FRITZ, A., and HALA, S. (1991), 'Children's Theories of Mental Life and Social Practices', paper presented at the Biennial Meeting of the Society for Research in Child Development, Seattle.

CHARMAN, T. (1997), 'Brief Report: Prompted Pretend Play in Autism', *Journal of Autism and Developmental Disorders*, 27: 325–32.

—— and BARON-COHEN, S. (1992), 'Understanding Drawings and Beliefs: A Further Test of the Metarepresentation Theory of Autism: A Research Note', *Journal of Child Psychology and Psychiatry and Allied Disciplines*, 33: 1105–12.

—— (1993), 'Drawing Development in Autism: The Development from Intellectual to Visual Realism', *British Journal of Developmental Psychology*, 11: 171–85.

—— SWETTENHAM, J., BARON-COHEN, S., COX, A., BAIRD, G., and DREW, A. (1997), 'Infants with Autism: An Investigation of Empathy, Pretend Play, Joint Attention and Imitation', *Developmental Psychology*, 33: 781–9.

—— (1998), 'An Experimental Investigation of Social-Cognitive Abilities in Infants with Autism: Clinical Implications', *Infant Mental Health Journal*, 19: 260–75.

CHATTERJEE, A., and SOUTHWOOD, M. (1995), 'Cortical Blindness and Visual Imagery', *Neurology*, 45: 2189–95.

CLARK, A. (forthcoming), 'Experience and Action: A Tension in the Appeal to Non-Conceptual Content?', *Philosophical Review*.

—— and GRUSH, R. (1999), 'Towards a Cognitive Robotics', *Adaptive Behavior*, 7: 5–16.

COHEN, L. J. (1989), 'Belief and Acceptance', *Mind*, 98: 367–89.

COHEN, M., KOSSLYN, S., BREITER, H., and DiGIROLAMO, G. (1996), 'Changes in Cortical Activity during Mental Rotation: A Mapping Study using Functional Magnetic Resonance Imaging', *Brain*, 119: 89–100.

COLTHEART, M., and DAVIES, M. (2000), 'Pathologies of Belief', *Mind and Language*, 15: 1–46.

CONRAD, J. (1900), *Lord Jim*, (London: Penguin Books, 1949).

COSMIDES, L., and TOOBY, J. (2000), 'Consider the Source: The Evolution of Adaptations for Decoupling and Metarepresentations', in D. Sperber (ed.), *Metarepresentations* (New York: Oxford University Press).

CRANE, T. (1992), 'The Nonconceptual Content of Experience', in T. Crane (ed.), *The Contents of Experience: Essays on Perception* (Cambridge: Cambridge University Press).

CRAVER-LEMLEY, C., and REEVES, A. (1987), 'Visual Imagery Selectively Reduces Vernier Acuity', *Perception*, 16: 599–614.

CURRIE, G. (1990), *The Nature of Fiction* (Cambridge: Cambridge University Press).

—— (1995a), *Image and Mind: Film, Philosophy and Cognitive Science* (New York: Cambridge University Press).

—— (1995b), 'Visual Imagery as the Simulation of Vision', *Mind and Language*, 10: 25–44.

—— (1998), 'Pretence, Pretending and Metarepresentation', *Mind and Language*, 13: 35–55.

—— (1999), 'Desire and Narrative: A Framework', in C. Plantinga and G. Smith (eds.), *Passionate Views* (Baltimore: Johns Hopkins University Press).

—— STERELNY, K. (2000), 'How to Think about the Modularity of Mindreading', *Philosophical Quarterly*, 50: 145–60.

CUSSINS, A. (1990), 'The Connectionist Construction of Concepts', in M. Boden (ed.), *The Philosophy of Artificial Intelligence* (Oxford: Oxford University Press).

CUSTER, W. (1996), 'A Comparison of Young Children's Understanding of Contradictory Representations in Pretense, Memory, and Belief', *Child Development*, 67: 678–88.

CUTTING, J. (1995), 'Descriptive Psychopathology', in S. Hirsch and D. Weinberger (eds.), *Schizophrenia* (Oxford: Blackwell).

DAHLGREN, S., and TRILLINGSGAARD, A. (1996), 'Theory of Mind in Non-Retarded Children with Autism and Asperger's Syndrome: A Research Note', *Journal of Child Psychology and Psychiatry and Allied Disciplines*, 37: 759–63.

DAMASIO, A. (1994), *Descartes' Error*, (New York: Avon Books).

DAPRATI, E., *et al.* (1997), 'Looking for the Agent: An Investigation into Consciousness of Action and Self-Consciousness in Schizophrenic Patients', *Cognition*, 65: 71–86.

DAVIDSON, D. (1980), 'Actions, Reasons and Causes', in his *Essays on Actions and Events* (Oxford: Oxford University Press).

DAVIES, M. (1981a), *Meaning, Quantification, Necessity* (London: Routledge & Kegan Paul).

—— (1981b), 'Meaning, Structure, and Understanding', *Synthese*, 48: 135–61.

—— (1987), 'Tacit Knowledge and Semantic Theory: Can a Five Percent Difference Matter?', *Mind*, 96: 441–62.

—— (1989), 'Tacit Knowledge and Subdoxastic States', in A. George (ed.), *Reflections on Chomsky* (Oxford: Blackwell).

—— (1994), 'The Mental Simulation Debate', in C. Peacocke (ed.), *Objectivity, Simulation and the Unity of Consciousness* (Oxford: Oxford University Press).

—— (1995), 'Two Notions of Implicit Rules', in J. Tomberlin (ed.), *AI, Connectionism, and Philosophical Logic* (Atascadero, Calif.: Ridgeview).

—— and STONE, T. (eds.) (1995a), *Folk Psychology* (Oxford: Blackwell).

—— (eds.) (1995b), *Mental Simulation* (Oxford: Blackwell).

DAVIES, M. and STONE, T. (1996), 'The Mental Simulation Debate: A Progress Report', in P. Carruthers and P. Smith (eds.), *Theories of Theories of Mind* (Cambridge: Cambridge University Press).

——(forthcoming), 'Mental Simulation, Tacit Theory, and the Threat of Collapse', *Philosophical Topics*, special issue in honour of Alvin Goldman, ed. C. Hill, H. Kornblith, and T. Senor.

——UDWIN, O., and HOWLIN, P. (1998), 'Adults with Williams Syndrome: Preliminary Study of Social, Emotional and Behavioural Difficulties', *British Journal of Psychiatry*, 172: 273–6.

——COLTHEART, M., LANGDON, R., and BREEN, N. (forthcoming), 'Delusions and Deficits', *Philosophy, Psychology and Psychiatry*.

DECETY, J., and BOISSON, D. (1990), 'Effect of Brain and Spinal Cord Injuries on Motor Imagery', *European Archives of Psychiatry and Clinical Neuroscience*, 240: 39–43.

——MICHEL, F. (1989), 'Comparative Analysis of Actual and Mental Movement Times in Two Graphic Tasks', *Brain and Cognition*, 11: 87–97.

——JEANNEROD, M., and PREBLANC, C. (1989), 'The Timing of Mentally Represented Actions', *Behavioral and Brain Research*, 34: 35–42.

DENHAM, A. (2000), *Metaphor and Moral Experience* (Oxford: Oxford University Press).

DEWEY, M. (1991), 'Living with Asperger's Syndrome', in U. Frith (ed.), *Autism and Asperger's Syndrome* (Cambridge: Cambridge University Press).

DOMINEY, P., DECETY, J., BROUSELLE, E., CHAZOT, G., and JEANNEROD, M. (1995), 'Motor Imagery of a Lateralized Sequential Task is Asymmetrically Slowed in Hemi-Parkinson's Patients', *Neuropsychologia*, 33: 727–41.

DRETSKE, F. (1997), *Naturalizing the Mind*, (Cambridge, Mass.: MIT Press).

DSM-IV (1994), *Diagnostic and Statistical Manual of Mental Disorders*, 4th edn. (Washington: American Psychiatric Association).

EDGINGTON, D. (1995), 'Conditionals and the Ramsey Test', *Proceedings of the Aristotelian Society*, suppl. vol. 69: 67–86.

EILAN, N. (1999), 'On Understanding Schizophrenia', in D. Zahavi (ed.), *The Self: Philosophical and Psychiatric Perspectives* (Amsterdam: John Benjamin).

ELLIS, H., YOUNG, A., QUAYLE, A., and DE PAUW, K. (1997), 'Reduced Autonomic Responses to Faces in Capgras Delusion', *Proceedings of the Royal Society: Biological Sciences*, B264: 1085–92.

EVANS, G. (1981), 'Semantic Theory and Tacit Knowledge', in S. Holtzman and C. Leich (eds.), *Wittgenstein: To Follow a Rule* (London: Routledge & Kegan Paul).

FARAH, M. (2000), *The Cognitive Neuroscience of Vision* (Oxford: Blackwell).

——GAZZANIGA, M., HOLTZMAN, J., and KOSSLYN, S. (1985), 'A Left Hemisphere Basis for Visual Mental Imagery?', *Neuropsychologia*, 23: 115–18.

—— WEISBERG, L., MONHEIT, M., and PERONNET, F. (1989), 'Brain Activity Underlying Mental Imagery: Event-Related Potentials during Mental Image Generation', *Journal of Cognitive Neuroscience*, 1: 302–16.

FEAGIN, S. (1983), 'The Pleasures of Tragedy', *American Philosophical Quarterly*, 20: 95–104.

—— (1996), *Reading with Feeling* (Ithaca, NY: Cornell University Press).

FEINBERG, I. (1978), 'Efference Copy and Corollary Discharge: Implications for Thinking and its Disorders', *Schizophrenia Bulletin*, 4: 636–40.

FINKE, R. (1989), *Principles of Mental Imagery* (Cambridge, Mass.: MIT Press).

—— KURTZMAN, H. (1981), 'Mapping the Visual Field in Mental Imagery', *Journal of Experimental Psychology, General*, 110: 501–17.

—— SHEPARD, R. (1986), 'Visual Functions of Mental Imagery', in K. Boff, L. Kaufman, and J. Thomas (eds.), *Handbook of Perception and Human Performance* (New York: Wiley).

FODOR, J. (1983), *The Modularity of Mind*, (Cambridge, Mass.: Bradford Books/MIT).

—— (1998), *In Critical Condition* (Cambridge, Mass.: Bradford Books/MIT).

FRITH, C. (1987), 'The Positive and Negative Symptoms of Schizophrenia Reflect Impairments in the Perception and Initiation of Action', *Psychological Medicine*, 17: 631–48.

—— (1989), 'Specific Cognitive Deficits in Schizophrenia', *Cahiers de Psychologie Cognitive/Current Psychology of Cognition*, 9: 623–6.

—— (1992), *The Cognitive Neuropsychology of Schizophrenia* (Hove: Erlbaum).

—— (1994), 'Theory of Mind in Schizophrenia', in A. Davids and J. Cutting (eds.), *The Neurospsychology of Schizophrenia* (Hillsdale, NJ: Erlbaum).

—— (1996), 'Neuropsychology of Schizophrenia: What are the Implications of Intellectual and Experiential Abnormalities for the Neurobiology of Schizophrenia?', *British Medical Bulletin*, 52: 618–26.

—— (1997), 'Language and Communication in Schizophrenia', in J. France and N. Muir (eds.), *Communication and the Mentally Ill Patient* (Bristol, Penn.: Kingsley).

—— and CORCORAN, R. (1996), 'Exploring "Theory of Mind" in People with Schizophrenia', *Psychological Medicine*, 26: 521–30.

—— and DONE, J. (1989*a*), 'Experiences of Alien Control in Schizophrenia Reflect a Disorder in the Central Monitoring of Action', *Psychological Medicine*, 19: 359–63.

—— (1989*b*), 'Positive Symptoms of Schizophrenia', *British Journal of Psychiatry*, 154: 569–70.

—— STEVENS, M., JOHNSTONE, E., and CROW, T. (1988), 'Acute Schizophrenic Patients Fail to Modulate their Level of Attention', *Journal of Psychophysiology*, 2: 195–200.

FRITH, U. (1989), *Autism: Explaining the Enigma* (Oxford: Blackwell).

—— (1991), *Autism and Asperger's Syndrome* (Cambridge: Cambridge University Press).

FRITH, U. and HAPPÉ, F. (1999), 'Theory of Mind and Self-Consciousness: What is it Like to be Autistic?', *Mind and Language*, 14: 1–22.

—— MORTON, J., and LESLIE, A. (1991), 'The Cognitive Basis of a Biological Disorder: Autism', *Trends in Neurosciences*, 14: 433–8.

—— HAPPÉ, F., and SIDDONS, F. (1994), 'Autism and Theory of Mind in Everyday Life', *Social Development*, 3:108–24.

GALLESE, V., and GOLDMAN, A. (1998), 'Mirror Neurons and the Simulation Theory of Mind-Reading', *Trends in Cognitive Science*, 2: 493–501.

GAURIGLIA, C., PADOVANI, A., PANTANO, P., and PIZZAMIGLIO, L. (1993), 'Unilateral Neglect Restricted to Visual Imagery', *Nature*, 364: 235–7.

GENDLER, T. S. (2000), 'The Puzzle of Imaginative Resistance', *Journal of Philosophy*, 97: 55–81.

GEORGIEFF, N., and JEANNEROD, M. (1998), 'Beyond Consciousness of External Reality: A "Who" System for Consciousness of Action and Self-Consciousness', *Consciousness and Cognition*, 7: 465–77.

GERRIG, R., and PRENTICE, D. (1996), 'Notes on Audience Response', in D. Bordwell and N. Carroll (eds.), *Post-Theory: Reconstructing Film Studies* (Madison: Wisconsin University Press).

GOLDENBERG, G., PODREKA, I., UHL, F., STEINER, M., WILLMES, K., and DEECKE, L. (1989a), 'Cerebral Correlates of Imagining Colours, Faces and a Map', *Neuropsychologia*, 27: 1315–28.

—— STEINER, M., WILLMES, K., SUESS, E., and DEECKE, L. (1989b), 'Regional Cerebral Blood Flow Patterns in Visual Imagery', *Neuropsychologia*, 27: 641–64.

—— MUELLBACHER, W., and NOWAK, A. (1995), 'Imagery without Perception: A Case Study of Anosognosia for Cortical Blindness', *Neuropsychologia*, 33: 1373–82.

GOLDIE, P. (2000), *The Emotions—a Philosophical Exploration* (Oxford: Oxford University Press).

GOLDMAN, A. (1989), 'Interpretation Psychologized', *Mind and Language*, 4: 161–85; repr. in M. Davies and T. Stone (eds.), *Mental Simulation* (Oxford: Blackwell, 1995).

—— (1992), 'In Defense of the Simulation Theory', *Mind and Language*, 7: 104–19.

—— (1993), 'Empathy, Mind and Morals', *Proceedings of the American Philosophical Association*, 66: 17–41; repr. in M. Davies and T. Stone (eds.), *Mental Simulation* (Oxford: Blackwell.)

—— (2000), 'The Mentalizing Folk', in D. Sperber (ed.), *Metarepresentation*, Vancouver Series in Cognitive Science (New York: Oxford University Press).

GOMBRICH, E. (1963), *Meditations on a Hobby Horse* (Oxford: Phaidon).

GORDON, R. (1986), 'Folk Psychology as Simulation', *Mind and Language*, 1: 158–71; repr. in M. Davies and T. Stone (eds.), *Mental Simulation* (Oxford: Blackwell, 1995).

——(1992), 'The Simulation Theory: Objections and Misconceptions', *Mind and Language*, 7: 11–34; repr. in M. Davies and T. Stone (eds.), *Mental Simulation* (Oxford: Blackwell, 1995).

——(1995), 'Simulation without Introspection or Inference from Me to You', in M. Davies and T. Stone (eds.), *Mental Simulation* (Oxford: Blackwell, 1995).

——(1996), ' "Radical" Simulationism', in P. Carruthers and P. Smith (eds.), *Theories of Theories of Mind* (Cambridge: Cambridge University Press).

——Barker, J. (1994), 'Autism and the Theory of Mind Debate', in G. Graham and G. Stephens (eds.), *Philosophical Psychopathology* (Cambridge, Mass.: MIT Press).

Goy, C., and Harris, P. (1990), 'The Status of Children's Imaginary Companions', Department of Experimental Psychology, University of Oxford.

Greenwood, J. (1999), 'Simulation, Theory-Theory and Cognitive Penetration: No "Instance of the Fingerpost" ', *Mind and Language*, 14: 32–56.

Grice, P. (1989), *Studies in the Way of Words* (Cambridge, Mass.: Harvard University Press).

Grush, R. (1995), 'Emulation and Cognition', Ph.D. thesis, University of California, San Diego.

Hacker, P. (1990), *Wittgenstein: Meaning and Mind* (Oxford: Blackwell).

Hacking, I. (1995), *Rewriting the Soul: Multiple Personality and the Sciences of Memory* (Princeton: Princeton University Press).

Happé, F. (1994a), 'An Advanced Test of Theory of Mind: Understanding of Story Characters' Thoughts and Feelings by Able Autistic, Mentally Handicapped and Normal Children and Adults', *Journal of Autism and Developmental Disorders*, 24: 129–54.

——(1994b), *Autism: An Introduction to Psychological Theory* (London: UCL Press).

——and Frith, U. (1991), 'Is Autism a Pervasive Developmental Disorder? Debate and Argument: How Useful is the "PDD" Label?', *Journal of Child Psychology and Psychiatry and Allied Disciplines*, 32: 1167–8.

Hargreaves, R. (1976), *Mr Forgetful* (Los Angeles: Price, Stern, Sloan).

Harman, G. (1999), 'Moral Philosophy Meets Social Psychology', *Proceedings of the Aristotelian Society*, 99: 315–31.

Harris, P. (1988), *Children and Emotion* (Oxford: Blackwell).

——(1992), 'From Simulation to Folk Psychology: The Case for Development', *Mind and Language*, 7: 120–44.

——(1993), 'Pretending and Planning', in H. Tager-Flusberg, S. Baron-Cohen, and D. Cohen (eds.), *Understanding Other Minds: Perspectives from Autism* (Oxford: Oxford University Press).

——(1996), 'Desires, Beliefs and Language', in P. Carruthers and P. K. Smith (eds.), *Theories of Theories of Mind* (Cambridge: Cambridge University Press).

HARRIS, P. (1998), 'Fictional Absorption: Emotional Responses to Make-Believe', in S. Braten (ed.), *Intersubjective Communication and Emotion in Early Ontogeny* (Cambridge: Cambridge University Press and Maison des Sciences de l'Homme).

—— (2000), *The Work of the Imagination* (Oxford: Blackwell).

—— (2001), 'The Veridicality Assumption', *Mind and Language*, 16: 247–62.

—— and KAVANAUGH, R. (1993), 'Young Children's Understanding of Pretense', *Monographs of the Society for Research in Child Development*, 58: 93–102.

—— and LEEVERS, H. (2000), 'Pretending, Imagining and Self-Awareness', in S. Baron-Cohen, H. Tager-Flusberg, and D. Cohen (eds.), *Understanding Other Minds: Perspectives from Autism*, 2nd edn. (Oxford: Oxford University Press).

—— BROWN, E., MARRIOTT, C., WHITTALL, S., *et al.* (1991), 'Monsters, Ghosts and Witches: Testing the Limits of the Fantasy-Reality Distinction in Young Children', *British Journal of Developmental Psychology*, 9: 105–23.

HEAL, J. (1986), 'Replication and Functionalism', in J. Butterfield (ed.), *Language, Mind and Logic* (Cambridge: Cambridge University Press).

—— (1994), 'Simulation vs. Theory Theory: What is at Issue?', in C. Peacocke (ed.), *Objectivity, Simulation and the Unity of Consciousness* (Oxford: Oxford University Press).

—— (1995), 'How to Think about Thinking', in M. Davies and T. Stone (eds.), *Mental Simulation* (Oxford: Blackwell).

—— (1996a), 'Simulation and Cognitive Penetrability', *Mind and Language*, 11: 44–67.

—— (1996b), 'Simulation, Theory and Content', in P. Carruthers and P. Smith (eds.), *Theories of Theories of Mind* (Cambridge: Cambridge University Press).

—— (1997), 'Indexical Predicates and their Uses', *Mind*, 106: 619–40.

—— (1998), 'Co-cognition and Off-Line Simulation: Two Ways of Understanding the Simulation Approach', *Mind and Language*, 14: 477–98.

HICKLING, A., WELLMAN, H., and GOTTFRIED, G. M. (1997), 'Preschoolers' Understanding of Others' Mental Attitudes Towards Pretend Happenings', *British Journal of Developmental Psychology*, 15: 339–54.

HOBSON, P. (1989), 'On Sharing Experiences', *Development and Psychopathology*, 1: 197–203.

—— (1993), *Autism and the Development of Mind* (Hove: Erlbaum).

—— OUSTON, J., and LEE, T. (1988), 'What's in a Face? The Case of Autism', *British Journal of Psychology*, 79: 441–53.

HOLTON, R., and LANGTON, R. (1998), 'Empathy and Animal Ethics', in D. Jamieson (ed.), *Singer and his Critics* (Oxford: Blackwell).

HOWE, M. (1989), *Fragments of Genius* (London: Routledge).

HOWES, C., and MATHESON, C. C. (1992), 'Sequence in the Development of Competent Play with Peers: Social and Pretend Play', *Developmental Psychology*, 28: 961–74.

HOWLIN, P. (1997), *Autism: Preparing for Adulthood* (London: Routledge).

——DAVIES, M., and UDWIN, O. (1998), 'Cognitive Functioning in Adults with Williams Syndrome', *Journal of Child Psychology and Psychiatry and Allied Disciplines*, 39: 183–9.

HUME, D. (1902), *A Treatise of Human Nature*, 2nd edn. (Oxford: Oxford University Press).

——(1987), 'Of Tragedy', in E. Miller (ed.), *Essays Moral, Political and Literary* (Indianapolis: Liberty Fund).

HUMPHREY, N. (1980), 'Nature's Psychologists', in B. Josephson and V. Ramachandran (eds.), *Consciousness and the Physical World* (London: Pergamon).

——(1998), 'Cave Art, Autism and the Human Mind', *Cambridge Archaeological Journal*, 8: 165–91.

HURLEY, S. (1998), *Consciousness in Action* (Cambridge, Mass.: Harvard University Press).

HUTCHISON, W., DAVIS, K., LOZANO, A., TASKER, R., and DOSTROVSKY, J. (1999), 'Pain Related Neurons in the Human Cingulate Cortex', *Nature Neuroscience*, 2: 403–5.

JACKSON, F. (1977), *Perception: A Representative Theory* (Cambridge: Cambridge University Press).

——(1999), 'All that Can be at Issue in the Theory-Theory Simulation Debate', *Philosophical Papers*, 28: 77–96.

JACOBS, D., SHUREN, J., BOWERS, D., and HEILMAN, K. (1995), 'Emotional Facial Imagery, Perception, and Expression in Parkinson's Disease', *Neurology*, 45: 1696–702.

JAEDICKE, S., STOROSCHUK, S., and LORD, C. (1994), 'Subjective Experience and Causes of Affect in High-Functioning Children and Adolescents with Autism', *Development and Psychopathology*, 6: 273–84.

JANKOWIAK, J., KINSBOURNE, M., SHALEV, R., and BACHMAN, D. (1992), 'Preserved Visual Imagery and Catergorization in a Case of Associative Visual Agnosia', *Journal of Cognitive Neuroscience*, 4: 119–31.

JARROLD, C. (1997), 'Pretend Play in Autism: Executive Explanations', in J. Russell (ed.), *Autism as an Executive Disorder* (Oxford: Oxford University Press).

——CARRUTHERS, P., SMITH, P., and BOUCHER, J. (1994), 'Pretend Play: Is it Metarepresentational?', *Mind and Language*, 9: 445–68.

——BOUCHER, J., and SMITH, P. (1996), 'Generativity Defects in Pretend Play in Autism', *British Journal of Developmental Psychology*, 14: 275–300.

JASPERS, K. (1993), *General Psychopathology* (Baltimore: Johns Hopkins University Press).

JEANNEROD, M. (1997), *The Cognitive Neuroscience of Action* (Oxford: Blackwell).

JOHNSTONE, E., and FRITH, C. (1996), 'Validation of Three Dimensions of Schizophrenic Symptoms in a Large Unselected Sample of Patients', *Psychological Medicine*, 26: 669–79.

JONES, K. (1996), 'Trust as an Affective Attitude', *Ethics*, 107: 4–25.

JOSEPH, R. (1998), 'Intention and Knowledge in Preschoolers' Conception of Pretend', *Child Development*, 69: 966–80.

KANNER, L. (1943), 'Autistic Disturbances of Affective Contact', *Nervous Child*, 2: 217–50.

KASARI, C., and SIGMAN, M. (1996), 'Expression and Understanding of Emotion and Atypical Development', in M. Lewis and M. Sullivan (eds.), *Emotional Development in Atypical Children* (Hillside, NJ: Erlbaum).

—— BAUMGARTNER, P., and STIPEK, D. (1993), 'Pride and Mastery in Children with Autism', *Journal of Child Psychology and Psychiatry and Allied Disciplines*, 34: 352–62.

KAUFMANN, G., and HELSTRUP, T. (1993), 'Mental Imagery: Fixed or Multiple Meanings? Nature and Function of Imagery in Creative Thinking', in B. Roskos-Ewoldsen, M. J. Intons-Peterson, and R. E. Anderson (eds.), *Imagery, Creativity, and Discovery: A Cognitive Perspective* (Amsterdam: North-Holland/Elsevier Science Publishers).

KAVANAGH, D. (1992), 'Recent Developments in Expressed Emotion and Schizophrenia', *British Journal of Psychiatry*, 160: 601–20.

KAZAK, S., COLLIS, G., and LEWIS, V. (1997), 'Can Young People with Autism Refer to Knowledge States? Evidence from their Understanding of "Guess" and "Know"', *Journal of Child Psychology and Psychiatry and Allied Disciplines*, 38: 1001–9.

KOSSLYN, S. (1994), *Image and Brain: The Resolution of the Imagery Debate* (Cambridge, Mass.: MIT Press/Bradford Books).

—— (1999), 'If Neuroimaging is the Answer, What is the Question?', *Philosophical Transactions of the Royal Society of London*, B354: 1283–94.

—— BALL, T., and REISER, B. (1978), 'Visual Images Preserve Metric Spatial Information: Evidence from Studies of Image Scanning', *Journal of Experimental Psychology: Human Perception and Performance*, 4: 47–60.

—— et al. (1993), 'Visual Mental Imagery Activates Topographically Organized Visual Cortex: PET Investigations', *Journal of Cognitive Neuroscience*, 5: 263–87.

—— THOMPSON, W., KIM, I., RAUCH, S., and ALPERT, N. (1996), 'Individual Differences in Cerebral Blood Flow in Area 17 Predict the Time to Evaluate Visualized Letters', *Journal of Cognitive Neuroscience*, 8: 78–82.

—— —— and ALPERT, N. (1997), 'Neural Systems Shared by Visual Imagery and Visual Perception: A Positron Emission Tomography Study', *Neuroimage*, 6: 320–34.

—— DIGIROLAMO, G., THOMPSON, W., and ALPERT, N. (1998), 'Mental Rotation of Objects versus Hands: Neural Mechanisms Revealed by Positron Emission Tomography', *Psychophysiology*, 35: 151–61.

—— PASCUAL-LEONE, A., FELICIAN, O., and CAMPOSANO, S. (1999a), 'The Role of Area 17 in Visual Imagery: Convergent Evidence from PET and rTMS', *Science*, 284: 167–70.

——SUKEL, K., and BLY, B. (1999*b*), 'Squinting with the Mind's Eye', *Memory and Cognition*, 27: 276–87.

KUHBERGER, A., PERNER, J., SCHULTE, M., and LEINGRUBER, R. (1995), 'Choice or No Choice: Is the Langer Effect Evidence against Simulation?', *Mind and Language*, 10: 423–36.

KUNZENDORF, R. (1990), 'The Causal Efficacy of Consciousness in General, Imagery in Particular: A Materialist Perspective', in R. Kunzendorf (ed.), *Mental Imagery* (New York: Plenum).

LAMARQUE, P. (1996), *Fictional Points of View* (Ithaca, NY: Cornell University Press).

LANG, P., LEVIN, D., MILLER, G., and KOZAK, J. (1983), 'Fear Behaviour, Fear Imagery and the Psychophysiology of Emotion', *Journal of Abnormal Psychology*, 92: 276–306.

LANG, W., PETIT, L., HOELLINGER, P., and PIETRZYLE, U. (1994), 'A Positron Emission Tomography Study of Oculomotor Imagery', *Neuroreport*, 5: 921–4.

LEEKAM, S., and PERNER, J. (1991), 'Does the Autistic Child Have a Metarepresentational Deficit?', *Cognition*, 40: 203–18.

——PERRETT, D., MILDERS, M., and BROWN, S. (1997), 'Eye Direction Detection: A Dissociation between Geometric and Joint Attention Skills in Autism', *British Journal of Developmental Psychology*, 15: 77–95.

LEEVERS, H., and HARRIS, P. (1998), 'Drawing Impossible Entities: A Measure of the Imagination of Children with Autism, Children with Learning Disabilities, and Normal 4-Year-Olds', *Journal of Child Psychology and Psychiatry*, 39: 339–410.

——— (1999), 'Counterfactual Syllogistic Reasoning in Normal 4-Year-Olds, Children with Learning Disabilities, and Children with Autism', *Journal of Experimental Child Psychology*, 76: 64–87.

LESLIE, A. (1987), 'Pretense and Representation: The Origins of "Theory of Mind" ', *Psychological Review*, 94: 412–26.

—— (1988), 'Some Implications of Pretense for Mechanisms Underlying the Child's Theory of Mind', in J. Astington, P. Harris, and D. Olson (eds.), *Developing Theories of Mind* (New York: Cambridge University Press).

—— (1994*a*), 'Pretending and Believing: Issues in the Theory of ToMM', *Cognition*, 50: 211–38.

—— (1994*b*), 'ToMM, ToBy, and Agency: Core Architecture and Domain Specificity', in L. Hirschfeld and S. Gelman (eds.), *Mapping the Mind* (Cambridge: Cambridge University Press).

—— (2000), 'How to Acquire a Representational Theory of Mind', in D. Sperber (ed.), *Metarepresentations* (New York: Oxford University Press).

—— and FRITH, U. (1987), 'Metarepresentation and Autism: How Not to Lose One's Marbles', *Cognition*, 27: 291–4.

LESLIE, A. and GERMAN, T. (1995), 'Knowledge and Ability in "Theory of Mind": One-eyed Overview of a Debate', in Martin Davies and Tony Stone (eds.), *Mental Simulation* (Oxford: Blackwell).

—— and ROTH, D. (1993), 'What Autism Teaches us about Metarepresentation', in S. Baron-Cohen, H. Tager-Flusberg, and D. Cohen (eds.), *Understanding Other Minds: Perspectives from Autism* (Oxford: Oxford University Press).

—— and THAISS, L. (1992), 'Domain Specificity in Conceptual Development: Neuropsychological Evidence from Autism', *Cognition*, 43: 225–51.

LEVINE, D., WARACH, J., and FARAH, M. (1985), 'Two Visual Systems in Mental Imagery: Dissociation of "What" and "Where" in Imagery Disorders due to Bilateral Posterior Cerebral Lesions', *Neurology*, 35: 1010–8.

LEWIS, D. (1983), *Philosophical Papers*, vol. i (Oxford: Oxford University Press).

LILLARD, A. (1993), 'Young Children's Conceptualization of Pretense: Action or Mental Representational State?', *Child Development*, 64: 372–86.

——(1998), 'Playing with a Theory of Mind', in O. Saracho and B. Spodek (eds.), *Multiple Perspectives on Play in Early Childhood Education* (New York: SUNY Press).

—— and SOBEL, D. (1999), 'Lion Kings or Puppies: The Influence of Fantasy on Children's Understanding of Pretense', *Developmental Science*, 21: 75–80.

—— ZELJO, A., CURENTON, S., and KAUGARS, A. (2000), 'Children's Understanding of the Animacy Constraint on Pretense', *Merrill-Palmer Quarterly*, 46: 21–44.

LOVELAND, K., and TUNALI, B. (1994), 'Narrative Language in Autism and the Theory of Mind Hypothesis: A Wider Perspective', in S. Baron-Cohen, H. Tager-Flusberg, and D. Cohen (eds.), *Understanding Other Minds: Perspectives from Autism* (Oxford: Oxford University Press).

LUZZATTI, C., *et al.* (1998), 'A Neurological Dissociation between Preserved Visual and Impaired Spatial Processing in Mental Imagery', *Cortex*, 34: 461–9.

LYONS, W. (1984), 'The Tiger and his Stripes', *Analysis*, 44: 93–5.

McDOWELL, J. (1994), *Mind and World* (Cambridge, Mass.: Harvard University Press).

McGINN, C. (1997), *Ethics, Evil and Fiction* (Oxford: Oxford University Press).

McGREGOR, E., WHITEN, A., and BLACKBURN, P. (1998), 'Teaching Theory of Mind by Highlighting Intention and Illustrating Thought: A Comparison of their Effectiveness with 3-Year-Olds and Autistic Individuals', *British Journal of Developmental Psychology*, 16: 281–300.

MAHER, B. (1999), 'Anomalous Experience in Everyday Life: Its Significance for Psychopathology', *The Monist*, 82: 547–70.

MARTIN, M. (1992), 'Perception, Concepts and Memory', *Philosophical Review*, 101: 745–63.

——(1993), 'Sense Modalities and Spatial Properties', in N. Eilan, R. McCarthy, and B. Brewer (eds.), *Spatial Representation* (Oxford: Blackwell).

——(1995), 'Bodily Awareness: A Sense of Ownership', in J.-L. Bermudez, A. Marcel, and N. Eilan (eds.), *The Body and the Self* (Cambridge, Mass.: Bradford Books/MIT Press).

——(forthcoming), 'The Transparency of Experience', *Mind and Language*.

MATRAVERS, D. (1997), 'The Paradox of Fiction', in M. Hjort and S. Lavers (eds.), *Emotion and the Arts* (New York: Oxford University Press).

MATTHEWS, G. (1969), 'Mental Copies', *Philosophical Review*, 78: 53–73.

MELLOR, H. (1978), 'Conscious Belief', *Proceedings of the Aristotelian Society*, 78: 88–161.

MELTZOFF, A., and GOPNIK, A. (1993), 'The Role of Imitation in Understanding Persons and Developing a Theory of Mind', in S. Baron-Cohen, H. Tager-Flusberg, and D. Cohen (eds.), *Understanding Other Minds: Perspectives from Autism* (Oxford: Oxford University Press).

MILLIKAN, R. (1993), 'Content and Vehicle', in N. Eilan, R. McCarthy, and B. Brewer (eds.), *Spatial Representation* (Oxford: Oxford University Press).

MILNER, D., and GOODALE, M. (1995), *The Visual Brain in Action* (Oxford: Oxford University Press).

MITCHELL, P. (1996), *Acquiring a Concept of Mind* (Hove: Psychology Press).

——(1997), *Introduction to Theory of Mind: Children, Autism and Apes* (London: Edward Arnold).

——ROBINSON, E., ISAACS, J., and NYE, R. (1996), 'Contamination in Reasoning, about False Belief: An Instance of Realist Bias in Adults but not Children', *Cognition*, 59: 1–21.

MITHEN, S. (2000), 'Paleoanthropological Perspectives on the Theory of Mind', in S. Baron-Cohen, H. Tager-Flusberg, and D. Cohen (eds.), *Understanding Other Minds: Perspectives from Autism*, 2nd edn. (Oxford: Oxford University Press).

MLAKAR, J., JENSTERLE, J., and FRITH, C. (1994), 'Central Monitoring Deficiency and Schizophrenic Symptoms', *Psychological Medicine*, 24: 557–64.

MOORE, C., JARROLD, C., RUSSELL, J., and LUMB, A. (1995), 'Conflicting Desire and the Child's Theory of Mind', *Cognitive Development*, 10: 467–82.

MOORE, D., HOBSON, R. P., and LEE, A. (1997), 'Components of Person Perception: An Investigation with Autistic, Non-Autistic Retarded and Typically Developing Children and Adolescents', *British Journal of Developmental Psychology*, 15: 401–23.

MORTON, A. (1980), *Frames of Mind* (Oxford: Oxford University Press).

——(1995), 'Game Theory and Knowledge by Simulation', in M. Davies and T. Stone (eds.), *Mental Simulation* (Oxford: Blackwell).

MUNDY, P., SIGMAN, M., and KASARI, C. (1993), 'The Theory of Mind and Joint-Attention Deficits in Autism', in S. Baron-Cohen, H. Tager-Flusberg, and D. Cohen (eds.), *Understanding Other Minds: Perspectives from Autism* (Oxford: Oxford University Press).

NASAR, S. (1998), *A Beautiful Mind* (New York: Faber & Faber).

NAYANI, T., and DAVID, A. (1996), 'The Neuropsychology and Neurophenomenology of Auditory Hallucination', in C. Pantelis, H. Nelson, and T. Barnes (eds.), *Schizophrenia: A Neurophysiological Approach* (Chichester: Wiley).

NEALE, J., BLANCHARD, J., KERR, S., KRING, A., and SMITH, D. (1998), 'Flat Affect in Schizophrenia', in W. Flack and J. Laird (eds.), *Emotions in Psychopathology* (New York: Oxford University Press).

NERSESSIAN, N. (1992), 'In the Theoretician's Laboratory: Thought Experiments as Mental Modelling', in D. Hull, M. Forbes and K. Okruhlik (eds.), *Proceedings of the (1992) Biennial Meeting of the Philosophy of Science Association*, vol. ii (Michigan: Philosophy of Science Association).

NICHOLS, S., and STICH, S. (1998), 'Rethinking Co-cognition: A Reply to Heal', *Mind and Language*, 13: 499–512.

——(2000), 'A Cognitive Theory of Pretense', *Cognition*, 74: 115–47.

——STICH, S., and LESLIE, A. (1995), 'Choice Effects and the Ineffectiveness of Simulation', *Mind and Language*, 10: 437–45.

—— and KLEIN, D. (1996), 'Varieties of Off-Line Simulation', in P. Carruthers and P. Smith (eds.), *Theories of Theories of Mind* (Cambridge: Cambridge University Press).

NORTON, J. (1991), 'Thought Experiments in Einstein's Work', in T. Horowitz and G. Massey (eds.), *Thought Experiments in Science and Philosophy* (Lanham, Md.: Rowman & Littlefield).

NOVITZ, D. (1999), 'Creativity and Constraint', *Australasian Journal of Philosophy*, 77: 67–82.

NUSSBAUM, M. (1995), *Poetic Justice* (Boston: Beacon Press).

OATLEY, K. (1994), 'A Taxonomy of the Emotions of Literary Response and a Theory of Identification in Fictional Narrative', *Poetics*, 23: 53–74.

O'SHAUGNESSY, B. (2000), *Consciousness and the World* (Oxford: Oxford University Press).

OZONOFF, S. (1998), 'Components of Executive Function in Autism and Other Disorders', in J. Russell (ed.), *Autism as an Executive Disorder* (Oxford: Oxford University Press).

—— ROGERS, S., and PENNINGTON, B. (1991a), 'Asperger's Syndrome: Evidence of an Empirical Distinction from High-Functioning Autism', *Journal of Child Psychology and Psychiatry and Allied Disciplines*, 32: 1107–22.

—— PENNINGTON, B., and ROGERS, S. (1991b), 'Executive Function Deficits in High-Functioning Autistic Individuals: Relationship to Theory of Mind', *Journal of Child Psychology and Psychiatry and Allied Disciplines*, 32: 1081–105.

PACHERIE, E. (1997), 'Motor-Images, Self-Consciousness, and Autism', in J. Russell (ed.), *Autism as an Executive Disorder* (Oxford: Oxford University Press).

PARSONS, L. (1994), 'Temporal and Kinematic Properties of Motor Behavior Reflected in Mentally Simulated Action', *Journal of Experimental Psychology: Human Perception and Performance*, 20: 709–30.

——— et al. (1995), 'Use of Implicit Motor Imagery for Visual Shape Discrimination as Revealed by PET', *Nature*, 375: 54–8.

——— GABRIELI, J., PHELPS, E., and GAZZANIGA, M. (1998), 'Cerebrally Lateralized Mental Representations of Hand Shape and Movement', *Journal of Neuroscience*, 18: 6539–48.

PAULIGNAN, Y., MCKENZIE, C., MARTENIUK, R., and JEANNEROD, M. (1991), 'Selective Perturbation of Visual Input during Prehension Movements', *Experimental Brain Research*, 83: 502–12.

PEACOCKE, C. (1985), 'Imagination, Experience and Possibility', in J. Foster and H. Robinson (eds.), *Essays on Berkeley* (Oxford: Oxford University Press).

——— (1994), 'The Issues and their Further Development', in C. Peacocke (ed.), *Objectivity, Simulation and the Unity of Consciousness* (Oxford: Oxford University Press).

——— (1999), *Being Known* (Oxford: Oxford University Press).

PENNINGTON, B., and OZONOFF, S. (1996), 'Executive Functions and Developmental Psychopathology', *Journal of Child Psychology and Psychiatry and Allied Disciplines*, 37: 51–87.

——— ROGERS, S., BENNETTO, C., GRIFFITH, E., REED, D., and SHYU, V. (1997), 'Validity Tests of the Executive Dysfunction Hypothesis of Autism', in J. Russell (ed.), *Autism as an Executive Function Disorder* (Oxford: Oxford University Press).

PERNER, J., FRITH, U., LESLIE, A., and LEEKAM, S. (1989), 'Exploration of the Autistic Child's Theory of Mind: Knowledge, Belief, and Communication', *Child Development*, 60: 689–700.

——— BAKER, S., and HUTTON, D. (1994), 'Prelief: The Conceptual Origins of Belief and Pretence', in C. Lewis and P. Mitchell (eds.), *Children's Early Understanding of Mind* (Hove: Erlbaum).

PETTIT, P., and SMITH, M. (1990), 'Backgrounding Desire', *Philosophical Review*, 99: 565–92.

PLODOWSKI, A., and JACKSON, S. (2001), 'Getting to Grips with the Ebbinghaus Illusion', *Current Biology*, 11: 304–6.

PODGORNY, P., and SHEPARD, R. (1978), 'Functional Representations Common to Visual Perception and Imagination', *Journal of Experimental Psychology: Human Perception and Performance*, 4: 21–35.

PROUST, M. (1992), *In Search of Lost Time*, trans. C. Moncrieff and T. Kilmartin, rev. D. Enright (London: Chatto & Windus).

PYLYSHYN, Z. (1981), 'The Imagery Debate: Analogue Media Versus Tacit Knowledge', in N. Block (ed.), *Imagery* (Cambridge, Mass.: MIT Press).

——— (1999), 'Is Vision Continuous with Cognition? The Case for Cognitive Impenetrability of Visual Perception', *Behavioral and Brain Sciences*, 22: 341–65.

RAILTON, P. (1997), 'On Hypothetical and Non-Hypothetical in Reasoning about Belief and Action', in G. Cullity and B. Gaut (eds.), *Ethics and Practical Reason* (Oxford: Oxford University Press).

RAMSEY, F. (1950), 'General Propositions and Causality', in his *Foundations of Mathematics and Other Logical Essays* (New York: Routledge).

RAVENSCROFT, I. (1998), 'What is it Like to be Someone Else? Simulation and Empathy', *Ratio*, 11: 170–85.

—— (1999), 'Predictive Failure', *Philosophical Papers*, 28: 143–68.

RECANATI, F. (2000), 'The Iconicity of Metarepresentation', in D. Sperber (ed.), *Metarepresentation* (New York: Oxford University Press).

REISBERG, D., CULVER, L., HEUER, F., and FISCHMAN, D. (1986), 'Visual Memory: When Imagery Vividness Makes a Difference', *Journal of Mental Imagery*, 10: 51–74.

—— and LEAK, S. (1987), 'Visual Imagery and Memory for Appearance: Does Clark Gable or George C. Scott have Bushier Eyebrows?', *Canadian Journal of Psychology*, 41: 521–6.

—— and MORRIS, A. (1985), 'Images Contain what the Imager Put There: A Nonreplication of Illusions in Imagery', *Bulletin of the Psychonomic Society*, 23: 493–6.

—— SMITH, J., BAXTER, D., and SONENSHINE, M. (1989), ' "Enacted" Auditory Images are Ambiguous; "Pure" Auditory Images are Not', *Quarterly Journal of Experimental Psychology: Human Experimental Psychology*, 41: 619–41.

REPACHOLI, B., and GOPNIK, A. (1997), 'Early Reasoning about Desires: Evidence from 14- and 18-Month Olds', *Developmental Psychology*, 33: 12–21.

RICHARDSON, J. (1999), *Imagery* (Hove: Psychology Press).

RIEFFE, C. (1998), 'The Child's Theory of Mind: Understanding Desires, Beliefs and Emotions', Vrije Universiteit te Amsterdam Ph.D. thesis.

RIGGS, K., PETERSON, D., ROBINSON, E., and MITCHELL, P. (1998), 'Are Errors in False Belief Tasks Symptomatic of a Broader Difficulty with Counterfactuals?', *Cognitive Development*, 13: 73–90.

RIPSTEIN, A. (1987), 'Explanation and Empathy', *Review of Metaphysics*, 40: 465–82.

RIZZOLATTI, G., FADIGA, L., GALESE, V., and FOGASSI, L. (1996), 'Premotor Cortex and the Recognition of Motor Actions', *Cognitive Brain Research*, 3: 131–41.

ROSEN, C., SCHWEBEL, D., and SINGER, J. (1997), 'Preschoolers' Attributions of Mental States in Pretense', *Child Development*, 68: 1133–42.

RUMSEY, J. (1985), 'Conceptual Problem-Solving in Highly Verbal, Nonretarded Autistic Men', *Journal of Autism and Developmental Disorders*, 15: 23–36.

—— HAMBURGER, S. (1988), 'Neuropsychological Findings in High-Functioning Men with Infantile Autism, Residual State', *Journal of Clinical and Experimental Neuropsychology*, 10: 201–21.

—— (1990), 'Neuropsychological Divergence of High-Level Autism and Severe Dyslexia', *Journal of Autism and Developmental Disorders*, 20: 155–68.

RUSSELL, J. (ed.) (1997a), *Autism as an Executive Disorder* (Oxford: Oxford University Press).

—— (1997*b*), 'How Executive Disorders Can Bring about an Inadequate "Theory of Mind"', in J. Russell (ed.), *Autism as an Executive Disorder* (Oxford: Oxford University Press).

RYLE, G. (1949), *The Concept of Mind* (New York: Barnes & Noble).

SARTRE, J.-P. (1940), *The Psychology of the Imagination* (London: Routledge).

SASS, L. (1994), *The Paradox of Delusion: Wittgenstein, Schreber, and the Schizophrenic Mind* (Ithaca, NY: Cornell University Press).

SCHIER, F. (1989), 'The Claims of Tragedy', *Philosophical Papers*, 18: 7–26.

SCHWARTZ, R. (2000), 'Self-Awareness in Schizophrenia: Its Relationship to Depressive Symptomology and Broad Psychological Impairment', *Journal of Nervous Mental Disease*, 189: 401–3.

SCHWEBEL, D., ROSEN, C., and SINGER, J. (1999), 'Preschoolers' Pretend Play and Theory of Mind: The Role of Jointly Constructed Pretence', *British Journal of Developmental Psychology*, 17: 333–48.

SCOTT, F., and BARON-COHEN, S. (1996), 'Imagining Real and Unreal Things: Evidence of a Dissociation in Autism', *Journal of Cognitive Neuroscience*, 8: 371–82.

—— LESLIE, A. (1999), ' "If Pigs Could Fly": A Test of Counterfactual Reasoning and Pretence in Children with Autism', *British Journal of Developmental Psychology*, 17: 349–62.

SCRUTON, R. (1974), *Art and Imagination* (London: Routledge & Kegan Paul).

—— (1983), *The Aesthetic Understanding* (London: Methuen).

SEARLES, H. (1988), 'Sources of Anxiety in Paranoid Schizophrenia', in P. Buckley (ed.), *Essential Papers on Psychosis* (New York: New York University Press).

SEGAL, G. (1996), 'The Modularity of Theory of Mind', in P. Carruthers and P. K. Smith (eds.), *Theories of Theories of Mind* (Cambridge: Cambridge University Press).

SEGAL, S. (1970), 'Imagery and Reality: Can they be Distinguished?', in W. Keup (ed.), *Origins and Mechanisms of Hallucinations* (New York: Plenum Press).

SELLARS, W. (1978), 'The Role of Imagination in Kant's Theory of Experience', in H. Johnstone (ed.), *Categories: A Colloquium* (University Park: Pennsylvania State University Press).

SERVOS, P., and GOODALE, M. (1995), 'Preserved Visual Imagery in Visual Form Agnosia', *Neuropsychologia*, 33: 1383–94.

SHEPARD, R., and COOPER, L. (1982), *Mental Images and their Transformations* (Cambridge, Mass.: MIT Press).

—— and METZLER, J. (1971), 'Mental Rotation of Three-Dimensional Objects', *Science*, 171: 701–3.

SIGMAN, M., KASARI, C., KWON, J., and YIRMIYA, N. (1992), 'Responses to the Negative Emotions of Others by Autistic, Mentally Retarded, and Normal Children', *Child Development*, 63: 796–807.

SIRIGU, A., DUHAMEL, J., PILLON, B., COHEN, L., DUBOIS, B., and AGID, Y. (1996), 'The Mental Representation of Hand Movements after Parietal Cortex Damage', *Science*, 273: 1564–7.

SMITH, A. (1976), *The Theory of Moral Sentiments* (1759) (Oxford: Oxford University Press).

SMITH, M. (1994), *The Moral Problem* (Oxford: Blackwell).

——(1998), 'The Possibility of Philosophy of Action', in J. Bransen and S. Cuypers (eds.), *Human Action, Deliberation and Causation* (Dordrecht: Kluwer).

SMYTH, M., PEARSON, N., and PENDLETON, L. (1988), 'Movement and Working Memory: Patterns and Positions in Space', *Journal of Experimental Psychology*, 40: 497–512.

SNYDER, A., and THOMAS, M. (1997), 'Autistic Child Artists Give Clues to Cognition', *Perception*, 26: 93–6.

SOBER, E., and WILSON, D. (1999), *Unto Others* (Cambridge, Mass.: Harvard University Press).

SODIAN, B., and HUELSKEN (1999), 'Young Children's Ability to Differentiate Pretense from Reality', paper presented at the the Biennial Meeting of the Society for Research in Child Development, Albuquerque.

SOUTHEY, R. (1894), *The Life of Nelson* (1813) (London: T. Nelson & Son).

SPARSHOTT, F. (1990), 'Imagination—the Very Idea', *Journal of Aesthetics and Art Criticism*, 48: 1–8.

SPERBER, D., and WILSON, D. (1986), *Relevance: Communication and Cognition* (Oxford: Blackwell).

SPERRY, R. (1950), 'Neural Basis of the Spontaneous Optokinetic Response Produced by Visual Inversion', *Journal of Comparative and Physiological Psychology*, 43: 482–9.

STALNAKER, R. (1984), *Inquiry* (Cambridge, Mass.: MIT Press).

——(1991), 'A Theory of Conditionals', in F. Jackson (ed.), *Conditionals* (Oxford: Oxford University Press).

STAMPE, D. (1987), 'The Authority of Desire', *Philosophical Review*, 96: 335–81.

STEPHAN, K., *et al.* (1995), 'Functional Anatomy of the Mental Representation of Upper Extremity Movements in Healthy Subjects', *Journal of Neurophysiology*, 73: 373–86.

STICH, S., and NICHOLS, S. (1992), 'Folk Psychology: Simulation or Tacit Theory?', *Mind and Language*, 7: 35–71; repr. in M. Davies and T. Stone (eds.), *Mental Simulation* (Oxford: Blackwell, 1995). Page numbers are to the reprint.

————(1997), 'Cognitive Penetrability, Rationality, and Restricted Simulation', *Mind and Language*, 12: 297–326.

STOCKER, M. (1981), 'Values and Purposes: The Limits of Teleology and the Ends of Friendship', *Journal of Philosophy*, 78: 747–65.

STRAWSON, P. (1992), 'Freedom and Resentment', in G. Watson (ed.), *Free Will* (Oxford: Oxford University Press).

STROUD, B. (1977), *Hume* (London: Routledge).

TAGER-FLUSBERG, H. (1992), 'Autistic Children's Talk about Psychological States: Deficits in the Early Acquisition of a Theory of Mind', *Child Development*, 63: 161–72.

——— and SULLIVAN, K. (1994), 'A Second Look at Second-Order Belief Attribution in Autism', *Journal of Autism and Developmental Disorders*, 24: 577–86.

——— (1995), 'Attributing Mental States to Story Characters: A Comparison of Narratives Produced by Autistic and Mentally Retarded Individuals', *Applied Psycholinguistics*, 16: 241–56.

——— and BOSHART, J. (1997), 'Executive Functions and Performance on False Belief Tasks', *Developmental Neuropsychology*, 13: 487–93.

TAYLOR, M. (1998), *Imaginary Companions and the Children who Create Them* (New York: Oxford University Press).

——— CARLSON, S. (1997), 'The Relation between Individual Differences in Fantasy and Theory of Mind', *Child Development*, 68: 436–55.

——— CARTWRIGHT, B., and CARLSON, S. (1993), 'A Developmental Investigation of Children's Imaginary Companions', *Developmental Psychology*, 29: 276–85.

TOMASELLO, M. (1995), 'Joint Attention as Social Cognition', in C. Moore and P. Dunham (eds.), *Joint Attention* (Hillsdale, NJ: Erlbaum).

——— (2000), *The Cultural Origins of Human Cognition* (Cambridge, Mass.: Harvard University Press).

——— KRUGER, A., and RATNER, H. (1993), 'Cutural Learning', *Behavioral and Brain Sciences*, 16: 495–552.

TREVARTHEN, C. (1998), 'The Concept and Foundations of Infant Intersubjectivity', in S. Braten (ed.), *Intersubjective Communication and Emotion in Early Ontogeny* (Cambridge: Cambridge University Press; Paris: Maison de la Science de l'Homme).

TYE, M. (1991), *The Imagery Debate* (Cambridge, Mass.: MIT Press).

VAN KREVELEN, D. (1971), 'Early Infantile Autism and Autistic Psychopathy', *Journal of Autism and Childhood Schizophrenia*, 1: 82–6.

VELLEMAN, D. (2000), 'The Aim of Belief', in his *The Possibility of Practical Reason* (Oxford: Oxford University Press).

VON HOLST, E. (1954), 'Relations between the Central Nervous System and the Peripheral Organs', *British Journal of Animal Behaviour*, 2: 89–94.

——— and MITTLESTAEDT, H. (1950), 'Das Reafferenzprinzip', *Naturwissenschaften*, 37: 464–76.

WALTON, K. (1990), *Mimesis as Make-Believe: On the Foundations of the Representational Arts* (Cambridge, Mass.: Harvard University Press).

——— (1994), 'Morality in Fiction and Fictional Morality', *Proceedings of the Aristotelian Society*, suppl. vol. 68: 27–50.

——— (1997a), 'On Pictures and Photographs: Objections Answered', in R. Allen and M. Smith (eds.), *Film Theory and Philosophy* (Oxford: Oxford University Press).

WALTON, K. (1997b), 'Spelunking, Simulation and Slime: On being Moved by Fiction', in M. Hjort (ed.), *Emotion and the Arts* (New York: Oxford University Press).

WARNOCK, M. (1976), *Imagination* (Berkeley: University of California Press).

WELLMAN, H., and WOOLLEY, J. (1990), 'From Simple Desires to Ordinary Beliefs: The Early Development of Everyday Psychology', *Cognition*, 35: 245–75.

—— CROSS, D., and WATSON, J. (2001), 'Meta-analysis of Theory-of-Mind Development: The Truth about False Belief', *Child Development*, 72: 655–84.

WHITE, A. (1990), *The Language of Imagination* (Oxford: Blackwell).

WHITE, G. (1788), *The Natural History and Antiquities of Selbourne* (London: Benjamin White & Son).

WIGGINS, D. (1998), 'Truth, Invention and the Meaning of Life', in his *Needs, Values and Truth* (Oxford: Oxford University Press).

WILLIAMS, B. (1973a), 'Deciding to Believe', in his *Problems of the Self* (Cambridge: Cambridge University Press).

—— (1973b), 'Imagination and the Self', in his *Problems of the Self* (Cambridge: Cambridge University Press).

WIMMER, H., and PERNER, J. (1983), 'Beliefs about Beliefs: Representation and Constraining Function of Wrong Beliefs in Young Children's Understanding of Deception', *Cognition*, 13: 103–28.

WING, L. (1991), 'The Relationship between Asperger's Syndrome and Kanner's Autism', in U. Frith (ed.), *Autism and Asperger's Syndrome* (Cambridge: Cambridge University Press).

—— and GOULD, J. (1979), 'Severe Impairments of Social Interaction and Associated Abnormalities in Children', *Journal of Autism and Developmental Disorders*, 9: 11–29.

WITTGENSTEIN, L. (1980), *Remarks on the Philosophy of Psychology*, vol. ii, ed. G. H. von Wright and H. Nyman (Oxford: Blackwell).

WOLLHEIM, R. (1973a), 'Imagination and Identification', in his *On Art and the Mind* (London: Allen Lane).

—— (1973b), 'The Mind and the Mind's Image of Itself', in his *On Art and the Mind* (London: Allen Lane); first pub. in *International Journal of Psycho-Analysis*, 50 (1969), 209–20.

—— (1984), *The Thread of Life* (Cambridge: Cambridge University Press).

WOLPERT, D., GHAHRAMANI, Z., and JORDAN, M. (1995), 'An Internal Model of Sensorimotor Integration', *Science*, 269: 1880–2.

—— MIALL, R., and KAWATO, M. (1998), 'Internal Models of the Cerebellum', *Trends in Cognitive Science*, 2: 338–47.

WOOLLEY, J., and WELLMAN, H. (1993), 'Origin and Truth: Young Children's Understanding of Imaginary Mental Representations', *Child Development*, 64: 1–17.

YIRMIYA, N., SIGMAN, M., KASSARI, C., and MUNDY, P. (1992), 'Empathy and Cognition in High Functioning Children with Autism', *Child Development*, 63: 150–60.

——SOLOMONICA LEVI, D., SHULMAN, C., and PILOWSKY, T. (1996), 'Theory of Mind Abilities in Individuals with Autism, Down Syndrome, and Mental Retardation of Unknown Etiology: The Role of Age and Intelligence', *Journal of Child Psychology and Psychiatry and Allied Disciplines*, 37: 1003–14.

——EREL, O., SHAKED, M., and SOLOMONICA-LEVI, D. (1998), 'Meta-analyses Comparing Theory of Mind Abilities of Individuals with Autism, Individuals with Mental Retardation, and Normally Developing Individuals', *Psychological Bulletin*, 124: 283–307.

YOUNG, A. (2000), 'The Neuropsychology of Abnormal Beliefs', *Mind and Language*, 15: 47–73.

YOUNGBLADE, L., and DUNN, J. (1995), 'Individual Differences in Young Children's Pretend Play with Mother and Sibling: Links to Relationships and Understanding of Other People's Feelings and Beliefs', *Child Development*, 66: 1472–92.

YUILLE, N., PERNER, J., PEARSON, A., PEERBHOY, D. (1996), 'Children's Changing Understanding of Wicked Desires: From Objective to Subjective and Moral', *British Journal of Developmental Psychology*, 14: 457–75.

Index